BAKER & TAYLOR

Strip City

Strip City

A STRIPPER'S

FAREWELL JOURNEY

ACROSS AMERICA

Lily Burana

B BURANA

talk miramax books

HYPERION

Library of Congress Cataloging-in-Publication Data
Burana, Lily.
    Strip city : a stripper's farewell journey across America / Lily Burana.—
1st ed.
        p. cm.
    "Talk Miramax books."
    "Portions of this book appeared previously in the October 1998 issue of GQ"—P.
    ISBN: 0-7868-6790-6
        1. Burana, Lily.   2. Stripteasers—United States—Biography.   I. Title.

PN1949.S7 B87 2001
792.7'028'092—dc21
[B]   2001039129

FIRST EDITION

10 9 8 7 6 5 4 3 2 1

To Gypsy—for being there at the beginning.

To Beth, Lynn, Elliot, and the
women of Operation Daisy Change—
for the illuminating detour along the way.

And to Randy—for being tougher than the rest throughout.

ONE

Spandex as a Second Language

It takes me several tries to get the bunny head thing just right.

As with much in life, it's a matter of positioning. You have to make sure you place the decal in the exact same spot every time, or you'll muck up the whole enterprise. I learned this the hard way. Careless application brought me, in succession, a three-eared bunny, then a bunny with too many eyes, then a blobby bunny with a club-ear and no distinct presence. Today, at the start of my tenth tanning session, I made sure the sticker was stuck just *so*, and when I'm done, I'll finally have what I am after: a small white patch in my tan, just below and to the left of my navel, in the shape of the Playboy bunny.

The girls who use the bunny heads are something of an amusement here at the busiest salon in Cheyenne, Wyoming. The plastic dish of decals sits next to the towels on a shelf by the cash register, in full view of every beautician and customer in the place. When a girl reaches into the dish, the women who run the shop look up from whatever make-over or pedicure they're doing and give one another a knowing glance. Oh, these ladies know that their job is to groom, not to judge—if you want your hair dyed a shade of copper-penny red that hasn't been seen since the days of "I Love Lucy" or your nails air-brushed blue and orange to show team spirit when you go down to Denver for a Broncos game, they'll oblige without comment. But something about a girl with the bunny tan sets the beauticians spinning. She's a little tacky, a little wild. The kind of girl who drives up to the salon in her Camaro fifteen minutes before closing, grabs a decal from the dish, and strides into the tanning booth for her ten-minute fake bake. Afterward, she's off to the Outlaw Saloon for a night of drinking, flirting, and, if the air is right, fighting.

That's not really who I am, but for my purposes, it's an image I can live with.

I have been making twice-weekly trips to the tanning salon for several weeks now. I started out pale as milk but I'm making significant progress toward my goal of a sensuous golden brown. Never mind that up close, my skin is starting to look knobby and taut—a little like the texture of a regulation football. The color is fantastic. From a distance, I'm the picture of health. I've never tanned in my life—I was a Goth as a teenager and didn't leave the house much during daylight in my early twenties, so all this dark, rich pigment is a novelty. I think it's great.

My dermatologist begs to differ.

I spent the morning getting yelled at in the skin clinic. I stopped by to see the doctor about a strange and sudden rash on my chin, and in an offhand moment I asked her, oh, by the way, if she would, please tell me about the effects of using a tanning bed.

It was an innocent question, and I simply was not prepared for the response. I gripped the edge of the counter in the examining room as the dermatologist dressed me down with vitriolic force strong as the heat from a blast furnace. "Oh, *tell* me you're not tanning," she moaned, closing her eyes and pressing her fingertips into her temples in frustration.

"Just a little," I lied, my eyes averted to the diagnostic posters on the exam room walls. Sebaceous Glands 101. Skin Occlusions At-A-Glance. Melanoma Made Easy.

"You seemed like such a smart person when you walked in here," she shrilled, "but after hearing what you've just said, I have to treat you totally differently!" She went on to tell me that by doing only ten tanning sessions a year—*a year*, she repeated for emphasis—I increase my risk of developing skin cancer seven times over.

The doctor spoke with the certain fury of a true believer, and she assured me that she had science to back her up. She called for her assistant to bring in a packet of information about indoor tanning. Slipping the thick sheaf of papers into a plastic sleeve, she said to me, "Do yourself a favor and stop right now. If you bought a package of tanning sessions that you haven't used up yet, give it to someone you hate."

With goggles to protect my eyes and a towel draped over my face, I lie in the tanning bed bathed in the eerie blue-purple glow. The industrial hum is oddly soothing, as if I'm a baby in a man-made womb listening to the muffled rhythms of the world outside. This snug, warm, thrumming space is all the universe I need. The white noise, the doctor told me, is part of what keeps tanning enthusiasts coming back, despite the known dangers. "Some people get addicted," she says. "Try meditation as a substitute."

In the packet she gave me is an article on the ills of tanning that says, "A tan is your skin's response to ultraviolet-induced injury; it's trying to tell you something. Just imagine if your skin could scream instead of tanning." I remember Fran Lebowitz writing about being on the phone with a Hollywood type, and describing him as "audibly tan." I am quite sure this is not what she meant. It would give a sensible person pause, this screaming-skin analogy. And if that wouldn't, the facts would: A tanning bed zaps the user with a day's worth of concentrated sun in ten minutes. Frequent use can cause premature aging, irreversible skin damage, and sun poisoning. One bad sunburn can equal years of accumulated exposure to natural sunlight.

But as far as risks go, tanning seemed pretty minimal compared to what I needed it for.

When a man gets engaged, his friends might throw him a bachelor party. They'll herd off to a club to see strippers, or order them in, and raise a glass to the groom—that poor sucker, that lucky bastard. The bachelor party is a raucous, ritual demarcation between the chaos of single life and the mature orderliness of pairing off. One final night with the antiwife before wedding your wife-to-be, it's a time-honored way of saying, "Goodbye to all that."

But what does a former stripper do when *she's* about to get married?

On my bed at home, I've carefully laid out everything I'll need for my trip: costumes, jewelry, makeup, hairpieces, brushes, combs, and curling irons—all the things that make a girl girly. Like a good tan, these tools of the trade are critical, because for a dedicated exotic dancer, form is just as important as content—if not more so.

It's a wonder that I made any money at all when stripping was my sole means of support. I was a bit of a slob. I'd wear the same costumes for a year. Instead of buying new outfits each month like many of the girls, I'd take their hand-me-downs. I had roots here, chewed fingernails there; I ate cookies for breakfast and, in general, was not much of a pro. But this time I am finessing every detail. With the knowledge that this upcoming trip is the last of the last, I'm building my ideal stripper persona from the ground up. Or rather, from the outside in. Starting with the wardrobe. Thus far, ready to be packed, I've got:

- Long spandex halter-top gowns and matching thongs in fluorescent pink, red, and leopard-print
- Black strapless evening gown with gold beading
- Black minidress with silver reflective squares on the front
- Baby doll minidress made of insect-print fabric
- Silver metallic thigh-high boots
- White patent thigh-high boots
- Gold iridescent platform sandals with long ankle straps that wrap around five times
- Clear Lucite platform mules
- Ankle-strap stiletto heels in white, gold, silver, and black
- Day-Glo orange-and-black zebra stripe bikini
- Pink velvet bikini sprinkled with rhinestones
- Hot pink bikini with white polka dots, trimmed with white bows
- Garters to tuck tips in

Add to that one bottle of wig shampoo; a wire wig brush; hair spray; hair gel; one large tub of body glitter; fruit-scented body spray; emery boards; nail glue; nail polish in turquoise blue, burgundy, gold, and silver glitter; tissues; cotton swabs; false eyelashes and adhesive; safety pins; bobby pins in two sizes; cocoa butter; a five-piece set of pedicure tools; Dermablend body concealer; lady razors; shave cream; deodorant body powder; a toiletry kit; my makeup. These are the bare essentials.

• • •

I have been engaged for six months, and I'm being called by some inner voice to go on my own bachelorette odyssey. I quit working as a stripper almost five years ago. When I stopped, I charged right into a new life as a writer, and never took a long look back. I left a lot of loose ends dangling and I didn't have the time or the emotional energy to take any kind of personal inventory. That period of my life is well in the past, and most would say I'm better off for it. But the past has a tricky way of not staying put. The idea of stripping my way around the country, an old fantasy of mine, has resurfaced. I've met several women who have done it, and I envied their adventures, their courage to hare off to a strange town with little more than a bagful of costumes and their own curiosity. Now, the thought of taking such a trip myself comes to me all the time—when I'm brushing my teeth, when I'm working at the computer, when I'm lying on the living-room rug watching TV with Randy, my intended. With a mate and a journalism career and a house to consider, I can't just pick up and leave for an open-ended venture, but I want to get out there somehow. I look at Randy sometimes and wonder, does my desire to do this mask a fear of settling down? If I married him tomorrow and hadn't gone out on the road, would I feel resentful?

But when examined closely, my yearning to take this trip is less about sweeping the path to the altar clear than it is about needing to settle this for myself. For my own sanity. Those inner voices can be pretty persistent, after all. Sometimes they seduce: "Wouldn't you love to see the clubs in Dallas?" Other times they nag: "You think you have your whole life to take a trip like this? Train's leaving the station, honey. Better get on it!" It's strange: When I quit, I wanted out so badly and now the pull is just as strong to go back in—a surprise to many. Myself, most of all. On the desire's surface is the basic hunger for adventure—the same impulse that sends people scaling Mount Everest or off on the Iditarod, despite the protestation of family and friends, and regardless—or perhaps because—of the danger and the length of the odds.

I miss the bright lights, the showmanship, the gamble. Beneath that lies a feeling of incompleteness: For all the time I spent as a stripper—six years, on and off—I still feel there's so much I didn't see, and even more that I don't know. At the very core of the urge, nesting deep like a secret seed beneath the thrill-seeking, the stage hots, and the curiosity, is the startling realization that I sleepwalked my way through stripping the first time. And while I've had ample exposure to what everyone else feels about stripping, what eludes me still, after so much time, is how *I* really feel about it. I don't want to enter the next stage of my life leaving six years of my past unresolved and incomplete. Like veterans compelled to revisit a battle scene or refugees who years later sojourn to the homeland, I need to go back in order to move on. That's why the desire for this is so pressing, I realize. It's nothing I can reason away. You don't always choose your journeys in life. Sometimes they choose you.

I can't play the carefree California hardbody type to save my life, and I'll never pass for a supermodel or a pouty-but-pure teen queen, so I don't draw much inspiration from the sex symbols of today. Finding a role model for my stripper self requires a look back in time, to the 1950s, when a vamp could be a vamp, and there wasn't nothing like a dame. When sex symbols had some hips, some thighs, and some mystique.

The obvious icon of the era is Marilyn Monroe, but she's never appealed to me that much. She seemed too vulnerable, too much a victim of circumstance. And too straight-up Hollywood. The girl for me is the campy Marilyn knock-off, Miss Mamie Van Doren. She is a classic vamp whose most notable achievement is making an impressive number of forgettable films. On the poster for her film *Born*

Reckless, Mamie stands staring into the distance, hands on her hips, wearing a cowboy hat, form-fitting blouse, criminally close-cut britches, and riding boots. The blurb reads: "She's every big-time rodeo prize rolled into one . . . pair of tight pants!" She also appeared in such projects as *The Girl in Black Stockings*, *High School Confidential*, *The Private Lives of Adam and Eve*, *Voyage to the Planet of Prehistoric Women*, and my favorite, *Sex Kittens Go to College*. Make no mistake, Mamie wasn't known as a woman of great intellect or grace. Or talent. As Paula Yates writes in her book, *Blondes: A History from Their Earliest Roots:* "With an important line like 'Over yonder,' Mamie could make a seven-minute scene just licking her lips and pointing in the wrong direction." But Mamie seems self-possessed and fun. Fast but fabulous, Mamie is a total rocker. So I'll take a pinch of Mamie, and mix it together with a lot of burlesque legend, Lili St. Cyr.

Lili St. Cyr, born Willis Marie Van Shaack in Minneapolis, gained notoriety as a stripper in the 1950s for her glamorous and inventive stage routines. She immortalized the bubble bath show and raised the stakes on burlesque gimmickry when she developed "The Flying G," an act that ended with her g-string, which was attached to invisible fishing line, zipping out over the audience just as the lights went out. But more than her trademark shows, Lili was known for her uncommon sophistication. While other women in the business invented giddy, packaged personae—Ann "Bang Bang" Arbor, "The Million Dollar Figure"; Pepper Powell, "The Titian-Haired Tantalizer"; or Bubbles Darlene, "America's Most Exciting Body"—she was simply Lili St. Cyr, a bombshell who adopted the name of a French military academy. If Mamie brought a little rock-n-roll freedom to uptight Hollywood, Lili suffused the sleazy world of striptease with some elegance.

The best stage name is already taken. "Daisy Anarchy" is the moniker of a well-known bottle-blonde virago in San Francisco. So

I have to come up with something else. Back in the early burlesque days, the second-tier, nonheadlining performers were called
soubrettes. They'd adopt stage names with kitsch value—Ada Onion
from Bermuda, Carrie de Booze from Canada, Lisa Carr from
Detroit, that sort of thing. The modern equivalents are called house
girls and they use straightforward first names: Keisha, Julie, Brittany,
Devon. But that's no fun. Even though I'm just a house girl, I want a
full name, something I've never used before, to go with my new,
custom-built stripper identity. But there are so many choices I don't
know where to start.

I guess you begin with what resonates, what sounds like who you
want to be. You can pick something wholesome: Kimberly, Jennifer,
Amanda, Kelly, Michelle. Something urban: Phoenix, Houston,
Dallas. Something Western: Cassidy, Cody, Cheyenne, Montana,
Dakota. Perhaps something exotic: India, Vienna, Geneva, Paris,
Egypt. Or something Gallic: Gigi, Lulu, Lola, Frenchy, Deja.
Something From Russia with Love: Natasha, Nikita, Katia, Katrina.
Something girly and sweet: Angel, Baby Doll, Bunny, Bambi. (And let's
not forget Lolita. Of course.) Something timely: Summer, Autumn,
April, June, May, December. Something weekly: Tuesday, Wednesday,
Friday, and Sunday. A name that's ripe for the picking: Cherry,
Strawberry, Peaches. I even met an Apple once. Something sweet:
Honey, Candy, Sugar, Cookie. Something spicy: Ginger, Pepper,
Cinnamon. Something fast and expensive: Mercedes, Porsche, Lexus.
Or something precious: Silver, Gem, Jewel, and Bijou.

For credibility's sake, I will avoid the whole Sandy, Mandy,
Brandy axis entirely.

There are names that are floral: Violet, Rose, Daisy, Wildflower,
Heather, Holly, Jasmine. Names that sound aristocratic: Page, Hunter,
Taylor, Tyler, Morgan, Victoria. Colorful names: Jade, Sienna, Blue,

Amber, Ebony. And tomboy names: Mel, Teddy, Bo, Charlie, Frankie, Joey, Johnny, Danni, and Sam.

Some names imply feline appeal: Tiger, Kitten, Kat, Cougar, Lynx, and Lioness. And some are things that are nice to touch: Velvet, Satin, Silk, and Lace.

I love the mythical and literary names: Penelope, Persephone, Circe, Ophelia, Cassandra, Daphne, Emma, Isis. And I have a special fondness for women who name themselves after biblical figures, for I appreciate homage to Lilith and Magdalene, the fallen women who preceded us all. I'm deeply moved by the story of Tamar, who attained righteousness through feminine wile, and I have to say, I never met a Jezebel I didn't like.

Maybe I should come up with a name of paralyzing wit, something like Kit Marlowe or Ann O'Dyne or Gloria Patri. But I'm attracted to a simpler, more obvious name: Barbie.

I don't have an adversarial relationship with Barbie. If anything, I'm Barbie neutral. I had plenty of Barbie dolls when I was a little girl, and I especially coveted the glamorous, super-dressy Barbies that came with evening gowns, handbags, and earrings you stuck into holes drilled into Barbie's head. But within days of taking the doll out of the box, I'd invariably start losing shoes, separates, little earrings. Her hair would bunch into an uncombable snarl and then I'd end up ditching Barbie altogether to chase after my older brother and sisters, who were always doing something much more fun than playing fashion show or make-believe prom. So I'm not choosing the name in order to alleviate some long-standing Barbie issues. It's just that in creating this stripper persona, I strive for the blondest common denominator, and what's blonder than Barbie?

Barbie. Okay, so the first name is taken care of. Now for a last name.

Barbie Doll—it's been done.

Barbie Dahl—stupid.

Barbie Winters—too cold.

Barbie Walters—that's funny. But no.

Barbie Wittgenstein—ugh, too pretentious.

Barbie Freud—that's kind of scary. Barbie Francis. Barbie Ferris. Barbie Ferrous? Barbie Frost . . .

Barbie Faust. That's it. That's perfect.

The timer on the tanning bed goes off. My ten minutes are up. I lift the upper canopy of the bed and sit up to check my tan lines. I peel off the bunny sticker—the white spot is more pronounced. I'm getting darker, I can definitely tell. Almost ready now.

I hurry into my jeans and sweatshirt, still tingling from the heat of the tanning bulbs. I leave the salon, jump in my truck, and drive down East Lincolnway, my skin shouting all the way home.

TWO

Runaway Love

Randy and I met because of the weather.

It is 1997, two years since I've moved back to New York City from San Francisco to jump-start my writing career. In that terrible way that you get what you wish for, a magazine sends me in search of a story that requires a cross-country drive for the entire month of December. I fare pretty well from New York to Iowa but by the time I am halfway across Nebraska, energy is flagging and I am feeling grim.

Somewhere near Ogallala, about six hours into that majestic, maddening prairie, I realize that half an hour has passed since I've seen a vehicle in either direction.

Oh, I think as I finally see a pair of headlights draw nigh in the eastbound lane, *so this must be where the West begins.*

Wyoming looms in the distance in the form of a tiny sawtooth ridge of mountain. If I can just get there and get some rest, I'll be fine. Near midnight, after eight hours on the road, I cross the state

line like a marathoner blasting through the ribbon—*I did it!*
I did it!—and pull into Cheyenne an hour later just as it starts
to snow.

The snow hasn't been too bad, not much accumulation, so I try
to leave town the next day. But I don't know—couldn't have known,
really—that the fifty miles of Interstate 80 between Cheyenne and
Laramie is one of the most dangerous stretches of highway in the
country. That little mountain ridge I saw as I drove into the state is
part of the peaks that surround the Summit—the highest point on
I-80, at over eight thousand feet—a treacherous clearing hacked
from the Laramie Range of the Rockies. Preceding the pass is a
wide-open landscape that sees more wind than a Yankee urbanite
could ever imagine. Even when it's not snowy, the road is often
closed just because of the gusts.

But the road is open, so I head out toward Salt Lake City just
after breakfast. As I edge onto the windy highway, blowing sleet
dashes the windshield, and snow clouds up and swirls off with an
angry hiss. Visibility is so poor, all the vehicles slow to a twenty-five-
mile-an-hour crawl. I watch, goggle-eyed with fear, as a gust of wind
catches a wood-paneled Jeep Cherokee and spins it around 180
degrees on the icy roadway, then blows it straight into a light post.
The post falls over the length of the Jeep, bashing a divot into the
roof, which crumples under the weight. I nose my car onto the
shoulder, jump out, and carefully pick my way across the road.

The driver is sitting upright, a rivulet of blood congealing to a
gummy red-black on his forehead. He's just a young kid.

"Hey man, are you okay? Do you need me to call 911?" I ask
when he rolls down the window.

"I'm fine, I'm fine." He waves me off with his left hand. His
right hand is torqued off the wrist—broken, I'm sure. "I already
called on my cell. They're on their way. But thank you."

I drive at a slow creep to the next exit and turn back toward
Cheyenne.

Shortly after noon, they close the highway for the remainder of the day.

I spend the afternoon touring the town, which at first glance appears to be mostly car dealerships and cute motels: the Hitching Post, the Home Ranch, the Thunderbird, the Ranger, the Lariat. I find the mall and poke around in there, get my nails done, then rent a room for the night, and spend the evening rearranging the contents of my luggage while watching cable.

The next day the highway is still closed. I can't face another evening by myself in front of the television. After dinner, I put on some jeans, a sweater, a pair of engineer boots, and my parka, and get in the car and head south. Ten minutes later, I am just beyond the 80 overpass on South Greeley Highway, drawn toward a two-stories-tall dummy of an oil derrick with a glowing star on top. Beneath the derrick sits a squat brick-faced building with grayscale rodeo murals painted on the front—a saddle bronc rider in mid-buck, and a roper bearing a calf in his arms with paternal tenderness. The sign out front reads JACK AND GLORIA HORN'S COWBOY BAR.

"Can I buy you a drink?"

I have only been in the bar for two minutes when a man pushes his way over and stands right in front of me. I step back and look him up and down: Beat-up buckaroo boots, skin-tight dark blue Wranglers, a tooled belt with a rodeo buckle, a faded denim button-down shirt, and a black cowboy hat with an Indian hatband.

His eyes are dark brown with a playboy glimmer, and he has the chubby cheeks, cleft chin, and black mustache of a young Ernest Hemingway. Muscled and obviously macho, he looks like low-grade trouble.

If I were out in New York and I saw a man like this, I'd think, "Okay, where'd this guy ride out of, Toon Town?" I'd look around for Allen Funt, like, this is a joke and it's on me, isn't it? The camera crew would pop out so everyone could have a good laugh at my expense. The guy would peel off his fake mustache and turn out to be an accountant masquerading as a cowboy to reel in the ladies for the amusement of millions of viewers nationwide.

But I'm not in New York, I'm in the capital city of Wyoming and this fellow is still standing in front of me, waiting for an answer while I fiddle with the zipper on my parka, dumbstruck.

Nice of him to offer me a drink. I am here alone, after all. But, me? Hook up with a honky-tonk player? I don't think so.

Then he gives me a hopeful smile, blinding white with a big black gap where one of his front teeth should have been.

I find myself softening. "Sure." I smile back. "A drink would be nice."

To be honest, it isn't love at first sight. Far from it. I only follow him across the cavernous room to his table—a couple dozen pairs of eyes following with me—and let him buy me a Diet Coke because I want to find out about the missing tooth.

"Well, it started when I was fighting with my sister when I was twelve and she was fourteen," he tells me over a Bud Lite. "She punched me right in the face and the tooth got loose. Then, ten years later I got kicked in the mouth while I was sparring during kick-boxing practice and the tooth came out."

I have to admit that's a pretty good story.

"Actually," he says, sheepishly, "the kick just loosened the tooth some more. It really came out the next day when I was eating lunch. I took a bite out of my sandwich, and when I looked down the tooth was sticking out of the bologna."

This being a weeknight, and a snowy one at that, the place isn't very crowded. People clustered loosely around the corners of the long bars just inside either entrance sit with their backs to the room. The televisions in the corner are mute, tuned to the broadcast of the National Finals Rodeo in Las Vegas. The voices coming from the speakers, singing upbeat country songs of love triumphal, barroom brawls, and redneck pride, brag to no one. The beer signs cast a rainbow of invitation on the empty wooden dance floor, announcing brand names beneath tubes of neon twisted into cowboy hats, guitars, and the silhouette of a man on the back of a bull.

When the band gets back onstage after the break, I tug on Randy's sleeve. "Let's go dance!"

We've run out of things to say—I've told him all I'm willing to about me, that I live in Manhattan, I'm just passing through for work reasons and I'm leaving tomorrow, and I've already learned that he has lived here all his life, he has an older sister and a younger brother, and he is two years older than me. That he rodeos in the summer and kick-boxes, and owns a local construction company. By the time my Diet Coke runs out, so does the casual bar banter and my interest.

Things change when we start dancing.

"I'm warning you," I tell Randy as we pass through the pole fence that corrals the dance floor, "I have no idea what I'm doing."

"Don't worry, I'll teach you."

This guy, it turns out, is a wild, wild dancer. As he whisks me to and fro, patiently guiding me through a basic West Coast Swing, his shoulders bunch up near his ears like he's doing a frug, while his feet do crisscross steps like a side-passing horse. Yet his moves are so tightly controlled he hardly assumes any space on the floor. I've never seen such economy of motion.

"Oh, sorry!" I yell over the music as I step on his feet yet again with my heavy engineer boots.

"Sorry!"

"Uh-oh . . . !"

"Sorry. Am I hurting you? Sorry!"

When Randy tries to teach me a two-step, I can't pick up my feet off the floor and still keep rhythm, so I shuffle along, one-two, *shoof shoof*. One-one-two, *shoofshoofshoof*, like I'm doing a modified soft-shoe. He notices that I'm struggling and sort of puts his weight behind his lead, shoving me gently across the floorboards like a push broom.

Later in the night, when the band comes back for another set, we're two-stepping past the stage and the singer looks down at us and says over the mic, "Way to go, Randy!"

"Everyone here knows each other, I take it."

"Small town," Randy whispers in my ear, keeping a steady rhythm as we shove on by.

I leave the bar at one with Randy's phone number in my pocket.

Turns out the next morning that the highway is still closed.

I can't say I'm disappointed.

That night, I meet Randy for dinner at the Albany, an old saloon in the heart of downtown Cheyenne. Most of the surrounding buildings are vacant—former hotels from when the town was built around the railroad in the late nineteenth century. Across the street is the old train station, its tall clock tower spire piercing the night sky. Passenger trains stopped coming through in the 1980s. The freights, wheels clacking heavily as they roll past, are all that's left.

Halfway through the prime rib I spring the stripper thing on him. Is my past any of his business? Not at this point, but I feel a major crush brewing and I know from experience that if someone can't handle this bit of background, we don't have a chance at moving from crush to relationship. Granted, it's not who I am anymore, but it's a damn significant part of who I've since become. If Randy fails this very important litmus test, I'll know to quash my infatuation and end the evening early. Which would suck, after those patient hours on the dance floor and the good manners and the adorable knocked-out tooth and all.

We're right down the street from the Green Door, the only go-go bar in town, which gives me an excuse to broach the subject.

"So what's that Green Door place like?" I ask, trying to keep my voice as even and neutral as possible. My tongue is thick in my mouth and I can't feel my lips. I hope my face isn't turning red, I don't want to give any indication of how much this matters to me. I push a piece of beef around on my plate with my thumb.

He doesn't flinch. I may as well have asked him about the weather. "Nothing special, really. A buddy of mine used to date a gal who worked there. She was all right—she didn't take any shit from anybody."

I like this response. He's not jumpy or critical or overexcited. Promising.

Reaching across the table, I take both of his hands in mine and gently rub the tender spaces between his knuckles.

I had a feeling he'd be down, but it's not something I can safely predict. There's nothing about a person—class, age, race, lifestyle, or personality type—that can accurately tip me off. All I can do is calmly float the subject out there and gauge the reaction. I can figure out how someone feels in a heartbeat—what does stripping teach you if not keen intuition based on body language? The posture will shift almost imperceptibly—moving closer in lechery or farther away in disgust or defense, and the face will register an impulse to recoil, leer, grimace, or smile before a muscle even moves. A flicker behind the eyes says everything. I don't think someone is a loser or a prude if they don't want to date a woman who has stripped—it's a lot to deal with. But I'm really clear that I need someone who is unfazed by that part of me. I don't require applause, or even approval. Just someone who can hang.

Well, I've cracked the egg, may as well reveal the whole truth. In the process of telling him in the most nonchalant manner possible that I was a stripper, I take a bite of mashed potatoes that goes straight down the wrong pipe.

"I just hope that you don't care," I say, coughing and reaching for my water glass.

"Why would I care? I think it's cool."

"Sometimes it was cool. Sometimes not," I say, clearing my throat and dabbing at my watering eyes with a napkin.

"Well, it doesn't matter," he says, his smile tough and sweet over the rim of his iced tea glass. "I think you're awesome."

Randy puts the glass down. I take his hands again and squeeze as hard as I can. He squeezes back and gives me a conciliatory wink.

A week later, I call him from a truck stop in Arizona.

"Hey, you know what? They have this special thing at the restaurant counter here. It's 'Truckers Only.' "

"Yeah, I know. Every truck stop is like that. It's so truckers never have to waste time waiting to be seated." His voice is light with amusement.

I was trying to be clever—sharing this little anthropological flourish from my travel like a slightly bored teenager holding up a fun, corny souvenir in front of her friends. Instead I feel a mild jerk of annoyance that my attempt backfired to reveal a basic ignorance. I could tell you about the seating politics of any trendy restaurant in New York, but I don't know jack about truck stops.

Randy, thankfully, isn't neurotic enough to hold such a trivial offense against me.

"So what will it take for you to come see me again?"

"I don't know," I tell him. "A plane ticket?"

And so it goes. I fly out to Cheyenne a month later for a six-day visit and end up staying six weeks. Then, three months later, I pack up my laptop and fly out with plans to stay for the whole summer.

• • •

I wouldn't say Cheyenne is unfriendly, but there's a vestigial coarseness to the place that betrays its renegade roots. It feels restless. Maybe it's the Air Force base and its migratory population. Or the ferocious wind that blows in off of the Rockies and beats the prairie senseless. It could be the myriad railroad tracks that cross the town from north to south and east to west. It may be the interchange between the two huge highways, 25 and 80, which run from New Mexico almost to Montana and New York to San Francisco, respectively. I'm not sure what it is, but there's something about this town that says Keep Moving.

This transient spirit is exalted in early August when the bikes start coming through en route to Sturgis, South Dakota, for Bike Week. At every stoplight on the shortcut to U.S. 85, prides of Harleys idle at low growl, saddle bags loaded and bedrolls strapped to the sissy bars. Gas stations teem with bikes filling up at every pump. To experience the full glory of this pilgrimage, you have to break free of town on 85 where the speed limit notches up to seventy-five miles an hour. There you see thousands of bikes riding staggered at top speed, past the grassy beige blur of nameless land and the small towns that hug the highway. Meridian, Hawk Springs, Lingle, Jay Em, and Lusk. Somewhere up near Newcastle, the sun-baked grasslands give way to the spruce-dotted red clay slopes of the Black Hills. You know you've arrived when the temperature drops ten degrees, a welcome gift courtesy of the abundant pines wicking heat from the air. The two-lane highway, for hundreds of miles a near straightaway, curves gracefully through the cool glades, past Lead and Deadwood, where it meets Highway 14 and goes on into Sturgis proper.

I was never much for bikes. As a ghoulie punk kid, the entire package—engine grease, calling women "old ladies," Lynyrd Skynyrd—seemed crusty and beat, and the racist cracker element set my teeth on edge. Then the Yuppies horned in and the biker lifestyle-as-commodity wrinkle made the whole thing seem even sillier: Harley-

Davidson coffee, Harley-Davidson baby clothes, even Harley-Davidson chocolate-covered peanut clusters. Born to Be Wild, Inc. Who needed it? But I was a self-satisfied snot who had always lived in tightly packed urban grids where I could frown stylishly at the whole scene without ever experiencing what's at the heart of it. When I got out into the Wyoming sticks and could tear around a bit on an open road, I understood. Peel away the totems, the predictable rebel conformity clause, and the purchasing push, and you strike the vein of a bike's appeal: It's as close to flight as a human being can get without having to leave the ground.

But we're not on a bike today—Randy and I are in his truck, speeding toward Sturgis, watching in awe and not just a little envy as the phalanxes of Harleys roar by. We're listening to the radio and eating boxed fried chicken. We pass a small plastic container of potato salad back and forth, and I search the stations for good music while Randy drives.

Ozzy Osbourne comes on. I turn it way up.

Resting my feet on the dash, I tap my toes. Randy drums his fingers on the steering wheel.

We've been a couple now for eight months and heavy metal had a cupid effect on us. When Randy confided that he really doesn't like country that much and would pick AC/DC over George Jones any day, I was relieved. It gave us a common territory, a shared language. Our love of really loud music gave us something to latch onto during my first visits to Cheyenne when it seemed like we had little more to go on than an abundance of chemistry and wishful thinking.

I crank the window open and hold my hand out, fingers splayed to feel the warm wind rushing through.

"You know," I muse aloud, relishing how the guitar solo complements the ranginess of the surroundings, the speed of the truck, "sometimes you've just gotta rock."

"That is the absolute truth."

• • •

Randy rented us a cabin at the top of a mountain in Lead. The owners, an elderly couple, meet us at the foot of the mountain and we follow them up the gravel-pocked road past gaily trimmed resort chalets and skeletons of old houses, abandoned once the Black Hills mines were exhausted years ago. Broken down to planks and shingles, their roofs collapsed after years of sighing under winter snow pack, they lean in wait for gravity to claim them.

The cabin, tucked into a densely wooded lot, smells of moths and liniment. We put our bags in the bedroom and I change clothes. Randy heads into the living room, which is outfitted in fake leather couches, plaid nubby slipcovered armchairs, and shellacked wood Christian affirmation plaques. When I come out and join him on the crinkly brown pleather couch, I notice he has poured champagne into the nicest glasses he could find in the kitchen cabinets—matching glass beer mugs. The air in the room is stagnant and hot.

Before I know what is happening, Randy drops down on one knee in the burnt-orange deep-pile shag carpet, takes a ring box out from under his cowboy hat, and asks me to marry him.

I want to daintily hold out my left hand and murmur a quivering, misty-eyed yes, but I don't. My hands fly to my face and I start laughing and crying at the same time. Because it is so unexpected. Because it is so sweet. Because it is so awful and perfect, with the leather-look upholstery and the old-people medicine-scented air and the slightly muggy embrace of the South Dakota night.

He slips the ring on my finger, and we kiss. Then we trek down the hill and into Deadwood, where we walk along Main Street, sharing the good news whenever we run into someone we know. In every bar, club, and casino, people toast our happy occasion over the ubiquitous refrain of "Sweet Home Alabama."

• • •

I wake the next day feeling like something is sitting on my chest, crushing me. Holding back the flimsy curtains made of cotton flowered sheets trimmed in red rickrack, I look out at the morning sun blazing through a stand of birch trees, the silvery bark bouncing the light into the canopy of leaves, making the forest a heaven of golden greens. Randy is still asleep, innocent masculine sweat sprinkling his brow. This ache in my chest is killing me. I'm such an asshole.

Randy lifts his head up from the pillow when he hears me sigh. "Is something wrong?"

"Oh, God. I can't marry you."

"What? What?! *Why?*" He sits up, his hair matted and going in a million directions.

"I'm not ready! I've only known you for a couple of months. Where will we live? I don't know if I want to live in Wyoming, and you don't know if you'll be happy in New York, and this is so sudden. I want to, but, it . . . it's just too soon!"

Randy lies back down and rolls over on his side, facing me.

"Well, if that's all it is, we can wait."

I take a deep breath.

"Just give me some time."

When we get back to Cheyenne and I call my mother in New Jersey to tell her, she is nonplussed. She's made it clear that seeing her children marry has never been a huge priority. Once in a while she reminds my siblings and me that she'd be perfectly content if, after finding the right partner, we bypass the formality of making it legal. Neither of my parents ever put any pressure on me in that regard, though occasionally, my mother will read about or see someone on TV who she thinks might be a good match.

"That Ted Nugent was on David Letterman the other night. He's very articulate, you know."

Ted Nugent. Oh good God, no.

"Mother, I am not interested in dating Ted Nugent."

"He doesn't look it, but he's really very intelligent!"

"Mom, I'm serious. I made a vow to never date anyone politically to the right of Barry Goldwater. Besides, he hunts."

"He's very handsome, though."

"Mom, he's married."

I can't blame my mom for agitating on my behalf, since I am certain she views my dating criteria as highly suspect. The only person I ever dated with whom she had any prolonged contact was my druggie high school boyfriend, Peter Doylan. Peter played guitar in a rather awful punk band and had a dyed-black mohawk. He also had a pretty big nose, so in photographs taken from head-on, with the mohawk showing up as just a centrally placed black tuft and the nose being what it was, he looked a lot like Bert from "Sesame Street." His greatest mortification was having the middle name Francis, so when anyone asked about the F, he said his name was "Peter Fuckin' Doylan." During the year that we were together, Peter was in and out of crash pads and in and out of work, so my mom must've been thinking that any musician with an actual job would be an improvement. She was probably right.

But Ted Nugent? I mean, really.

"Wy-*O*-ming?" my friends in New York exclaim when I tell them that I've decided I'd rather relocate to Cheyenne than attempt the formidable task of carving out life *à deux* in the city. "Why the hell are you moving all the way out to Wy-*O*-ming?"

I don't quite know what to say. How to explain to them that ever since I returned from my cross-country trip, Manhattan seems different? Less exciting and more confining. Plus, I am becoming increasingly annoyed with my New York self. I lived there for a couple years as a punky teen dropout, and the city then seemed scary and magnificent. But now, after having returned as an ambitious twenty-something media-type-in-training, I find myself looking around at everything with an unsatisfied sniff. I'm too easily irritated and bored, and I'm disturbed by the arrogance that that implies. I feel as if I've gotten to the bottom of the New York mystery that has enchanted me since I was a small child. So if it is indeed true that I know everything that is worth knowing, and I have solved the metropolitan puzzle known as New York City, then why stay? I want to be someplace, and be surrounded by things, that I don't immediately recognize and greet with contempt.

Randy told me he proposed in order to show me that our time together wasn't for naught. I decided to move to Wyoming for the same reason. That, and the roaches. Sometime during our torrid cross-country affair, the roof in my Chelsea apartment building cracked and sprang a leak, fostering an infestation of two-inch-long flying cockroaches. While having a phone conversation with Randy, during which I had to put down the phone three times to chase—shoe in hand—after a giant roach, I decided that Wyoming had to be better than this. I didn't want the halcyon days of new love queered by clouds of Raid.

When I move in with Randy, we don't attain immediate domestic bliss. I have to kick and scream a little. I wish I were an easier person to live with. I can effortlessly go all giddy and foolish over a throwaway affair, because there's no compromise in a dead end. But I'm thornier when there are future prospects, because I get nervous.

I want to fall in love but I don't want my life to be subsumed. My independence is the key to my sanity, and I'm loath to see it jeopardized even though I long to be held and kissed and fussed over and to do the same for someone else, too. I know you can have it all, but how?

I've seen countless smart, inspired women slip under their mates' feet—in terrific haste or by attrition, but always to the same sad end—and I am scared of that happening to me. So I try to strike that critical balance between love's submission and personal autonomy, but my execution is pretty hairy. When I dated an artist, it turned into a constant battle over which one of us was Yoko (not me!). When I was involved with a Marxist fanzine publisher, we always bickered over what I considered to be his oppressive politics. I don't want to be a battle-ax, but I always feel I have to resist being squashed and I'm not sure how to refine my approach. Is this a typical modern woman's dilemma? I don't know, but it's certainly *my* dilemma.

I'm not nearly so bad with Randy. I'm more confident now about how to keep Stepford Wifery at bay. But there's still this defensive *thing* that I do. Every so often I have a hiccup of New York–style snobbery about some bullshit matter, like not being able to find the MC5 in the record store, or the fact that salads in the restaurants around town are still at the *no tengo arugula* stage. One time when we were driving somewhere in the truck I rolled my eyes because he didn't know who Eustace Tilley was. It was the first time I turned that attitude on Randy, and the last.

He came completely uncorked. "Do you know the difference between a two-by-four and a two-by-six?" he yelled.

I sat there dumbfounded. I'd never seen him lose his temper before, at least not with me.

"Well, *do you?*"

Silence.

"I didn't think so! So don't treat me like I'm stupid, because I know plenty of things that you don't!"

In Wyoming, they call that fixing someone's wagon. Thereafter my wagon was suitably fixed.

Most of the time, though, we have a pretty great time. We travel back East together now and again, and I introduce Randy to museums and restaurants. So far he likes the low-key Mafia hangout in the West Village best. When we're home, I spend the day at the desk in the spare bedroom working on articles, while Randy goes to the job sites to line out his men. Come summer, I ditch work and tag along whenever he goes to a rodeo for a wild horse race. Even though I spent the first rodeo with my hands clapped over my mouth in fright watching the mugger and shank man on his team steady the untamed horse as it burst into the arena so Randy could saddle it and attempt to ride it across the finish line, I find them fun. The only thing I actively dislike is the steer wrestling—men grabbing the animal by the horns and twisting its neck until it falls—*boomp!*—in the dirt. I appreciate all the rest, though—the God-fearing cowboys with crosses stitched into the flank of their chaps, the mud, the rodeo queens with their satin sashes and sky-high lacquered hair, the bulls milling around in the stock pens and firing from the chutes, snorting and spinning.

Love can't sustain solely on "exotic other" confectionery. For it to last there has to be more—a singular quality that makes it a love that not just intrigues but lets you sleep better at night. In an interview, a well-known CEO described what he'd sought in a mate back when he was single. He said he wanted a woman so resourceful that if he ever found himself in a Third World prison, she'd know exactly how to go about getting him freed. To him, the most prized characteristic is capability. To me, it's bloody-knuckled devotion. The moment that I really believed Randy and I would make it in the long run was when he said to me, "I may not win every fight I'd get in to defend you, but I'd die trying." I realized in an instant that this streetwise chivalry was what I'd been looking for my whole life. Not because I need so much to be protected by a m-a-n but because that's also how *I* feel. My loyalties may be few, but they are not subtle. He would go to the wall for me, and I for him. No one would dare try to disrespect or harm either of us in the other's presence. Not if he valued his windpipe.

One can list a hundred reasons why our relationship could work, and a thousand more why it shouldn't, but what remains is that it does. It works. We're both always ready to charge at the world, yet we've managed to hollow out a restful pocket to retreat to together. This is the real deal, even if to the rest of the world we just look like two souls joined at the attitude problem.

Now it's mid-January, six months postproposal and four months since I gave up my Manhattan life. Randy and I live in an old railroad flophouse. The entire building was moved off the original foundation, put on a flatbed, and trucked into town from its site by the tracks. The house is confused—it was designed and added upon so haphazardly we can't tell whether it was meant to be a miniature Victorian or Mission-style bungalow. Perfect for us.

We sit on the living-room floor together as I make plans for my trip. With the atlas and a dog-eared copy of the *Exotic Dancers Directory* open before me, I'm trying to put together a workable itinerary. I don't want to dance totally nude, so Georgia is out of the question, along with Washington, D.C., Oregon, Montana, and Alaska (I will have to reconsider the "no nudity" rule for Alaska. God, I'd hate to have to skip it). I'm past the point where customer contact seems worth it, so I'll aim for places that don't get any more extreme than table dancing—which eliminates a large percentage of clubs. Thankfully the strip-related media has advanced to the point where I can look this stuff up in a guide, or consult Web sites, which list everything from club hours, to levels of physical contact and exposure, to directions from the nearest airport. I don't know how I would have planned this trip if I'd wanted to take it ten years ago.

When I circle a club in the guide, Randy slides the book around to see what I've picked. "Why there?"

The answer varies: I want to see that state. I've heard a lot about this club. I like the name.

Randy focuses more intently on my list.

I ruffle his freshly cropped hair. "Are you okay? Do you not want me to go?"

"Of course I don't want you to go! But I understand why you feel like you have to. I can't stop you."

"Would you try to stop me if you thought you'd succeed?"

"No," he says, ruefully. "I trust you. I have to. I have to or I'll lose you."

I know Randy well enough to tell the difference between his separation anxiety and his genuine despair. If I sensed that he truly objected to me going on this trip, I wouldn't. But then, if he were the type to object to such a thing, I doubt we'd have hooked up in the first place. We share a bone-deep understanding of each other's daredevil streak, and we both know that sometimes satisfaction must be wrested from risk. Between the rodeo, the kick-boxing, and the stripping, neither of us has ever had to ask the other, "Why?"

But understanding doesn't ensure ease. Even though Randy would never stand between me and my aspirations, he worries what the pursuit might do to me, to us. And while I wouldn't sacrifice what I need to do just for his appeasement, sometimes I worry about losing him nonetheless. I close the atlas and push my notepad aside for a while.

The road trip is traditionally the undertaking of those on the cusp, people who have nothing to lose. I myself have everything to lose; I need to take this trip and at the same time I need to make sure it's all still here when I get back—mate, house, career. After some negotiation with Randy, I decide it'd be best to break the journey down into brief jaunts, maybe ten days at the longest. A drive here, a round-trip flight there, spread out over the course of a year.

Randy is the main reason why I'm being careful about this expedition, but he also helped confirm my decision to make it in the first place.

I asked him once, "Why do you think guys go to strip clubs? Not the ones who go every once in a while, but the ones who are there day after day?"

"Well, usually a guy gets all hung up on a certain dancer, and he thinks that if he comes in to see her often enough he might have a chance."

"What do you mean, 'a chance'? A chance that she'll go out with him?"

"Well, yeah!"

"You are *kidding!*"

His illumination, this insight that hope, of all things, is part of the engine that drives the strip club economy, really gave me pause: Man, if I didn't clue in to something as simple as that, what else have I missed? I can wax rapturous about what makes a woman take off her clothes for money, or break down the rudimentary political ramifications of topless dancing. But beyond my own defensive analysis, I really don't have any idea how it *works.* There are gaps in my consciousness you could drive a truck through. If I expect to get any smarter about this business, then I'd better get out there. Now it seems less a pipe dream than a mandatory assignment.

Is it even remotely possible to figure out the personal and professional complexities of stripping, while at the same time being back in the game to see how they play out in different areas of the country? And can this be accomplished in the course of a single year?

What will it take, I wonder, to lay this matter to rest, once and for all?

Somewhere in the atlas lies the answer.

THREE

Pure Talent

The real scandal in my working as a stripper is that I can't dance. It's just not a talent I've ever possessed. When I was in grade school, I took an afternoon course that offered instruction in all the dance steps from the movie *Grease*, and I struggled in vain to learn a basic cha-cha. As an adult, I made a point of avoiding aerobics classes after grapevining the wrong direction into an entire row of classmates one too many times. But lacking terpsichorean skill never hurt me that much. The first time I auditioned at a bona fide strip club—not a go-go bar or a peep show where you stand and shimmy, but a place where you have a stage to yourself and are expected to use it with style and sex appeal—I was nervous to the point of nausea, memories of childhood stumbles and aerobics class carnage in my head. I sat on the staircase backstage at San Francisco's notorious Mitchell Brothers O'Farrell Theater with six other auditioning hopefuls and tried to steady my knees. The manager came back to where we were hiding behind the curtains, propped one foot on the lowest step, and rested his elbow on his knee so he could lean down to talk us. I'll never forget his shoes, cobra-skin moccasins with the heads still attached. "Got 'em for twelve dollars American in Thailand last year," he said, flexing his toes to make the snakes' heads weave back and forth. "They make them while you wait." But more incredible than his shoes was what he told us about our impending audition: "Don't worry about how you move out there. Ninety percent of the women who work here can't dance." That wasn't exactly true—in fact, his assessment was as rudely unjust to the veteran dancers as it was meant to be reassuring to us wannabes—but I felt a little more at ease. When my turn came in the amateur contest lineup, I got up on shaky legs, loped around the stage for the length of Aerosmith's "Love in an Elevator," and took first place by an audience-applause vote. I won a little trophy and twenty-five bucks. And a job. Which is pretty good winnings from a dance contest for somebody who can't dance.

But now, several years and a career coda later, I'm no longer comfortable with being barely competent. If I'm to return to dancing, I want to be as good as I can—or at least better than I was. So what does a woman do when she wants to improve and expand herself in an area of study? She goes to school. Stripper school.

The Pure Talent School of Dance in Clearwater, Florida, is the nation's only academy for professional exotic dance. There are plenty of personal enrichment courses that will teach you how to strip for your lover—Learning Annex–type evening classes where for two hours you can practice twirling a silk scarf and rolling your hips in a conference room with the table and armchairs pushed to the walls. But a real stripper can't properly practice footwork on industrial-grade carpet. She needs ample solid flooring, a floor-to-ceiling mirror, poles, and, if she has any pride at all, a light source other than a bank of fluorescents glowering overhead, exaggerating every pore, lump, and ripple. She needs professional help in professional surroundings.

The Pure Talent School brochure promises to aid students in every area I'm hoping to improve:

- Dance Instruction
- How to Be the Star in Your Club
- Costuming and Music Selection
- Pole Techniques
- Stage Presence

There's also less-urgent instruction in makeup, diet, fitness, and financial planning. Pure Talent is not an inexpensive school—the five-day course costs 750 dollars. But if I come away looking less like a goof onstage, it'll be worth it.

The last week in January, I kiss Randy goodbye at the curb at Denver International. I land in Tampa, hauling with me a small carry-on bag of regular clothes and Randy's hockey duffel stuffed with costumes. The duffel almost wrenches my arm out of the socket when I throw it over my shoulder at the baggage carousel. While I wait at the rental car counter, I keep the bag on the floor and move it along with me by nudging it with my foot.

In line behind a dozen harried businessmen in wrinkled suits and tourist families with mountains of luggage, I'm fidgeting foot to foot, nervous because the Journey Has Begun. But I'm glad, too, to get under way after planning for so long. I grab the keys and drag my bags across the paved parking lot to my nerdy economy car. The evening is soft and warm, like the breath of a child—a welcome relief from the dry cold of home. The Wyoming winter is an endurance test—winds gust at night with such force they wake me out of a dead sleep and the storms fell trees, overturn semi trucks, and make a mockery of any snow fence. There is no Currier and Ives cuteness, very little to charm you through the long dark months. I'm so pleased to be in some friendly air for a change. Driving across the Courtney Campbell Causeway at sunset, my eyes move toward the horizon as the sky goes baby blue to pink to purple to the blue-black water of the bay.

While in Florida, I am staying with my friend Jeanette's parents, who moved down from New Jersey eight years ago. Jeanette and I met in gym class on the first day of our junior year in high school. A world-traveled Bronx girl, she had just transferred from Memphis, Tennessee. As a spectral white, six-three redhead dressed in head-to-toe black with three earrings in each ear, she stuck out like a sore thumb among the Jersey girls, buffy and blonde-highlighted from their days down the shore. So did I, having spent the last day of summer vacation on my friend Laurie's bedroom floor, bleaching out my hair. We sat down next to each other in the stands and became instant allies. For the next two years, we were the ringleaders of our school's small band of freaks, salving each other's wounds, shaving each other's head, and trying to stay out of trouble. We succeeded. Most of the time.

Jeanette flew in from Los Angeles to meet me at her parents' house, where she and her mother, Cathy, come to the door and fold me into a huge hug. Cathy is the quintessential cool mom—her home has always been a refuge, noisily exotic with Indonesian shadow puppets, carved fruitwood screens, and a continuous march of far-flung friends dropping in for dinner, dessert, or a poker game. I knew I could state my Florida business without fear of judgment or pesty inquiry. When I told her about the school for strippers she thought it was hilarious, and rolled out the red carpet.

"You don't get to wear a hot-pink sequined cap and gown at the graduation, do you?" she asks hopefully.

I wish.

The first day of school, I drive across the causeway with an escort of pelicans circling overhead.

Tampa Bay—famous for its beaches, famous for its strip clubs!

That's the station I.D. of a local classic rock station. Florida has the third highest concentration of strip clubs in the country, and the Tampa/St. Pete area is particularly dense. Amidst the well-groomed subdivisions with names like Harbor Woods and Grove Estates, the strip malls, and the beaches with powdered-sugar sand are more than twenty-five clubs. Down on Dale Mabry is the most famous of all—the rather appallingly named Mons Venus. Mons' notoriety stems from a unique blend of world-class babes and nasty action— two elements that are generally mutually exclusive in the strip club universe. These gorgeous girls do totally nude, full-grind lap dances with ample fondling privileges, making a visit to Mons something of a rite of passage for the adventurous club gourmand.

The school is held at a much tamer place—a tony gentleman's club right off Route 60 called Scarlett's. Class starts at noon, and the club doesn't open until five, so we'll have the run of the place while we study.

Twelve of us sit in fancy armchairs placed in a semicircle around a far corner of the stage. You'd never peg us as exotic dancers, in our sweatsuits and street wear, sipping from paper cups of coffee or drawing deeply on cigarettes. We greet each other nervously, then take out our pens and notebooks as a very pregnant woman sits down on the side of the stage and introduces herself. She is Ann Marie Hayek, the owner of the Pure Talent agency.

School is in session.

Ann Marie, a wholesomely pretty blonde with an easy, deep-dimpled smile, used to be a dancer herself, touring the country with a dance revue she booked and managed called the Dream Girl Centerfolds. Now thirty-five, she minds the careers of sixty feature dancers who travel all over doing week-long guest stints at various clubs.

"I want to congratulate you on being committed to your careers and coming here," she says in a measured, kindergarten teacher voice. "I'd like you to introduce yourself, tell us where you're from, whether you're working now or not, and what you hope to get out of attending this school."

There are two classes of stripper—the house dancer and the feature entertainer. House dancers are the bread-and-butter girls of stripping. House dancers (or house girls) typically work in one club for a six-to eight-hour shift. Some clubs pay house dancers a nominal hourly wage; however, most dancers are treated like independent contractors and work only for tips. Sometimes house dancers, like me, turn into "road girls" and move between clubs, but most stay put. Features are a more exotic breed of exotic dancer. Most start out as house girls and evolve into features when they hear the call of the road—and the money. Features travel the country booking into clubs for limited engagements—from three days to a week. Features receive special publicity, perform choreographed and costumed theme routines, earn a weekly rate which varies depending on their professional profile, and can earn extra money by selling promotional merchandise like autographed Polaroids taken with customers, videos they have appeared in, and posters. A top feature earns much more than a house dancer; however, her initial investment in costumes, props, and merchandise is much greater, and the travel can be exhausting. The Pure Talent class is evenly divided between house dancers and working and aspiring features.

Veronica and Page are two young girls from North Carolina—both corn-fed, with long, wavy light brown hair. They've only been dancing for six months, they drawl out slowly, and they both want to learn better stage technique.

Angela, a local, is married with two kids. Pushing her blonde bangs back with one hand, she shyly tells everyone she's never danced professionally before, but plans to start once she's through with the course.

Dark-haired Alisha worked for six years at Jill's in Wheeling, West Virginia. She says she loves dancing.

"Why?" Ann Marie wants to know.

"Because it's like a party," Alisha replies. All eyes are upon her while she speaks, as she's so uncommonly lovely. With wide, dark blue eyes set deep in her demure, heart-shaped face, she has the quietly devastating beauty of Vivien Leigh. She now works in Fort Lauderdale and hopes to learn new dance steps.

Thumper—"Yes, it's my real name"—has worked as a dancer for five years. She's transitioning into being a feature entertainer and wants to learn how to be more theatrical. This coltish, twenty-three-year-old redhead will also be our pole tricks instructor.

Lexus, lithe and blonde-bobbed, took dance classes as a child. In a rich, husky voice that's quite startling coming from her pale, cheerleader-cute countenance, she says she started dancing in Philadelphia and now works in central Pennsylvania. Her goal is to learn the basics of transitioning from house dancer to feature.

Anna, like me, is one of the older girls in the class. Her gypsy-green eyes are lined in smudged black kohl, giving her the desultory look of a veteran rock goddess. After clasping her small lips carefully around a menthol cigarette while lighting it, she says she's been dancing for eleven months in Kentucky. She wants to increase her self-confidence.

Teresa, a shy and curvy brunette, speaks so softly we can hardly hear her. Ann Marie takes pains to smile warmly at her and coax her to speak up. She danced four years ago in Tampa until her daughter was born. She's not dancing right now, she says, but hopes to return to the business.

Holly, seasoned as a house dancer, is just getting her feature career started. She's a classic spitfire—long red hair, tiny on the bottom and bodacious on top. She's a thirty-year-old married mother of two and her husband, a cheerful, stocky Mexican in thick, black-framed glasses, is sitting by her side. They drove here from their home in Texas, and can only stay for four days of school, because Holly is booked at a club in Flint, Michigan, next week.

Gabrielle is a very thin woman with matte black hair and piercing blue eyes. Feature dancing is in her sights. In her four-and-a-half years in the business, she has worked in Texas, Michigan, and Florida. She now lives in the area and is chauffeuring Lexus around for the week.

My turn: "I'm Barbie. I'm going to spend a year dancing my way around the country. I used to be a house dancer, and now that I'm getting back into it, I decided to come here because when I was doing it way back when, I was never very good."

When we're finished, Ann Marie introduces our dance instructor, Jade Simone Sinclair. Jade, deeply tanned with rippled abs smartly showcased between white hip-slung sweat pants and a yellow jog bra, has an irrepressible boingy quality. Her brown bushy ponytail bobs as she addresses her students. "I just want you to know that I was once a house girl just like y'all."

(She's from Texas.)

"I have made all the mistakes you can make. I have fallen flat on my butt onstage. I have tripped. I have nothing to hide from y'all, because we're in this together. We're going to have a lot of fun this week, and I'm here to help you in any way that I can." She smiles as she speaks, the corners of her mouth pinched and straining in affable flexion.

We go over the different types of dances:

Strip-o-grams and bachelor parties—usually a choreographed routine done either solo or with another dancer in a private setting. A set fee is usually charged for a certain predetermined amount of time (half an hour to two hours). Then dancers can take tips from partygoers for additional acts, such as whipped-cream shows, lotion shows, or lap dances. Contact and specialty shows should be discussed up front. Dancers often hire their own security for parties.

Stage—dancing on the stage in a club, either solo or with other dancers, for one to three songs while patrons watch. Customers may or may not be able to tip dancers personally. If they can, rules vary as to where they may put the tips (on the stage, in your hand, in a garter around your thigh, under your g-string, between your breasts), depending on the club's policy.

Table—a one-on-one dance between you and a customer, either in the public, main floor area of the club or in a private VIP section. Usually done while standing in front of the customer, on a platform by the table, or in the space between the customer's feet. Body contact may or may not be permitted, but usually it is limited to leaning your hands on his shoulders or knees for balance.

Lap/Couch/Bed—these are "friction" or "contact" dances, where the dancer rubs her body along the customer's, either by sitting in the customer's lap, straddling him, sliding against him while standing, or, as in the bed dance, lying down. I tune out the description since I've already decided that I'm not working in any contact clubs. But "bed dance" is a new one to me—sounds very extreme. Yikes.

After a half hour for lunch, Jade gets onstage, bounces on her toes, and claps her hands together. "Now let's get you moving!"

We stand in two rows on the stage and practice our walk. One at a time, we travel the length of the stage toward Jade, who stands at the end, coaching.

She calls us baby doll, honey, cutie pie, and babe.

"Okay now, cutie, as you come toward me, I want y'all to give me hips and eyes. It's all about the eyes."

"That's right, baby doll, work that butt. You've got a great butt—slow and sensual now."

"Honey, great walk! Very high energy! Ooh, I can tell, honey, you've been on the runway before!"

"Now slow down, slow down, baby girl. You're going to be my Mae West. Make them work for it. Slide your hands down your belly. Yes!"

When it's my turn, I walk toward her, dragging my toes, moving as slowly as I can. I bring my eyes up from the floor to meet her gaze and wink.

She slaps my arm playfully and says, "That's it, cutie pie, you're going to be in my next video!"

By the end of the first day, we're much more relaxed. Jade flirted us right out of our defenses—no wonder she earns enough as a dancer to buy a new luxury car every year!

When I get to Jeanette's parents' house after dinner, I fall dead asleep.

• • •

On the second day Jade teaches us a few simple dance steps, then we break out our costumes and perform onstage, just as if we were working in a club. The deejay drops in to cue up our music and introduce each of us before we dance, as is usually done. Everyone looks petrified—this isn't dancing for a bunch of horny, tipsy men who are just grateful to watch women ready and willing to strip down, regardless of skill. This is being exposed before a jury of our peers, the naked-in-the-classroom nightmare come true. We know the difference between good striptease and bad, and if our pinched moves, chewed lips, and wooden smiles are any indication, I'd say every one of us is afraid of coming up short.

In my black-and-silver minidress and silver stilettos, I clod-hop around the stage to a Crystal Method song, stiff and self-conscious like the rest of the girls. Scary as this may be, it's a good sight more efficient than the typical "learn as you go" means of learning to strip: First an aspiring dancer needs to dredge up the nerve to get onstage in the first place, quieting the anxious "what if" questions ("What if someone I know sees me?/I look like an idiot?/my parents find out?") with visions of heaps of cash on the stage, or maybe a few stiff drinks. Then, once she's worked awhile, she crafts a profitable image and over time, the moves are finessed. All of this is fostered through observation, dressing-room tutelage, trial and error, and practice, practice, practice. Any scared, awkward girl will get slick and smooth if she keeps at it long enough.

When I get in the car after school, I yank off my hairpiece. I open the windows to get some cool air on my itchy scalp. At an intersection, I glance over and see Lexus and Gabrielle in the next lane. They look at me funny, trying to figure out if I'm the girl they know from class. I pick up my hairpiece and shake it at them. They laugh, the light changes and we turn off in opposite directions.

• • •

On the radio is a song I used to dance to all the time. The deejay comes on: "That was by Madonna, released ten years ago this week." It can't be . . . the song doesn't seem that old. Then it hits me. My god, it *has* been ten years. In stripping things can change overnight, and a girl can reach obsolescence even faster than that. Ten years. And so much has changed, especially outside the business. Most notably, being a stripper isn't such a big deal anymore. Maybe this is because every other video on MTV has strippers in it. Or maybe the claims of massive moral decay are true, and decadence-wise, stripping seems like relatively small potatoes. Or maybe we can thank Courtney Love. I don't know. But in the past decade the stripper seems to have gone from a social outcast to a thonged "whatever." The strip club business is booming. The publisher of the *Exotic Dancer Bulletin* estimates that there are 250,000 exotic dancers working today. And the number of clubs in the United States has skyrocketed to roughly 2,500, an increase of almost 30% since the late 1980s.

When I get back to Jeanette's house, she's at the glass-topped mahogany breakfast table with her mom, younger brother, and neighbor, playing poker.

"How was school today, dear?" She looks up from her hand. There's a pile of nickels on the tabletop, next to her red plastic tumbler of juice.

"Let me show you what I learned!" With my hands on my hips, I attempt the kick-ball-step combination Jade taught us. Kick your right foot, step quickly onto the ball of your left, then step out to the side with the right.

Jeanette laughs, auburn ringlets bouncing. "What the hell is that? *Riverdance*?"

"No, wait, wait, let me take off my shoes." Clunk, clunk go my black suede platform slides on the terra-cotta tile.

Kick-ball-step. Now it looks even worse because I can't blame the shoes. The neighbor looks at me as if I've just fallen from the trees.

"Stripper school," Jeanette explains.

"Ah," he says, eyeing me warily.

Tomorrow will be better.

Scarlett's is an "upscale" club. The nicer places aren't billed as "classy" anymore. Managers of clubs that court white-collar clientele are style conscious enough to get with the vernacular of the times. "Classy" is a blue-chinned guy with a half-chewed cigar in his mouth saying, "Hey, honey, fix your eye patch before you go onstage. This is a classy place!" "Classy" is a Classy Lady T-shirt. "Classy" is, basically, a KICK-ME sign.

At Scarlett's, the lighting is low and sultry like a jazz club, dark cloths cover the tables, the carpet and upholstery are immaculate, and the main stage that spans the room's center has a transparent square in the middle so you can see down to the elegant foyer below. It's a very nice touch, but we have to be very careful when we do our routines because there's a nonlevel seam between the wood and the Plexiglas. One of the girls in class already tripped on it once.

On day three, Jade teaches us a portion of a routine to the Commodores' "Brick House"—a series of cross-steps and side-steps. She leads us across the stage in formation and we waddle behind like baby ducks after Mama. But the real lesson of the day is eye contact. The class manual reads: "You have to fully understand why men come to a club to begin with. They want to see beautiful women, fantasize about them, and enjoy conversation with them. They want you to pay attention to them."

So as we all get ready for our individual stage time, we're told to "push our personalities out." We're reminded: It's all about the smile and the eyes.

I do full Barbie drag onstage: platinum hairpiece down to my behind. Hot pink gown and thong, clear Lucite platforms, rhinestone choker, and earrings. Pink beach towel with a cartoon Barbie framed by starfish, shells, and a couple sea horses, to lie down on when I do my floor work. False eyelashes, frosted lipstick. The whole bit.

Our dancing goes much better today—we're all more confident. Over the music, everyone whistles and cheers each other on. Stripping is hard and we know it's hard, and flattery is a critical lubricant. We're used to affirmation in cash and here we get none, so a kind word goes a long way. When a girl gets offstage someone says, "You look so great up there, I can't believe you haven't danced in four years," or "Wow, there is no way anyone could tell you haven't done this before." Ann Marie sits with her feet resting on the side of the stage, smiling as she takes notes on a yellow legal pad. Jade sits by her side, watching us, giving lascivious winks or an occasional thumbs-up.

I'm particularly excited because this is pole-work day. Thumper leads us over to the small—tiny, really—stage in the corner, the only one with a pole on it. She teaches us how to shinny up the pole ("Don't do this in a dress or in bare feet. You need your skin and the shoes for traction"), cross your legs around the pole, then lean backward and slide down.

This looks really stupid when inexpertly done. As I find out firsthand.

"Lean back, I'll spot you!" Thumper commands, coming in close.

"Uh . . . ," I say, trying to cross one leg over the other way up there. I'm suddenly aware that I'm wearing nothing but heels, a thong, and a torn-up old bra. I look at myself in the mirror and try not to wince at the range of cellulite puckering up where my thighs strain against the pole.

"No, really, do it! Lean back."

"Thank God clubs aren't lit like this all the time," I say, stalling for time as I wrinkle my nose at my reflection.

"Would you just *do* it?" Thumper huffs like a fourth-grader issuing a decree from her official position as Queen of the Treehouse.

I lean back and the skin on my inner thighs makes a terrible noise—-*squeeeeeeeeeeeeee*—against the pole as I slide slowly down.

The second trick goes better—grabbing the pole at mid-chest level, kicking my legs up over my head, spreading them, and sliding to the stage upside down—because I already know how to do it. My only decent stunt.

But Thumper teaches me a twist: While upside down, I hook my ankles behind the pole, move my arm down the pole toward the floor, and flip around so I'm facing the pole. Then I put my hands on the stage and slide down head first.

Very cool.

"You can also push yourself back up the pole and wiggle down like an inchworm," she says.

I try the first variation again and lose my grip, almost landing right on my face.

Think I'll save the inchworm thing for later.

As the makeup artist lectures us how to do hair and cosmetics for the stage, Ann Marie and Jade call us out to the hall one at a time for our evaluations. I know they're not going to tell me anything nasty—would you say something bad to someone who paid 750 bucks to take your class? Still, I dread my turn.

"Well, Barbie . . ." Ann Marie begins.

Oh God. She's going to tell me to give it up. I'm a heinous geek. A has-been and never-was all at once.

"We just can't believe you haven't been dancing all this time. You move so well."

My cheeks are burning.

Jade nods. "You know what you remind us of?"

I shrug, smiling.

"Did you ever see *Austin Powers*? You know those FemBots? You remind us of them."

My heart thumps, threatening to leap right out of my chest. A FemBot. Retro. Girly. Plasticky. Lethal. Yes. I couldn't be more flattered if they'd compared me with a Bond girl.

Ann Marie agrees, "It's clear you have your look *down*. Maybe, though, you could try to harden your appearance a bit sometimes."

I'm sure what they're saying is just to build me up, but, hey, that's the point and it's working. The sloppy, brittle-tough image I retain of myself is shrinking to an insignificant dot.

I float out of class on a Barbie-pink cloud.

Day four. Time to learn how to crawl. I remember watching a man teach models how to walk on the runway. The opposite leg and shoulder should move forward at the same time: right leg, left shoulder. Left leg, right shoulder. The same thing applies to a crawl: left knee comes forward at the same time as your right hand. We all try this, at Jade's urging, followed by rolling over onto our backs and arching into sexy, statuesque poses, then sitting up. My lower back cracks and pops. I slide my fingers along the floor behind me as I sit up, arched and aching.

When it's time for individual shows, Alisha struts onstage in a suit, tie, and fedora. Once she's stripped of all but her necktie and hat, she takes off the tie, threads it between her legs, wraps it around her hips, and tucks in the end, fashioning a g-string. Jade taught us how to do this, and when she sees Alisha execute the trick perfectly, she looks so honest-to-god happy I think she might cry. Jade has been such a good teacher this week, coaxing the shy students like

Angela and Melissa, slowing down the fast ones like Lexus and Holly, and making each of us feel good about our personal style—be it glamorous, innocent, or nasty. Considering that one aspiring feature entertainer in the class was taught exotic dance by a woman so mean she earned the nickname "Hitler in Heels," we're very lucky to have had such expert instruction.

I only half-listen to the afternoon's lecture from the personal trainer because I've decided to blow off fussing over the minutiae of diet and fitness while I'm on the road. I know how I get when I dance, stressing every ounce, every angle—a typical impulse, I realize, since you're severely naked out there and have plenty of time in the dressing room and onstage to compare and get overcritical—but I don't want to get sucked backed into that nit-picky trap. I've decided to try limiting my body anxiety to worrying about my tan and my nails—two things I can easily control, two areas of maintenance that seem reasonable. I've already watched one of my classmates pick all the meat out of her sandwich at lunch and throw away the bread ("I only eat carbs once a week," she said to the girl next to her), and I don't want to get crazy about weights and measures. I've got too many other things I want to pay close attention to, things far more important than the ever-changing state of my ass.

Day Five: Graduation Day. The girls who want to do another routine change into costume and get up onstage, but I am pretty sore from dancing three days in a row for the first time in forever, so I sit this one out.

The lecture for today addresses the topic of "longevity in a short-lived business." The gist of Ann Marie and Jade's advice: Think of yourself as a professional athlete. Save your money, because you've got a short run at this. I don't know that the idea sinks in with the younger girls but Holly agrees, saying, "The first day you work is when you should start saving for your last."

At the end of the afternoon, Ann Marie and Jade call us up one by one so Ann Marie can hand each of us a completion certificate. Afterward we crowd together while Ann Marie's husband, Jim, a smart-looking fellow in chinos, an Oxford cloth shirt, and silver wire-framed glasses, snaps a class photo. I hold my certificate in my hands, admiring the smart black plastic frame and my stage name printed on it. "Barbie Faust" is official. Credentialed, even. For me, this is a first. When I was seventeen, I received my high school diploma from an adult education program in the mail, rolled up in a cardboard tube. I unrolled the sheet of fake parchment, looked it over once, and stuffed the diploma back in the tube. I threw the tube in the lower cabinet of the teak secretary in my parents' living room, and that was that. This is as close as I've ever come to a graduation ceremony.

I'm ready to head out into the world. I think.

FOUR

Pueblo, Colorado

Spring comes to Wyoming, bringing with it the fattest robins I have ever seen. Unsure how to balance their great weight, they bobble around the yard and take to resting on the fence along the driveway. When they aren't in repose, they work over the ground, pecking for worms. One damp, gray mid-April afternoon, I count more than a dozen robins between the back door and the garage, their plump red chests in stark contrast to the leaden sky and the trees still just in bud. I don't know how they manage to fly, they're so heavy—more than two sitting together bow the telephone wire that runs from the main line to the house.

Randy and I celebrate the season by getting our own bike, a beautiful '74 shovelhead that we bought off of a wiry retired Air Force engineer named Sam. His back could no longer withstand the jarring ride of a hardtail, so we took the rickety old growler off his hands. Riding, I come to find, isn't easy for me, either. The bike is a noble beast, but lands so hard that whenever we come up to a bump in the road, Randy yells "Bump!" over his shoulder so I can post up by bracing against the foot pegs to spare my cervical vertebrae the distress of my head slamming into my neck with the force of a big fat pumpkin pitched from a rooftop.

We spend the first warm evening of the year riding out Happy Jack Road to the lakes. A small herd of antelope graze on a low rise in the distance, then take off at a quick spring when they hear the bike rumbling up. In a few weeks these slopes will bloom with thousands of tiny purple and blue wildflowers. Twenty miles west of the city, the plains end and the road ramps into the mountains, where Granite Springs reservoir sits glassy and undisturbed a mile outside the entrance to Medicine Bow National Forest. The late day sun slants through the pines, mingling orange light and black shadow on the pebbly ground.

Tall reeds grow at the lake's edge. We walk around the rim in silence, holding hands and searching for flat rocks to skip across the water.

"Are you all packed?" Randy asks me, skipping a rock off the surface of the lake, *plip plip plip*.

"More or less. I still need to get a padlock and some no-slip things for my shoes."

We settle into a weighty silence, both preoccupied with feelings too complicated to articulate.

I am leaving for the first round of clubs tomorrow afternoon.

After several weeks of poring over maps, combing Web sites and trade magazines, and culling recommendations from my dancer friends across the country, I've a loosely fashioned itinerary. I'm starting with a short, four-stop road trip: Pueblo, Colorado, to Las Vegas, then Dallas and El Paso, Texas. Later on in the summer, I plan on flying to the Exotic World Museum in California. Then at the end of August, Randy and I will fly up to Alaska. I had originally fancied making the entire journey by myself, but one night I was at the Outlaw talking with Rob, a guy on Randy's wild horse racing team. "Let me get this right," Rob said, shaking his head good-naturedly and rubbing the buzzed blond hairs on the back of his neck, "You want to go off to Alaska by yourself? To strip. Where there's big outdoorsy guys everywhere and all that oil money?" Rob brushed a wisp of beer foam from his mustache and cracked his straight white teeth, laughing. "Let me tell you, if I were Randy, there is no way in hell I'd let that happen."

Rob was right. Once Alaska was on the table, there was no way around Randy's resistance. So I cashed in my frequent flier miles, got him a ticket, budgeted more time so we could sightsee, and called it our working vacation.

I'll take most of the fall off, as that's my high season as a journalist, then when it gets colder and Randy's work slows down, I can explore the clubs of New Jersey around Thanksgiving and Randy can fly out for the holiday with my family. Jeanette invited me out to Los Angeles to tour the clubs, so come winter, when Wyoming starts to get miserable, I'll go out California way and warm up a little. In between stops, I can investigate the two Cheyenne clubs: the Green Door, the little go-go place downtown, and the Clown's Den, the topless honky-tonker way down South Greeley Highway, on the Colorado state line. This venture is going to be bloody expensive, even if I stay on the Motel 6 strata. I need to make this quest break even. Thankfully, stripping is a lucrative sinecure. That's what brought me to it in the first place, heaven knows.

Traffic on 25 South is a mess—there are five substantial jams between Aurora and Colorado Springs. By the time I hit Pueblo, two hours behind schedule, I've had enough time idling in the truck to put on my makeup, plus the hairpiece.

Aloha Glorya's is on North Main Street in downtown Pueblo, a discreet façade that blends right in with the other storefronts. My lateness is a blessing because I'm in too much of a hurry to be nervous. I pull open the heavy front door, and with my costume bag over my shoulder, I stride right in.

The club is a cute little party box, a single room with diamond tuck wall covering, carved wood tiki statues adorning the bar, and blue and pink streaks in the carpet that glow under the black light. And dark, of course. They're all so very dark. It's as if light would stall the growth cycle of whatever's seeded in these places and must be banished. Directly across from the entrance, in a carpeted conversation pit, a petite, dusky-skinned girl rolls around on a low, circular vinyl-topped table. She's topless, with diminutive, brown-nippled breasts that pay gravity no mind. She shifts onto all fours, then sits back on her heels so the flesh of her haunches dimples unprettily, as a bearded middle-aged man in a John Deere cap sits watching with his hands pressed between his knees. She looks back at him over her shoulder, her expression pleading in its sexiness and disdainful all at once, and he places a twenty-dollar bill on the table, delighted.

I smile at this tableau, so fleeting and familiar, with her showing more than she means to, him only seeing what he wants anyway, and the grace encircling them both for their respective show of will.

A thin man with a wiry gray mustache materializes out of the darkness. "Can I help you?" The silver steer skull bolo tie fastened loosely under his collar glimmers, catching the light from the horseshoe-shaped bar to the right of us.

Shifting my costume bag on my shoulder, I force a brighter smile. Out of my mouth comes an automatic phrase that I haven't uttered in a long, long time. "Yes, I'd like to audition."

• • •

I wonder if the good folks at McDonald's have any idea of their significance in the lives of strippers. Whatever the situation—whether someone is picking on you for your choice of job, or you're sick of dancing and need to convince yourself that it's worth coming in to work—the justification of choice is, "Well, it beats working at McDonald's!" I've never worked at McDonald's, or any fast-food restaurant, so I can only assume that this is true. I have, however, had a number of tedious, ass-busting jobs, mostly when I was in high school: cleaning lady, supermarket cashier, department store clerk. So I know a bit about scraping people's crap off of toilets, wearing mildly humiliating smocklike uniforms, and shuffling and refolding product for an indifferent corporation. I also know about trading all that for a job where you can make in one night what you used to earn in a week, or a month. Or two months. When you consider the sacrifices of social stature, privacy, and peace of mind, it is a rather big trade-off to make, but when the choice is limited to a McDonald's-type job or stripping, I can't fault a woman for making the money decision. I sure wouldn't mind making bank tonight.

The manager shows me to the stairway leading up to the dressing room. As I climb the stairs, my anxiety mounts. Although I've not had the displeasure of the experience, I've heard about clubs where the girls run off newcomers, not wanting their money threatened or their turf encroached upon. I hope things will be okay if I enter in low-relief. When I meet the women who work here, I will smile, self-deprecate, and dispense compliments like a salesman hands out business cards.

The dressing room is actually three—a large room with a long table and chairs, a smaller room fitted with a deeply gouged, double-sided mirrored vanity, and a locker room that's the size of a large closet. Two women sit at the vanity, smoking cigarettes. They both turn to look at me.

"Hi," says one, a skinny girl with a choppy brunette bob. She has homemade tattoos on either shoulder—a four-leaf clover with LUCKY inked in uneven hand beneath it on the left, and a letter *C* on the right. "Are you new?"

"Yeah, I just came in for an audition. How's the money here?" I say, pointing to the chair next to hers.

Lucky nods for me to take the seat. "Sucks," she says, stubbing out her cigarette in a fluted plastic ashtray.

"No way, really?" I pull a couple dresses from my bag. The black minidress with the mirrored squares on the front, the minidress with the bugs.

"I worked yesterday from three o'clock until midnight and made three fuckin' dollars."

My eyes widen. "You're joking, right? It couldn't have been that bad." I pull my sweatshirt over my head and take off my jeans. "Which dress?" I ask, holding them both up.

"The bugs. And I'm serious. Three dollars. You would not believe how slow it's been here lately. I usually make good money when my regular comes in, but he's in jail."

"My doctor guy is supposed to come in tonight," interjects her friend, Kitten, a short, plump redhead with fine lines at the corner of her mouth. "I really hope he does. He hasn't come in for two weeks and I am seriously hurting."

When I stand up in just my underwear to pull on the dress, Lucky looks me over, fumbling with an unlit Salem. Her fingernails are covered in acrylic tips painted with chipping red polish. Two tips are missing, the underlying nails bare and ragged. "You've got a good body," she says, coolly. "You're nice and thick."

Here we go. Back to the arena where every aspect of my body is up for scrutiny. I'm not skinny, and without dieting, I never will be. So I don't know why having this pointed out bothers me so much. "Thick" isn't an insult, I guess. It's just not what I want to hear.

"I could do better," I say, steering the appraisal back to her. "I wish I were thin like you."

She observes her reflection in the mirror, turning to the side, placing her hands on her plainly visible ribs. I'm the size of two of her put together. She seems pleased by what I said.

Slipping my feet into red stiletto heels and straightening my dress, I say, "Well, I guess I'd better get downstairs. I'll see you guys later. If they hire me."

"Of course they'll hire you. Won't they?" Kitten says to Lucky.

"Oh, for sure," Lucky nods, exhaling a plume of mentholated smoke.

Nice girls. Good.

Lucky and Kitten were right. The standard-issue three-song audition on the main stage goes by in a flash: First song in the dress, out of the top by the end of the second song, topless for the third. There are only ten or so women working in the club, and half of them sit at the stage for my audition and tip. The Mexican guys at the tipping rail seem energized by having them in their midst. Hoots and dollar bills all around. When I get offstage the manager tells me I can stay and work for the rest of the night.

There aren't many customers in Aloha Glorya's, so after a couple turns onstage and two hours of absolutely nothing to do except gossip with the other dancers, I head to the bar and ask for a soda.

A beefy middle-aged Asian man in chinos and a polo shirt swivels around on his bar stool. "Hello, I'm Arthur. You must be new!"

I hop up on the bar stool next to his and he buys me a drink. He tells me he stops in every day after work in his manufacturing concern, then proceeds to recite a list of the things he owns—two houses, three Harleys, a customized vintage Corvette. Plus, his business is worth several million dollars. And that, you see, is why he can't divorce his frigid, pain-in-the-neck wife. If he does, she'll get everything. His solution? Rental girlfriends.

He peels off two twenty-dollar bills and puts them under my glass. Then he leans in close, touching my arm. "What would you say to a proposition?"

At this question, something primal stirs inside of me. A long-dormant instinct is waking up and feeling the air. Sandra Dee has left the building and hustle mode has begun.

I rest my hand on his thick, hairless forearm. "What do you have in mind?"

"We could get together sometimes. You wouldn't have to work here. I could put you up someplace and support you. I promise it would be worth your while."

"Hmmmm, interesting!" I say, looking into my drink, smiling slightly. I have no intention of taking him up on his offer, but he doesn't have to know that.

My mind flashes on an earnest women's studies student I once met at a cocktail party. During a conversation about the sex industry, she swirled her vodka violently around in her glass and exhorted, "Well, stripping isn't as hypocritical as the rest of the culture, which denigrates sex but uses it all the time to sell stuff. At least stripping is *honest!*"

I would say that stripping is blatant in its purpose but I wouldn't call it honest. More than anything else, the point on which this business turns is suspension of disbelief. That's show biz. Plato said, "That which deceives may be said to enchant."

At this moment, I am about to become one enchanting motherfucker.

"Oh, that's an intriguing offer, Arthur," I purr, draining my glass, "but I just don't know you well enough."

As if on cue, he pulls out a hundred-dollar bill and slips it under the garter around my thigh. "I've made the same arrangement with a couple of women who've worked here and they've all been very happy. They get some extra money, then go back to where they came from, and it works out well for everybody concerned." He speaks with the money-clip cool of an executive sketching out a business plan.

Now I want to see how far I can push this. If I liked Arthur, I'd be restrained by guilt. I would feel terrible about leading him on and play it clean. But it's hard to work up sympathy for a self-professed serial cheat. I feel almost vindicated taking him for all he's worth. This isn't bilking an old lady out of her pension fund. This is relieving the pressure in a philanderer's obviously straining wallet.

"I'm sure you're a very generous man, Arthur. But so much of what I hear in these clubs is all talk." Careful to suggest but not promise, I am leveraging my Maybe with another woman's Yes—a classic stripper feint. I don't particularly like this part of myself, but I'm impressed by my own audacity. I never attempted such a stunt when I was doing this for a living, I was afraid I'd scare the guy off. Funny how much nervier you can be when it's not for necessity but sport.

Arthur folds up another hundred and presses it into my palm, confidently. "Well," he says, getting up off the bar stool and stretching, "I should skedaddle. It's getting late. You think about what I asked and I'll see you soon."

Not likely, I think, crunching down on an ice cube. I turn round on my bar stool and watch his broad back as he leaves the club. Grimy yellow streetlight shows through the open door.

Considering the setting, I'm not insulted by Arthur's proposition, but by the same token, I'm hardly flattered, because it has nothing to do with me. For Arthur, the art of the deal is key: What do I have to do to buy this girl? It's simple dollar-cost averaging—for every seventy-five girls he drops a couple hundred bucks on who say no, maybe the seventy-sixth will say yes.

I return to the dressing room to patch my makeup and a buxom dancer in a tropical print bikini sidles up to me at the mirror. The furrows in her forehead deepen as she raises her eyebrows, trying to look aggressively neutral. "I saw you sitting with Arthur for a while. He likes you, huh? You'd better watch out."

"Why, what's the deal with him?"

"Oh, he's a total dick," she sneers, fluffing her long poufy wheat-blonde hair with chubby fingers. "He'll pester you forever to screw him and if you give in, he'll be really mean to you from then on."

I tell the girl I'll take what she said under advisement. There's an oft-quoted adage: "When you go to a strip club, you might get screwed, but you won't get fucked." I finger the hundreds wrapped around my garter, feeling scuzzy and superior at the same time.

What surprises me about tonight is not how slow it is or how quickly I get back into the swing of things, but how I feel as if I never left. So many years away and I realize now that I still feel, have felt all this time, like a stripper. Like I fit in. Everything is strangely similar to what I remember, like a childhood home that has remained exactly as it looks in my memory or an old acquaintance whose face has been untouched by time.

All the dancers start filing into the dressing room to get ready for the full-dress introduction. This would be a good time to clear out for the night. Since I just dropped in for an audition, I doubt the manager will care if I want to leave early. The girls crowd into the locker room, zipping each other into dresses and complaining about what a waste of time it is to put on evening gowns and parade across the stage when there's no one out there to be introduced to.

"Ouch!"

I look in the locker room and one girl has another pinned to the floor with her knee and she's biting her ass. The pinned girl is roaring with laughter while her grappling partner tears at the hem of her blue polyester gown with her teeth.

The bitten girl rises up off the floor, grinning and twisting around trying to see her butt cheek. "You fucker," she shrieks, her eyes alight with glee, "you left a mark!"

The stage fee is twenty-five dollars a shift. On my way out the door, I settle with the manager. He asks how I did tonight.

"Okay. But not great. Is this a typical Friday night for your club?"

"It's been slow," he says, apologetically. He opens a notebook ledger to mark down that I've paid.

I steal a quick look at the ledger and see that a number of the girls are running a tab on their stage fees, some as high as a hundred dollars. That means four shifts when they didn't earn enough to part with twenty-five dollars. Assuming it's always this bad, or this bad even half the time, a girl might be better off working at McDonald's after all.

I see it before I even know what I am seeing. The accident, I mean. In the southbound lane of the freeway on the outskirts of Pueblo, the traffic sits at a complete standstill, pale yellow headlights queued up as far as the eye can see. The scene of the crash is eerily still. No sirens, no horns, just the loud diesel chug of a generator running an overhead bank of blinding blue-white disaster lights. The highway is lit up like a football stadium. An unintelligible voice crackles over the radio in one of the squad cars.

All three lanes are covered in broken glass. A red sedan, every window smashed. The front end accordioned almost to the backseat, it faces backward in the lane. A tow truck waits on the side of the road to load and haul it away. A silver hatchback, the rear and passenger side totally crumpled, rests on the bed of another tow truck. In the center lane, stretched horizontally across, a putty-colored tarp drapes over a long, narrow form. I squeeze my eyes shut for a second and clutch at my chest. That's a body under there.

I want to get off the freeway immediately. I spot a motel with a VACANT sign a couple hundred yards ahead so I take the next exit and double back on the frontage road. I sign in and drive around the outbuildings scanning for my room number. Just my luck, the building with my room in it is located at the very end of the long parking lot—right across the highway from the crash site. Half the motel room doors stand open, and a group of children gathers at the concrete guardrail to watch the emergency crew clean up the wreck. Standing in a row, barely tall enough to see over the divider, their faces are blasted to a featureless white by the intense light, their heads like turnips lined up on a garden fence.

The parking lot is full of old camper trailers and station wagons loaded down with hastily packed possessions—clothes stuffed in plastic trash bags, pots and pans in cardboard boxes, heaps of grotty toys.

I flick on the light, a single lightbulb screwed into an ancient four-bulb ceiling fixture. The room is just as depressing as the scene outside. I should have asked to see it first, but I was in such a panic from seeing the accident I didn't think. Cigarette burns pock the bedspread and the television cable is torn from the wall. Fist-sized dents mark the plaster walls, and the door has no chain, sliding bolt, or deadlock.

That the Reagan-era bone-colored telephone works seems a miracle. I punch my calling card numbers on the sticky gray pushbuttons. Now I'm only eleven digits from home. Randy picks up on the first ring, which makes me smile.

"You took the phone into bed, didn't you?" I say after I hear his eager hello.

"Are you kidding? Of course I did. How are you? *Where* are you?"

"I'm in Pueblo. At the Misery Motel," I crack, trying to come across light. I don't want to sound like a girl crying to Daddy because she skinned her knee.

"Are you going to be okay staying there?"

"Mmm, yeah," I fib, not wanting to alarm him.

He sounds assured, ready to shift gears. "How'd you do tonight?"

"Oh, you would *not* believe it. Awful! Awful, awful, awful. Like two hundred bucks and I think I did better than anyone there."

"Of course you did!"

Aww!

I hear a whisper of sheets. He's changing position. "So," he hesitates, "did you meet anybody?"

Meet anybody? Oh, the poor guy. I'm not the only one having a tough night.

"No"—I drop my voice down to the comfort register—"of course not. I miss you and I'm sorry you're not here."

"I love you,"

"Love you, too."

"Miss you,"

"Same here."

"Bye."

How strange those words sound. So safe. Routine. Simple. They make the distance between us seem greater. I place the receiver back in the cradle. A seam of icy white shines between the stiff, nicotine-stained drapes.

Love you. Miss you. Bye.

Perched warily on the side of the bed, I hear the generator hum from the crash site. The air in the room tastes like suicide. I feel a guilty stab of self-recrimination about the awfulness of the room, the guiltiness magnified by the absurdity of such a feeling when there's a dead person lying two hundred yards away.

I find my bearings and regroup. I cannot spend the night here alone. I will find a nicer place up the road and leave for Las Vegas first thing in the morning.

FIVE

Las Vegas, Nevada

Susan Sontag is wrong—there is only taste, and Vegas. It's a 24-7 excursion of neon-lashed moral vacuity, God bless it, and no place typifies the soul of this town—or lack thereof—better than Cheetah's. Every man I know who's been there—whether he's infatuated with strippers or is the more common curious skeptic—has had an absolute blast, so I figure why not me, too? Cheetah's was made famous as the nudie springboard for Nomi Malone, the googly-eyed sex whippet in the film *Showgirls*. But it's not a fully nude club, as I discover. In fact, dancers at this open-24-hours establishment have to wear two g-strings, to keep any errant pubic hairs from peeking out and giving pissed-off vice cops an excuse to yank the club's liquor license.

If you want to work in a strip club or a casino in Las Vegas, you need a sheriff's card. To get a card, a club has to hire you and give you an application signed by a manager. Then you bring your paperwork and I.D. down to the office on Fremont Street, take a number, and wait. And wait. Standing in line, number in hand, with all the aspiring blackjack dealers, casino maids, and bartenders, the strippers are easy to spot—we're the only ones in full hair and makeup at nine in the morning. The reason why the line is slow goes something like this: "I'm sorry, Mr. McGilicuddy, but you need to list *all* of your arrests in the past seven years. You only listed the one in 1995, and we can see in the database that you have eight more." I've never had to register with the sheriff anyplace I've worked, and even though I've never been convicted of a crime, I'm paranoid that I won't pass muster for some reason. Then a man comes in wearing a maroon sweatshirt on his head as a do-rag, and a backward pastel seashell-print hospital gown over a grey trench coat and he gets a card, so I figure I'm in the clear. I hand over my paperwork, pay my thirty-five bucks, get a mug shot taken, and give them a full set of fingerprints. By the time I scrub off the printing ink with the citrus-scented granular hand cleanser, my laminated card is ready and I am good to go in Vegas.

Cheetah's is literally all smoke and mirrors, and there must be at least sixty women working the floor tonight. Here's a foxy Mexican girl in hot pants, lace-up boots, a baseball cap over her luxurious ponytail, and a baby-T that says SEXY. A perky, cropped bumpkinette flounces by in a red-and-white gingham Daisy Mae bikini while two Jheri-girls mingle in rainbow-striped Day-Glo hip huggers and matching calypso tops. There are lots of implants here, some of which look lumpen and sad, others that have an admirable impudent thrust. Real breasts may have more cachet, but they're so squishy and vulnerable looking, I wonder sometimes if it wouldn't be nice to have a few inches of saline and silicone bubble-wrap as armor between me and the elements.

There's a bacchanalian thump to this place that's irresistible. The deejay slides from techno to rap to disco to heavy metal with ease and sonic acuity. He seems to favor the metal, which I appreciate, since a lot of the upscale clubs won't play anything heavier than Van Halen. Not even Metallica, which blows. To forbid the glorious Wagnerian pomp of Metallica is a gross misread of the male libido— their songs are the most righteous manifestation of testosterone-fueled virtuosity and aggression. The guitar is presented with the same respect that an artist's brush lavishes on an odalisque, and guys go nuts when they see a pretty little girl take on a song as big and brutal as "Enter Sandman." To deprive them of that spectacle is nothing short of a shame.

A commuter class of dancers comes from around the country to work in Vegas, especially during conventions when the city over-flows with expense account money. Tonight, the dressing room is alive with out-of-towners hoping to cash in when the latest batch of corporate junketeers comes out to play. The women compare where they're from—Alaska, Washington, New Hampshire—while they curl their hair, apply their makeup, have a smoke, and in my case, read the rules.

The house rules at Cheetah's specify no grinding, no lap humping, no touching the customer's crotch. But here, as in a lot of clubs, there are two sets of rules—those that they tell you and those that you actually work by. I wedge my way into a leopard-print dress and double-decker g-strings and bound out of the dressing room just in time to see a girl turn away from her customer, place her ankle on his shoulder, and slide her leg back until her crotch is right in his face. How am I to compete with a girl who wraps herself around a man like a jade necklace? I must be radiating nerves, because I can't get a dance to save my life, even though the club is mobbed. Finally, Paulie, a burly body-builder, catches my eye and offers to buy me a drink. I ask him where he's from. Colorado. What's he doing in town? Bachelor party. Has he been here before? No, first time. Then it's my turn. Have you worked here long? No, sure haven't. How old are you?

Do I lie about my age? Honey, I lie about everything. Highly impolitic, I concede, but what about this profession isn't? My job is not to be who I am, but what the average strip club customer wants, and those two things are, I'm resigned to admit, quite different. Sure, some guys might find my loopy urban pedantry attractive, but they aren't the men who frequent strip clubs. Men who come to the clubs want to be soothed, catered to, and stimulated . . . but not too much. The governing principle of stripping is Thou Shalt Not Threaten. So when I dance, I'm not an engaged, cranky ex–punk rocker with a stack of published articles and the larger portion of my twenties behind me. I'm a twenty-six-year-old milk-fed girl from Minneapolis who's come to town to help her sister take care of her newborn. And a Pisces, should you care to ask. All this chicanery has a purpose apart from pleasing the men—it protects me. Like, if they find me repulsive, they're not rejecting the real me, they're rejecting this shimmery tart-let who looks like she sprang fully formed from the head of RuPaul.

Once I'm done with Paulie, I turn away from the table and see a girl reclining in her customer's lap, her head thrown back, her per-fect small breasts vaulting heavenward. As she grinds on him she runs her hands up her torso and pinches her plump, caramel-colored nipples. I stand there riveted to the spot as if I've been struck between the eyes with a poison dart. Not because I'm repulsed, mind you, but because it's just about the sexiest thing I've ever seen. I stare at them for a good long time and then I think, *Man, if I see this every day at work, I'll become seriously demented.* It's sexy the first time, but how long until I see something like that and shrug, So what? I don't want to be inured to lust.

Stripping didn't used to be so touchy-feely, but in the past ten years, it's become a full-contact sport. I understand this evolution from an economic perspective—there are a lot more clubs, hence, a lot more competition, and as stripping becomes more acceptable, local legislations relax. And if adult entertainment thrives by offering something beyond the pale of convention, the look-but-don't-touch fleshiness of today's culture has to be done one better by adult venues and that means hands-on treatment. It makes sense, but I can't lie—if increasing contact is the trend, I worry what the next generation of strippers will have to do to keep up. It's hard enough rearranging your psyche so you can comfortably work half-naked in front of strangers, but touch is something quite apart. Touch changes everything.

Not making any money, and not being willing to do the contact dances to get it, I am left with nothing to do but work myself into a jealous snit. I spend an hour stalking among the tables watching the girls, conjuring up all sorts of hypothetical scenarios in which Randy would choose one of these women over me were he given the chance. I want to throttle the customers, shake the money tree till the very sap flies out. When I complain to two sweaty men in suits that I can't make any money, one of them says, "Well, you need to grab these guys by the crotch to get their attention." He tries for a ribald laugh but it ends up an embarrassed yelp.

I used to be able to do the wild stuff, but in the time I've been away from dancing I've gotten in touch with my inner prude. I don't know if it's because I no longer have the defenses to deal with being touched by a stranger, or that I simply no longer have to do it, but I can't. So realizing this, do I leave the club? No, I do not. Do I pay for it? Yes, I do.

By 1 a.m., I'm wiped out, my quadriceps shrieking and my "no contact" rule torn and bleeding. The table dances here—which are performed only in the center of the club (for privacy, the heavy-contact lap dancing is relegated to the seats at the perimeter of the room and in the VIP area)—are too close for comfort. I pledged to myself that this stripping odyssey would be a break-even proposition, but getting the needle back to zero requires thrusting my breasts into men's faces—not what I'd planned on doing. "Oh yeah, an ambitious girl can get awful beard burn in her cleavage working here," a zaftig British girl sighs sympathetically in the dressing room as she dabs antibacterial ointment on her scratched decolletage. Of course, I could maintain greater distance between myself and the customer, do my table dancing totally clean, but that would mean going home broke. These are very educated consumers, and with dozens of girls only too eager to peddle their wares, the men watch closely and choose with great care.

I could've gone to another club, too, but I picked this one because the reviews sounded fairly conservative. I can't imagine what I might find elsewhere if this is what passes for tame in this town.

I'm consumed by wild hunger, and after settling with the house, I leave Cheetah's in search of food. I decide to try the Stardust. There's elaborate planning behind the layout of casinos—the clocks are hidden and it's very hard to find an exit. This is supposed to encourage people to stay and gamble their lives away, but in my compromised state the crooked unnavigability of the casino floor just makes me want to torch the place. I finally find the Stardust's #@&% coffee shop, which has a cloying tropical theme—it's called the Cranky Parrot or the Rusty Pirate or something. As I wait for my food, I realize I've been ground down by the sleaze factor—it's so obvious that I got in too deep yet I refused to admit it. Dancer-cum-performance artist Jill Morley calls it "go-go head"—you get so amped up on the ego, the money hunt, and the "I can do anything" daring that you don't know when to quit. Hoisting the fork to my lips with a hand heavy as lead, I inhale an entire Prime Rib Special—hot rolls, salad, soup, slab of meat, peas and carrots, mashed potatoes, gravy, giant Diet Coke—in mere minutes. My hunger goes way beyond the physical yet I don't seem to be tasting much. From my fingertips to my taste buds, it appears I've gone quite numb. Then, when I get up to settle my bill, I start to burn. I feel like my skin has been peeled off and I'm transparent; that anyone who looks at me—the waitresses, the man in the hotel lobby, the family in the elevator—can see me for what I really am: a weak and greedy person. Bad Boundary Barbie.

I'm not sure why it is that a bad night stripping is a million times worse than a bad day at any other job. Maybe it's the sinister voice in your head asking you, *if you can't make it doing this, what the hell else is there?*

I head back to my room at the Circus Circus and sink into fitful sleep.

The next morning, I lie on my back on the bed in my rented room, vibrating with a bad case of seller's remorse. Sore and spaced-out, I feel like I've been dropped back into my body from a great height. I'd give anything to take back the night before. Choosing a hotel with a circus motif was a bad call. Wherever I look, I'm assaulted with ominous good cheer—screaming colors, jeering clowns. Every move I make seems like it's accompanied by a laugh track and the toot of taunting calliopes. I spend the early part of the morning trying to work up the energy to walk over to the hotel's Pink Pony coffee shop, but I just can't face the restaurant's bright red carpet with white and pink carousel horses, so I order room service.

I hang my head off the bed as I talk to my friend Eleni in L.A. Every girl needs a friend she can call with her most screwed-up, esoteric conundrum. Someone who not only sympathizes but isn't the least bit fazed by either the stupid thing you did or how bent you feel. For me, that's Eleni. She's never stripped—she looks like a twelve-year-old boy, albeit a heavily tattooed one. But she's been through her ration of shit and I trust her with my girl drama.

"I can't believe this happened," I tell her. "I set strict limits from the get-go, and just like that, I undid them. And for what? It's not like I need *that* much money!"

"Aw, honey, listen. You have to look at it the way a recovering alcoholic looks at having a drink. You slipped." Her voice is careful and soft.

"You're right. I know you're right."

"I know you feel like you let yourself down, but you can use it as a marker for how far you've come. It was just one night."

"Yeah, but then why doesn't it feel like progress? I feel like if I *am* going to bend the rules, I ought to just suck it up and deal." But she's got a point. Why should I abide something that I don't feel right about? I could be tough, since strippers know from tough, and marshal through compromising situations without complaint, or I could be strong and avoid such situations entirely.

"Be nice to yourself," Eleni says. "Don't go back to work there!"

I promise to heed her advice, even though my first instinct is to march right back in there. "All right, you bastards, I'm here, and I will prevail! Hand over your money!" But she's right. Don't try to reverse the situation, just walk away.

When I hang up the phone, I catch sight of my reflection in the mirror. I look wild-eyed and pale. Tired. The "shouldn't have" face.

The room service waitress comes in, takes one glance at the up-ended costume bag on the floor—shiny boots and little dresses and crumpled singles strewn about—and makes me immediately. The look she gives me—a sympathetic smile followed by a brief, courteous nod—says it all. She knows the drill. She knows what I've come to town to do and that I'm not in good shape today. She leaves the tray on the desk and closes the door behind her carefully so it doesn't make a sound.

I think I'll try Club Paradise.

Before I can work at Club Paradise, I need to get my sheriff's card back from Cheetah's, so I drive over there first thing the next day, feeling somewhat better but still pretty raw. I'm blinking in the darkness of a strip club at 8:30 a.m., and the breakfast crew in this place is quite a slice of humanity. Casino workers and cab drivers just off of their all-night shifts sit curled over their Bloody Marys, the roil of night given over to the quiet of new day. Morning stays safely on the other side of the tinted doors, leaving the inside of the club sleepy and black as a cave. The dancers on duty, barely visible in the darkness but for their Day-Glo party clothes, seem to glide silently over the carpet. You're in Bukowski country.

I find the house mom shuttling around the dressing room putting grooming supplies on the counter, saying something about how she just started her shift and she's trying to get organized and could I give her a break and wait. With my skin still thin from the night before last, I'm irritated that's she's more concerned with arranging hair spray and breath mints than with helping me. I bang out of the dressing room in search of a manager. By the time I find the manager in the office, I'm practically foaming at the mouth, which he aggravates by doing that pantomime remote control clicking gesture at me, that, "I'm trying to turn you off" thing. This sends me sailing right over the edge.

"I need my sheriff's card now and the house mom just totally witched out on me . . ."

"Calm down, honey," says the manager who just tried to channel surf me. "Just calm down."

"No, I won't calm down!" I'm screaming now. "Because a house mom is supposed to tend to the dancers' needs and being a bitch is not in her job description!"

I have officially lost it. I've never so much as raised my voice in a club and now I'm having a total diva meltdown in front of the top brass. I fling open the office door, storm back to the dressing room, demand my card, tap my foot, and huff loudly while the mom fishes it out. I grab the card and leave without saying thank you. I've got to get a grip. The point of this trip is to sort the bright and complicated fragments of striptease. This trip is not about money. It is not about resuming bad habits. No more "go-go head" for me.

As the day wears on and I walk along the Strip, past virtual Venice and virtual Paris and virtual New York, it occurs to me that my fragile emotional state might be partly due to the Vegas Creeps. Whenever I come here, at first I feel a magpie's delight at all the shiny surfaces, but after about forty-eight hours I grow leery of the blinking lights and chirping slot machines and steak-n-shrimp dinners had on the cheap after midnight. The manufactured fun starts to get frustrating. I end up wanting to claw off the wallpaper, melt the tinsel into puddles of silver, tear apart all the scale models of big, meaningful cities. I want to scrape down to the soul of the Strip and there isn't one. Vegas isn't evil, but it's maddening for lack of moral reverb. Indulgence is the coin of the realm here, but what good is pleasure without the contrast of propriety? Just tinny decadence in a neon cavern and it makes me a little crazy.

"It's because this place was built in the middle of a desert, you know," Don says. Don is the manager of Club Paradise, and he's sitting next to me at the bar, listening intently as I describe the Vegas Creeps. The night is young and there aren't many customers in the place yet, so we have time to share a drink, me in my black beaded evening gown and him in an expensive navy suit. The club is sprawling and elegant—the two of us are dwarfed under the high ceiling hung with elaborate chandeliers. Don continues: "People come to Vegas to do what they can't do at home. They come here, dump their psychic garbage, and the desert just sucks it right up. Then when they leave, all that negative energy stays here."

Don looks weary—he doesn't seem to have the thick skin or the hard-headed business sense you need to climb the ranks of management in this industry. And he cops to it. His big dream is to work in music promotion. But as long as he's there, he says, I'm welcome. "You can come back here and work anytime you'd like, but I can understand why you might not want to. This place is just a huge void, built around loss. It sucks people in and takes everything they've got."

He taps the filter end of a Marlboro Light on the bar, then flips the cigarette into his mouth and sucks the tiny flame from his lighter into the tobacco. Don is a young man but his eyes contain decades of sadness.

I've got to get the hell out of Vegas.

SIX

Dallas, Texas

The epicenter of strip culture shifts periodically. In the early 1990s, Tampa's outrageous lap dancing generated the most buzz, then Houston's sheer volume of clubs (more than thirty in the city limits) made that city the hot spot, and now that Houston has passed an ordinance that requires three feet of space between dancers and customers, the locus of stripping hype has shifted north to Dallas.

Dallas is a matured cow town, sprawling and flat, with a small, centralized skyline surrounded by ropy gray tangles of freeway that wind round and fling you off in whatever direction you need to go. The tidy thing about Dallas is that most of the major strip clubs are on or near the same road, Northwest Highway, a.k.a. "Pervert's Row," so you can just drive along the strip and check out whatever looks promising. Now, I'd heard that stripping is different in Dallas— a town known for big money, big party atmosphere, and a big air of high-status masculine entitlement. But nothing in my most lavish macho man dreams could have prepared me for the Lodge. From the minute the valet took my car, I knew I'd found a new level of luxe. Most gentlemen's clubs are an interior design travesty, all polished brass and potted ferns—a motif once referred to as "Bennigan's with tits." This place, however, is another story. As the name suggests, the club is tricked out like a giant hunting lodge—the walls sided in lodgepole pine, the carpet an egregiously tasteful leopard pattern, a stuffed bear poised for attack in the foyer. The main stage is a wonder: A cave built around a black polyurethane platform, with a small waterfall running down one side. Exotic animal heads line the perimeter of the ceiling—the exit sign is wedged into a mounted hippo's mouth. The restaurant area boasts cases full of rifles, crossbows, pistols, and old hunting trophies. Clearly, the management courts patrons of a type somewhere between Gerry Spence and J. R. Ewing. If strip clubs are the last bastion of dudesmanship, the Lodge pitches that sentiment into butch overdrive.

The manager who hires me is a baby-faced jarhead with a mind for discipline and a gift for idiom. When he impresses upon me that "lewd" dancing—flashing, tugging on my thong, any contact with the customer that goes beyond touching his knees or shoulders for balance—will not be tolerated, he looks me square in the eye and drawls, "Don't even think about bending the rules here, 'cause that dawg don't hunt." No lie, in the office they have a corkboard filled with Polaroid photos of women they've fired, some with the word *lewd* scrawled, Prynne-like, under their names.

He also tells me that the music women can dance to is restricted to selections that will "be pleasing to their demographic—affluent men age thirty-five to fifty-five." No rap, no alternative, no heavy metal. Ah, one of those clubs where they keep the wild side carefully groomed.

It's a gown club—a place where your nails have to be perfect (they checked mine), your costume formal (evening dress—prom queen style, not streetwalker), and your heels a certain height (nothing less than three inches). They're very serious about all of this. Micromanagement is a fairly recent development in strip clubs, but if a place caters to a corporate clientele, it hardly seems inappropriate to institute corporate practices.

I do my rotation: two songs each on the main, bar, and restaurant stages. The men who sit stage-side in the fancy upholstered armchairs are a mixed bunch. Some are generous with their attention and tips, others couldn't care less whether I am there or not. I hate that "Hey, I'm dancing here" feeling that slinks around in the face of indifference. But that feeling dissipates when I notice the customers' eyes that are upon me. In my dancing days, I've been looked at all sorts of ways—the furtive glance of a shy guy, the predatory gawp of a trick, and the friendly leer of a party boy, but until now, never with the pampering gaze of a would-be lover. These men court and woo like none I've ever met.

"Marry me, our children would be gorgeous," says Johnny Pepsodent as he tucks a buck. "My divorce is final soon," is the pitch of a dapper entrepreneur. "Can I come back then and take you to Tiffany's?" I always thought the point of coming to a strip club was to get away from commitment, with a carefully orchestrated "Him up *here*, her down *there*" social dynamic. But the sorority-girl spin the dancers get here seems to bridge the gap. In this kind of environment, working presents a potential slippery slope between a job and a relationship.

Dangerous. But it also charges the air.

Later in the shift, I'm dancing in the restaurant area of the club. The stage is nothing more than a small raised platform set amidst the tables, and right in front of me a group of men in elegant suits is having a business dinner. Unsmiling and rigid, they wear their entitlement like a shroud. One of them, a middle-management type in his early thirties, watches me intently as he dines on a steak. He doesn't look cruel, or even needy, in fact, his face is placidly handsome and kind, but watching him eat as he looks at me gives me a chill. Locking gazes, we are bound together by primal rhythm—my undulating and his chewing.

I shudder and turn my back to the table. The only other man near the stage is pointedly looking in the other direction. Fine. I'd rather be ignored than consumed.

The big money here isn't made doing table dances, but rather sitting around with the customers, chatting, eating, and drinking—like trophy wives for hire (minus the sex, of course). This creates an air of Lobster Palace swank, and it's pretty fun, if a little bit hard to figure out. I'm sort of bad at small talk, and my money radar is severely underdeveloped, so I spend the time between sets tucked into an armchair next to a dreamy-eyed rancher who talks to me about hunting and dog breeding. It's almost too sophisticated to be truly sexy, this club, but it is quite a break from the rat race. I fully understand why a guy might be drawn here. The Lodge is the most physically beautiful reinforcement of male privilege I've ever seen.

I squeeze my way through the crowd at Baby Dolls Saloon the next night, because word of mouth has it this is Party Central. Baby Dolls grosses more on liquor than any strip club in the state, and it's one of the industry's few havens for country music fans. I break into a broad smile as the sound system begins blasting John Berry's "She's Taken a Shine," a song that's fresh as ozone and sunlight. Two black cowboys are standing by one of the stages, handing out singles and singing every word. This place is more my style than the Lodge. It's loud and rowdy, with a great sense of sensual freedom and Texan largesse.

The manager shows me around the club, beginning upstairs in the dressing room. "We don't load the girls down with rules here because we want you all to make money and be happy . . ."

I'm not paying attention because my gaze is riveted to the two tanning beds, gleaming white under the fluorescents—there's a girl in one of them, baking away as she talks on her cell phone. There's also a wrap-around vanity, fitness equipment, a beautician for hair and makeup, a house mom to watch over the girls, and—gasp, sputter—a manicurist. The typical strip club dressing room is nothing more than a meat locker with a mirror and a coat rack, so thoughtful details like this blow me away.

The only hitch at Baby Dolls is that you can't wear a t-back or thong; you have to wear a tanga-cut bottom, which still shows the entire behind, but is about two inches wider across the top. It seems a silly distinction, but local municipalities are always forming ad hoc committees to dicker over what constitutes a buttock or a breast or a nipple, and how much—down to a fraction of an inch—a dancer can show. There's a nipple issue here, too. They have to be covered, and Baby Dolls has a canny solution: liquid latex mixed with iridescent opaque powder.

"Do you know how to do latex?" asks the house mom, a big old tough gal who frankly scares me some.

I shake my head no.

Pick a color, she tells me. I look at the choices: gold, bronze, copper, and dark copper. Um, dark copper. She pumps the Elmer's glue–like latex into a relish cup, and scoops in a small amount of sparkly powder with a Q-tip. Once it's mixed to the color of Thousand Island dressing, she swabs it in circular motion onto my nipples.

"Give it five minutes to dry, and don't start working until they're done, because they have to be covered," she warns. "It'll peel right off at the end of the night." I wander the dressing room, saying hi to the girls, alternately fanning my latex and admiring the visual effect of all our gilded nipples. One Filipina with a huge set of implants chose gold powder, giving her the mighty rack of Croesus. Too cool.

This ain't no gown club, so once I'm dry, I dress to hustle. I tease my hairpiece to stratospheric heights, snap on my rhinestone choker—*sine qua non* by now—buy a fluorescent pink tanga from the house mom, and zip on a dress I named The Tentacle of Love. The hottest of pink spandex, it reaches my ankles and is slit up to mid-thigh. The shoulder straps are white to match the rows of rubber-ized oblongs that dot the fabric, and the rubberized bits glow under black light. It's nothing I'd consider wearing in civilian mode, but when you work in near-darkness, you need to play big just to show up. Besides, this is about courting the peripatetic male gaze, not about the imprimatur of Polly Mellen.

"Love that dress!" whoops the Arkansas businessman who buys my first table dance. I say thank you, tuck the twenty into my gar-ter, nudge his knees apart and start dancing in the space between his feet. His fingers start creeping up my thighs. I brush them away. More dancing. More creeping fingers. Finally, I grab his hands and pin them to the arms of the chair and finish the song that way. Of course he doesn't want another dance, because I'm a priss. Almost all the dances thereafter go like this, but the manager had warned me that some dances could be "handsy." "Handsy" is some-thing of a euphemism. "Grope fiesta" would be more accurate, but you can set your own limits here and still do okay. You just have to settle for a minimum of repeat business. Still, I manage to recoup my travel expenses in a few hours while wriggling just out of the customers' reach.

Dancing onstage here is totally awesome, but it's a workout because there are eight stages you have to dance on consecutively, which takes about forty-five minutes. The only problem with the stage rotation is that you might get trapped onstage during a song you hate, which is what happens when a little Black girl comes on-stage to "The Devil Went Down to Georgia." Sure, she looks great in her hot pants and halter top trimmed in flame appliqués, but those lyrics, "*Chicken in a bread pan. Pickin' out dough*" are so anti-erotic and *what the fuck*.

I'm not sure if it's the booze or the Texas machismo that makes the men here want to spend money, but they sure do fork it out.

They like to tip girls onstage as well as at the tables, which usually isn't the case in a place that does a high volume of table dances. When a guy steps to the edge of the stage—most of which are three feet high, making the girls look positively giant—we do a little smiling dip and shimmy before he tucks in the tip. It's good policy, really, to do something that conveys, "I see you," before taking a guy's money. Nothing is worse than a preoccupied stripper staring off into space, lost in her own private orbit. That disinterest bores its way into a man's heart. To appear interested in the Baby Dolls boys is no chore, though, because they're so enthusiastic. By the time I get to the eighth stage, my garter is full-to-groaning with money. I look down at the singles wreathing my thigh and picture myself at the bank, trying to deposit four hundred dollars in ones and smiling weakly at the teller. "Oh, I'm a waitress."

I would dance to country music all the time if I could, but not everyone likes it as much as I do. I ask a man for a dance, he says yes. The next song begins, "A Lot More Action" by Toby Keith.

"No, no." He grabs my arm to stop me. "Wait until the song is over. I can't stand country music. I had a terrible one-night stand in Nashville once and ever since then I can't stomach the stuff."

Fair enough.

This guy is pretty cool. Turns out he's an orthopedic surgeon with a practice in town. He asks if I've ever seen foot surgery.

"I've got one tomorrow. Would you like to come?"

When I work, I get all sorts of offers, some strange, most predictable—every dancer does—but this was the most unusual by far. I have a pretty weak stomach, but when given the chance, I always want to see fetal Siamese twins pickled in a jar, or a TV show with the world's largest tumor, even if I end up queasy and sorry I ever looked. So, naturally, I'd love to see the inside of a human foot. I'm tempted, I really am. But I'm also engaged. And I think, given the context, foot surgery would be cheating. I have to pass.

A couple sits at a table along the back wall, and when I get off-stage the man motions me over by waving a twenty and slurs, "It's for her." When I see the notepad on the table, I realize his speech is a little off because he's deaf, and so is his girlfriend. This isn't so much a charity case as a recruitment opportunity, so I climb down off my prissy horse and pull out all the stops. It takes real nerve for a woman to come to a strip club and it's a form of female misbehavior I think should be richly rewarded. So I work it—belly to belly, breast to breast. I nuzzle her neck, inhaling her scent. It's so rare to get any kind of approval from women not involved in this line of work, I want to draw her excitement deep into my lungs, as if to keep it with me always. If I rubbed up against this woman any harder, I'd end up standing behind her, and she really seems to enjoy it. Here's to claiming new territory, sweetie. Sisterhood *is* powerful.

I have such a fine time at Baby Dolls that as I drive back to my hotel room at 2 a.m., I am high on the whole business. There's worse ways to earn your keep. You can make your own hours, the money is plentiful, and on a night like tonight, it's a great party and a fat ego-buzz.

But morning is the great equalizer—a good night usually begets a crispy day after. When I wake up, I'm so bone-wrackingly sore I can barely stand upright, and after eight hours of chronic politeness and idle chatter, I am unable to form a coherent thought. My mind feels trashed—like a broken tape, snapped and flapping stupidly on its reel. I stand in front of the mirror, scraping the raccooned mascara from under my eyes, just letting my thoughts settle where they may. The drive to El Paso. Check-out time at noon. Finding a big omelette for breakfast. And money. Last night's money.

After dragging my bags to the car, muttering and cursing at their heft, I go back to the room and sit on the bed, listening to Travis Tritt on the clock radio and methodically sorting last night's haul.

First, I separate piles of twenties, tens, fives. Ones in stacks of twenty each. Each of the bills facing the same direction. It's got to be the same way every time, this stabilizing ritual. Handling this much currency gives me a primitive sense of contentment. There's something so satisfying, so intimate about the riffle of bills and the odd perfumey smell they take on from passing through all those sweaty fingers, fabric softener–scented pockets, leather billfolds, metal tills.

Almost seven hundred dollars.

From the world's hands to my wallet.

It's good to be back.

SEVEN

Mommy's Little Monster

Distance is different west of the Mississippi. If "far" to a New Yorker is Columbus Circle to Wall Street, and to a Midwesterner it's Fargo to Beloit, then to a West Texan, "far" is, I think, El Paso to the moon. I call the motel where I'm booked for the night and ask how long to get there from Dallas. "Oh, the drive isn't too bad," says the gal at the front desk, "by taking I-Twenty to I-Ten, it's about six hundred miles." Rough calculation: nine hours, if I don't lollygag at lunch.

The sights: A discount western-wear outlet luring shoppers with a giant inflatable cowboy boot staked to the ground like a docked blimp. Homemade memorial wreaths and white crosses, *descansos*, plunged into the grass at roadside, plentiful enough to move a morbid person to keep tally with hash marks on the steering wheel. A blur of dwellings. An abandoned town, now just windborne sand, a gas station, and a name: Sierra Blanca.

With that many miles to log, once that which the eye sees ceases to amuse, what can the mind do but wander? Wander back and back and back, to where it all began.

There is a blinking neon sign that says GIRLS GIRLS GIRLS because there has to be. There are mirrors everywhere. The gouged linoleum floor is swept with a moving pattern of swirling silver dots, cast down from the mirror balls that turn round on the ceiling. The walls are red and yellow—happy colors, fast-food restaurant colors. Everywhere the gaze might rest hang photographs of naked girls, smiling gamely as they bend and twist in corny, lurid poses. Flashy disco music is forced through the speakers, pumped in at top volume to give the place rhythm, life. The atmosphere is stubbornly festive, as if repeatedly emphasizing its own cheerfulness would make it somehow believable. The sweat-bloated air smells of grime and Clorox.

While most eighteen-year-olds are starting college or picking up a trade, I am here, amidst the porn theaters, the live sex shows, and the cluttered, brightly lit shops that sell fake I.D.s and Chinese throwing stars, in the vicious heart of Times Square. This is Peepland. This is where I work.

I could blame it on New Jersey. When I was twelve my family moved there. Not to the broken-down boardwalks and smoke-belching factory towns of Springsteen country, but farther west to the low sloping foothills where white-collar families raise college-of-their-choice children. You don't hear much about this area—Madison, Chester, Bernardsville, Tewksbury, Livingston, Jefferson Township—a region beyond the reach of the turnpike, and therefore immune to the "what exit" joke. It's almost an entirely different state than the steel-and-grit parts they call Jersey.

New Jersey is the last stop after numerous executive peregrinations. The moves are hard on my family, given its size. I'm sure things were easier for my parents at the outset. There is a photograph of my mother and father, taken early in their marriage, with my brother and eldest sister on their laps—my brother, Tad, a jug-eared tot in black woolen shorts and a button-down shirt, my sister Barbara a newborn, her tiny form lost in a delicately embroidered christening gown. My father, at the time attending graduate school in Cambridge, Massachusetts, is beaming down at my brother, handsome in his dark suit and skinny tie. My mother, with her black hair in a short pixie cut, smiles coyly at the camera, prim in a black jacket with a Peter Pan collar and matching black skirt from Peck and Peck. My parents look smart and tidy, like they've got the world on a string. Whenever I see that photo, I think, *they really should have stopped there.*

But they don't. My family moves to Sweden and my mother gives birth to three more children, my sisters Annette and Kelly eleven months apart, then, five years later, me. After two dark-haired children from two dark-haired parents, my sisters and I are an aberrance of blondeness, prompting much family ribbing about Swedish mailmen. But the three of us all have father's close-set, heavy-lidded elfin eyes and mother's forbidding pointy chin. We belong.

When I am still an infant, we move back to the States. As we grow, the five kids form our own universe—a solar system loosely arranged in orbit around my mother. My father is the chief bread-winner, but like so many, he's a phantom dad—more absent than home, more aggravated than content. So he moves among the planets as a separate, belabored presence, whirling out of sight as quickly as he appears—a vital satellite, a scowl of moondust.

Since I'm the youngest by a wide margin, I am frequently ditched by the older kids; who don't want to be saddled with the baby. So my mother and I form an inseparable pack of two. I am happy to be a hip-pocket kid. I stand so close to her side as she works in the kitchen that whenever she moves her arm, her elbow strikes my forehead, which doesn't hurt and makes us both laugh. An indulgent mother, she makes me feel like I am her favorite and never does anything to contradict my assumption that this is truth, not wishful thinking.

In idle moments, my family will impress their hopes upon me.

"She should go to Harvard like Dad and be a philosophy major."

"She should go to NYU and study acting. They have an excellent drama department."

"She will do whatever she wants," my mother says, then later tells me she wishes I'd take up the drums.

They fuss over my future as if I am the family's last great hope. The exact outcome is uncertain, but that I will grow up to do something grand, turn into someone significant, is not in doubt.

What I turn into is an all-American misfit, a sullen, moonfaced ghoul. Come fourteen, I hate school and hate New Jersey, and don't want to do anything but listen to the radio, go to the city, and read. At my English teacher's behest, I launch into the junior outcast's canon—Hesse, Salinger, and Plath, who quickly becomes my favorite. Holden Caulfield seems to me a captious little pecker, but I love Esther Greenwood—that she was so full of promise yet so full of despair makes perfect sense to me. I consult "The Colossus" and "Ariel" for spiritual succor as if they are the Testaments.

Whenever I get to the end, I clasp the books to my chest, look out my east-facing window, and silently vow, "Someday."

When my Dad gets home from work, I drift downstairs and join my parents for dinner. My father takes off his glasses and rubs his eyes, his brows, thick and bushy as Brezhnev's, furrowing as he scours his eyelids with his knuckles. Another day run through the Lomanator. As the only child left under their roof, I observe my parents closely. My father always seems exhausted, and my mother gives off the melancholy impression that she is bigger than any suburb that might contain her. Between watching them and watching my siblings wander aimlessly between college and the real world, I figure if that's what obedience gets you, then the hell with it.

I develop terrible insomnia and stay up well past two, devouring books and plotting my next escape to New York. When I finally sleep, my dreams are filled with visions of the city. I walk the streets downtown and people with great plumed hairdos and surreal outfits nod at me, as if they know me intimately. Doors open and strangers invite me into their home. I know I have to move there eventually, but how?

Every school day, I drag myself out of bed fifteen minutes before I have to run for the bus and start my morning ritual: Plug in the curling iron. Wash my face and brush my teeth. Dress in something black. Spread white makeup stolen from my sister Annette, who had a brief stint in clown school, in a thin layer over my face and neck. Meticulously apply a coat of Hazel Bishop's "Black Minkberry" lipstick, to stain my lips a deep, deep red. This is the greatest cosmetic, the only cosmetic—chalky and cheap, ninety-nine cents a tube at Woolworth's, it lasts all day and is the exact color of dried blood. Next, outline my eyes with black liquid liner, all the way around with points at the corners. Spray my bleached-blonde bangs with Aqua Net Super Hold (in the white can) and curl my bangs, half under, half back, until the hair hisses and burns. Tease the bangs until they stand up in a flaxen pouf and spray again.

If Goth is my look, then punk is my life, for I was just slogging along in a fugue state, not fully alive, until I heard it. It completely turns me around. Books are one thing, but here is this music that sounds as torn-up raw and tangled as I feel inside, and it has something dangerous and weighty to impart. This isn't just "fuck you."

This is "fuck you" with a philosophy, and I organize my life around the stuff. I become so wedded to this identity that when someone calls me a poseur in the hall at school, I burst into tears. After school, I scan the radio dial—from WFMU in East Orange on one end to WPRB in Princeton on the other—in search of the hardcore bands that I like: Dead Kennedys, Circle Jerks, Suicidal Tendencies, Youth Brigade, Minor Threat, FEAR. The record that really blows me away is Social Distortion's "Mommy's Little Monster." Once I get my hands on a copy, I listen to it every day. It is my refuge, my gospel, my hope. I sit on my bed, punching my fist in the air as I sing along. I would say I began straining at the parental leash, but *what* leash? With no real call to rebel against anything at home, I simply rebel against everything else.

My parents smile bemusedly at their bullheaded child. They are pleased that I am developing a social conscience, so they are patient with me—a patience I will test repeatedly, starting with the day Jeanette and I get arrested in the city at a No Nukes demonstration. Jeanette, in a group of protestors who were blocking the sidewalk, was being swept into the paddy wagon, and I couldn't let her go to jail by herself (what would I tell her mother?), so I stepped forward and let them take me, too. We spent the night in the juvie cell, while the other protestors were thrown in the regular lock-up. We remained alone, but they kept cramming more women into the group cell—streetwalkers ("My God, they're barely wearing any clothes!" Jeanette and I whispered to each other, peering through the bars as they were led past), dealers, petty thieves. Later on they put someone else in with us, an older woman with long blonde hair. She'd been caught shoplifting costume jewelry at Bloomingdales and was sobbing inconsolably. The guards knew the other women in the lock-up would make good on their threats to kick her ass if she didn't stop crying so they moved her to our cell, where she spent the night sitting cross-legged on the floor, rocking back and forth, raking her fingers through her hair, and crying some more. Our case was dismissed the next morning and Jeanette's mom picked us up from the courthouse and took us to the Second Avenue Deli, where we sat, gray-faced and contrite, as we ate our latkes.

But such trials are few and far between. Most of my spare time is spent with friends roaming the nearby towns for something to do that doesn't incite mixups with jocks or other local meatheads. We search everywhere for a friendly corner—punk shows, gay discos, midnight showings of *The Rocky Horror Picture Show* and *The Hunger*. Maybe a road trip to see the Ramones at Trenton City Gardens, whatever we can get. If it's the only territory you can mine, you will find someplace to fit in. You will dig toward sanctuary.

Sometimes there are all-ages shows at the Showplace in Dover, a dumpy low-ceilinged box across from the Kmart. The Showplace is known more for its weekday lunch special featuring go-go dancers than anything else, but they'll advertise any feature they have in hopes of attracting some business to the miserable old place. When my boyfriend Pete's band played there, the sign out front said MEN-TAL ABUSE on one side and GO-GO LUNCH on the other. My friend Laurie, a temperamental, spiky-haired twenty-six-year-old who has been my idol ever since the night she cut in front of me on line for *Rocky Horror*, has been inside during the day and seen the go-go lunch for herself. One night while she touches up my roots in her kitchen, squirting my scalp with the gritty blue bleach solution, she tells me about it. "I went in to get some flyers and this dancer was wearing a stretched-out old leotard that she had pinned across her chest and it wasn't even a safety pin, it was like a badge, turned around backwards. It was so sad!" We cluck and murmur, united in girlish pity, glad that we aren't losers in bad leotards grinding away in front of a bunch of slack-jawed businessmen.

Then Laurie brightens. "Which is a cooler name for my band, the Vampiristics or Lust for Blood?"

"Lust for Blood is good," I say, "because it's like 'Lust for Life.' "

"See, that's what *I* think!"

The conversation heaves further and further away from the subject of stripping, and it never comes up again.

The distractions I am able to find in New Jersey help me muddle through the days, but it is the trips to New York that I live for. When the bus gets to that point on Route 3 where the Manhattan skyline unfurls—from the stately high-rises of Riverside Drive all the way down to the Twin Towers, my heart flutters at the majestic sight and my insides unclench. Oz dead ahead. I don't have to do anything outrageous to be happy—just being there is enough. I walk around Astor Place with Jeanette, looking at the junk people have spread out on blankets in hopes of selling, or follow Laurie around as she shops for records at Free Being and Sounds. Once in a while we go to a show—a hardcore matinee at CBGBs or Rock Against Racism in the park. Most memorable of all the shows we see is the triple bill of Reagan Youth, Murphy's Law, and the Dead Kennedys at the World Theater on 2nd Street, where Jello Biafra kisses me backstage. He grabs my arm, pulls me to him, and mashes me full on the mouth. It is like being kissed by the lips of God. A sweaty, warbly-voiced, preachy-preachy God. A pivotal moment. I spend endless hours in study hall writing letters telling him how much it meant to me and that he is the only one who could possibly understand me, man. I don't mail any of the letters but Jeanette finds a few in the locker we share and immediately confiscates them for future blackmail purposes.

I show up the first day of senior year in dirty clothes, a white petticoat with a black fishnet handkerchief skirt over it, a man's undershirt with the collar torn off, grubby tights, and black pointy-toed boots. I slept forty-five minutes the night before. My stomach hurts constantly and the doctor is afraid I might have an ulcer.

I walk the halls at school in a somnambulant haze. I know I get from class to class, from school to home and back, but I don't know how. I'm preoccupied with images that play over and over again in my head:

Standing in a ballroom in the vintage black-velvet dress my sister Annette painstakingly tailored and fitted with a tulle and lace fishtail, and hearing a classmate say, "I thought you were supposed to bathe before you came to the prom."

My orderly father, exasperated, trying to make sense of my daily recitation of complaints about my life. "If you don't want people to make fun of you, then why do you look that way?"

My mother curled up with her legs tucked under her on the yellow plaid loveseat in the family room, appraising my ever-worsening grades with a portentous, "Don't limit your options."

Sitting on the gym floor with a bunch of friends when a paper airplane sails down from the bleachers and lands right in the middle of our circle. I pick it up and read the message scrawled on the wing. "Freaks Suck."

The weeks drift past. A day when no one throws anything at me is a triumph. A day when no one screams an insult at me never happens.

I am a tough kid, but not a bulletproof one. I know inside of a month that I am not going to make it.

A swishy New Wave kid is my savior. Kevin is a friend of Laurie's, an occasional member of our *Rocky Horror* posse. When I first met him I thought his personality—at once bitchily unctuous and terribly jumpy—was formulated as a reaction to living in the closet, but I eventually ascribed it to his massive speed consumption. He has beautiful, birdlike hands with unusually long fingers that don't so much reach for things as dart at them. His nails are bitten to the quick and covered in chipped black polish. One night after the movie, while everyone is at the Howard Johnson's in Hibernia eating french fries bought with change fished from under couch cushions and scrounged from the bottoms of our linty pockets, he tells me he dropped out of school because he'd gotten harassed so badly for being gay and is about to graduate from an adult high school way out in Newton.

"Is it difficult?" I ask him.

"Naw. You just have your parents sign you out of school."

"No, no, I mean the work."

"Oh! It's totally easy. It's all multiple choice."

This is it, my ticket out. The trick will be getting my parents on board. I can't just go to them with an entreaty to spring me from my academic prison—I'll have to have a good reason, reinforcements, a Plan B. I quickly zero in on my ace in the hole: acting. I've already chewed up the scenery with leads in every school play, and spent weekends going to acting classes, auditions, and working on movies as a rent-a-punk. Leaving school would give me that much more time to pursue my career and hone my craft (convincing them that this is a good idea may well be my most rigorous improv exercise to date). Mom and Dad are shocked, but after continuous heavy petitioning on my part, they grow less averse to the idea, provided the school backs me up. So we sit down with the guidance counselor and she assures them that while it's risky for any child to leave school, in my case she doesn't consider it a huge liability. "We're sure she'll be just fine," she says, sliding the papers over for my parents to sign. I can't believe that anyone would give their blessing to a dropout. Either she is a weirdo or I am the luckiest kid alive. It doesn't occur to me till much later that both could be true.

All the freaks descend on Jeanette's house for the dropout celebration of the century. We howl along to Bauhaus records and smoke Marlboros in the backyard. Jeanette's father, an accomplished pastry chef, bakes a cake with an icing illustration of me. I'm standing at a podium holding up an Oscar saying, "It all happened after I left high school!"

Three mornings a week, I drive into Sussex County to the pastoral town of Newton, where the adult high school is set up in a dilapidated modular. My teacher is a doddering old man named Wally. Wally has about three greasy strands of gray hair in a combover, a stutter, thick glasses, and two club feet—you can tell walking pains him terribly. He shuffles around in those big black shoes of his, bringing me study guides and freshly sharpened pencils to circle the answers in the test booklets. My other teacher is Marilyn, a soft-spoken middle-aged woman who wears a pink knit cardigan with tissues tucked into the cuff of one sleeve. Wally and Marilyn are used to dealing with children who are at their wit's end and they treat me very gently.

Marilyn asks me one morning why I left school. I want to tell her about how every day, my guts churn with rage because I feel trapped. Because I hate the tiny girl world into which I was born, with its emphasis on being groomed for acceptance—hands clasped, hair combed, ankles crossed. Because I can't stand one more comment on who and what I should be, and how I'm failing. But I can't form the words. I can only watch her face blanch as I look into her eyes and say, plain as toast, "Because I could."

Each day when I come home from school, I look out the window in my room and silently pledge, *Soon.*

Soon.

The day I pass my multiple-choice final exam, months before I would have graduated had I stayed in school, I say to myself, *That fixes it. I'm free. I will go to the city. I will become somebody, make my parents proud.*

I will show them all.

I arrive in a hard and bright New York. It is still the city of my dreamscape, but by now, the late 1980s, the worm has turned and there is no cheap quarter for runt bohemians like me. Even the East Village, still riddled with drugs and crime, is absurdly expensive. I have six hundred dollars I've saved from my after-school jobs, which isn't much by Manhattan standards, but I am undeterred. My friend Deb, who plays guitar in a much-maligned band called False Prophets, leaves for a two-month European tour and sublets her apartment to me and our mutual friend, Atom, a loveable teenage Communist with an abundance of nervous energy and a severe case of acne. The False Prophets' roadie, Jane, a strapping peroxide blonde from Wisconsin, drives out to New Jersey in the band's van and helps me move my boxes and a big piece of foam to use as a mattress into the two-room apartment on East 10th Street. Atom and I squabble about who gets which room. Neither is worth fighting over—one is the size of a closet and receives no light, and the other is a kitchen with a bathtub in it and a creaky, precarious loft bed over the stove and reeking refrigerator. After a bribe of Chinese food, Atom takes the kitchen.

For the first few weeks, I walk around the city feeling like I've just been shot out of a cannon: *Whoa, okay, well, that was intense. Now what?* To orient myself, I mark Tompkins Square Park as ground zero. If I were looking for someone, chances are I could find him or her roaming Saint Marks Place, sitting on one of the benches just inside the entrance to the park splitting a forty-ouncer or a Foster's lager with twelve other kids, on the payphone at Saint Marks and A making calls with a stolen calling-card number, or down in the squats on 9th between B and C.

Right away, various family members begin making their way up the treacherously crooked and narrow staircase in the building on East 10th: sisters unloading coolers full of food into the fridge; Atom, P.C. down to his diet, wrinkles his nose at the hotdogs (he eats a couple buns with mustard, though). Dad proffering cardboard boxes of old plastic dishes and flatware—the tines of the forks slightly bent. I'm on the phone home all the time—my parents are worried in the way that only parents can be. Am I eating enough? Am I working yet? Do I need towels? Sheets? They want their arty kid to conquer New York, not vice versa. But I tell them everything's okay. And in my newness as a city-dweller, I believe that it's true. Such is the arrogance and optimism of eighteen.

I take a job as a salesgirl in a SoHo boutique. The owner, Helga, a high-strung forty-five-year-old German woman with an orange crew cut, lets her vast array of animals—half a dozen dogs, fifteen cats—roam the store. At night, she loads the dogs into her minivan to take home, but the sales help has to chase down the cats so they can be locked into cages in the basement. When we're not cat-wrangling, we "style" the clients—fussy, soft-bellied housewives from Fort Lee and Bedford who are eager to be fawned over and dressed up in something that might recapture a husband's eye.

I instantly befriend the boutique's window dresser, Rachel, an ebullient, curvy orthodontist's daughter from Grosse Pointe, Michigan, who came to New York to make it as a sculptor. She sucks in her cheeks and tosses her curly, shoe-polish-black hair around as she mocks the other salespeople—a tedious brood of aspiring actors and fashion designers imperiously swanning about the store in their giant shoulder pads. She'd motion me into the stockroom where we'd stuff as many shoulder pads as we could under our bra straps—I think our record was eight apiece, four on each side—to see if anyone got the joke.

"Great shirts, ladies," Helga would say in her Teutonic lisp, swishing past in one of her ghastly tropical-colored leather pantsuits.

Rachel and I develop a passionate, crushlike friendship. We go to moody, smoke-and-incense-filled nightclubs where I sit on the couch with her head in my lap and her arms looped around my neck. Rachel looks up at me wondrously, her eyes a lambent, sky-high blue, sighing, "You're like a womb to me, Lily!" At twenty-five, Rachel seems sophisticated and almost magical. She has a curious magnetism that draws all manner of hard cases—junkie poets, performance artists sold on their own transgressive postures, snide British industrial musicians, me—who recognize something in her guileless receptivity that inspires them to drop their defenses and pour their hearts out. In return for their confidences, Rachel treats her friends as if they each possess some amazing quality of which she couldn't possibly tire.

I am not making enough money at the boutique for luxuries like cabs, so I walk everywhere. Each day I make the round-trip on foot from 10th Street and Avenue A to the corner of Spring and Greene Streets, watching the rubbishy funk of the Lower East Side melt into the continental charm of SoHo. After work, I collapse on my foam mattress like an amphibious creature panting on a rock, exhausted by running from land to water and back. I'm actually relieved when Helga fires me.

In late November, Rachel and I spend a night out at Limelight. As I dance in my red fifties prom dress with the shredded crinoline skirt and black pillbox hat, she watches me with a mixture of appraisal and awe. "You would be such a good stripper!"

"No way," I say, and spin away from her. She's said this to me before. She and her roommate Carrie used to work at a peep show in Michigan when they were in art school together, so I guess she feels she's an authority on the subject. But what's it to me? I couldn't possibly do that.

Then, closer to Christmas when we're on the dance floor at Save the Robots at five in the morning, Rachel tells me again that I'd be a good stripper. I don't say anything.

By now, I've been in New York for six months. I have already moved three times, been through five roommates, and taken on and lost one irritating job. I have combed the city for waitressing work, which proves unfruitful, I'm too young to work in a bar, another retail job won't pay me enough to survive, and when I fill out an application at the Art Students League to work as a life drawing model, nobody calls me. I am out of money and almost out of options.

I put on a black felt cowboy hat to hide my hair, which has grown past my shoulders, the blonde striped with black and purple. I don't know what to wear, so I dress in what I think might be someone's version of sexy—low black suede boots that buckle on the side, purple stockings topped in black lace, black bra, panties, and garter belt, a long black sweater and knit skirt and over that, a black suede jacket trimmed in fringe. I look like an extra from "Bonanza" fed through a punk rock shredder.

"Wow, great outfit!" Rachel bubbles when she comes into my apartment, her cold, red nose poking over the top of her black-and-white keffiyeh. I hustle her through the door and onto the street before I can chicken out. We crunch along the snow-covered sidewalk, then head down the wet cement steps to the subway, where we catch the R train to Times Square station. As the train rattles along the tracks, Rachel rubs my sweaty hand between hers.

I'm so anxious I have to keep wiggling my toes to make sure they're still there.

Forty-second Street teems with holiday shoppers loaded down with shiny bags full of gifts, commuters swinging their briefcases as they beeline toward the Port Authority, men in leather jackets and knit caps selling watches out of cardboard boxes and milk crates. I pray I don't run into anybody I know. Rachel holds on to my arm as we wend through the crowds, dodging blowing newspaper and patches of blackened slush. I concentrate on putting one foot in front of the other, taking gulps of the raw, cold air.

On the south side of 42nd, halfway between Seventh and Eighth Avenues, stands Peepland, the façade ornamented with a giant glittering eyeball peering through a key hole. Without hesitation, Rachel swings open the blacked-out glass door. Keeping my gaze fixed on her back, not daring to look around, I follow right behind.

My nostrils prickle at the harsh whiff of industrial cleanser. It's so quiet. I hear muffled movie sounds, moaning, and bad sex music coming from the video booths that line the large room like so many broom closets, and a faint backdrop of disco music, but the men drift wordlessly by. Nobody makes eye contact, nobody makes a sound.

Finally, a rotund black man in a change-maker's apron comes over to us. His upper lip is covered in blisterlike beads of sweat. "Can I help you?"

"We're here to see about jobs?" Rachel says. The upward tone of her voice is the first indication of her nervousness.

"Come with me."

He leaves us standing by a change booth surrounded by bullet-proof glass like a bank teller's window. Inside sits a dark, brooding man with a low, Cro-Magnon brow, counting quarters.

A few moments later, a middle-aged man opens the door next to the booth. His salt-and-pepper hair is thick and wavy. He's wearing tan wide-wale corduroy slacks, a yellow cotton V-neck sweater, and woven leather loafers. A thick gold watch gleams against his deeply tanned skin, a luxurious detail in these crude surroundings. "Hi, ladies. My name is Mick. Are you here for work?"

Rachel and I both nod our heads.

"Do you have identification?"

We nod again.

Mick motions for the guy in the change booth to buzz the door and shepherds us through.

"Okay, come with me and we'll get those copied."

As Rachel and I follow Mick up to a messy, dust-filled office, he talks over his shoulder.

"We don't pay anything but you keep all your tips. The work is pretty easy. You don't have to touch the guy's joint or nothing." He emphasizes the word *joint* as if to imply that he understands that penises are gross and that nobody in their right mind would want to touch one.

He leads us back to the main floor, then down a flight of stairs to the basement where the disco music is coming from. Everything pops and flashes—a huge neon sign of a winking naked woman sitting spread-legged, electric labia to the wind, with tits that blink to mimic swaying back and forth, giant rotating quarters hung from the ceiling, mannequins in filmy lingerie perched up high, surveying the scene below with blank gazes, and everywhere the sound of tokens—jingling in pockets, dropping into slots, flooding jackpot-style into twenty-gallon buckets as a short, gruff-looking red-haired man empties the coin boxes in the booths.

Our booth is four feet square, red, with a window covered by a yellow plastic screen in the middle, about the size of a full-length mirror. Next to the window are a phone and a small slot, just big enough to slide money through. There is a black vinyl-upholstered bar stool with a high back outside the door, where I sit in my funny lingerie, while Rachel, now stripped down to a black thrift-store merry widow that strains to cover her Russian peasant voluptuousness, stands next to me, trying to entice a man our way. "Would you like a show, sir? Double trouble, twice the fun!" I am grateful to be with her, this expert pitchwoman. My friend.

I hear the *chink* of tokens being dropped in a slot and the yellow screen slides up. Our first customer, a bearded, crazy professor-looking guy with curly black hair and Coke-bottle glasses, the *Times* tucked under his arm, is staring right at us, plainly visible through the Plexiglas pane.

"Hey! I thought you said these places used one-way glass!" I hiss at Rachel under my breath, panic escalating.

"How was I supposed to know this place doesn't?"

"Ew! If I have to see these guys, I don't want to do it!" I start to reach for my street clothes, which are piled in the corner.

"Oh, come on! I'll stay with you the whole time. How bad can it be?" Rachel has a vested interest in seeing this work—she wants to quit the boutique.

The man knocks on the window with the handset and motions to say, "Hey, what about me?"

Rachel picks up the phone on our side of the booth and introduces us to him by our stage names. She picked Gypsy, because she likes to travel, and I chose Polly, as in Poly Styrene, the singer from X-Ray Spex. "What would you like to see, sir?" she asks him, voice dripping with saccharine.

"I, uh, would like to see you, uh, together."

The yellow partition slides down. The sound of more tokens in the slot. The window opens again.

"Well, baby, we can do what*ever* you like, but you have to be sweet to the slot." Rachel wheezes lustily, pointing to the opening in the wall.

For every increment of flesh the man requests—my top off, her top off, my stockings, her shoes—Rachel just keeps tapping the slot.

By the time Rachel and I get out of the booth two hours and five customers later, we have 120 dollars to split. I can't believe it. Sixty dollars. I'm rich!

Instead of turning to the peep show I could have gone back to New Jersey, but in my view, returning home would have been tantamount to failure and I couldn't have that. In the way that fear cleverly masquerades as pride, I convince myself that working at Peepland is the best thing for me. I can handle it. Besides, it's only for a few weeks. Then I'll find something else.

I know the threshold I have crossed, that I have entered a dangerous and possibly damaging world. This is not cosmetic defiance like being a hardcore kid; a very serious taboo has been broken, and there is no turning back. This is scary, but in a small, sleazy way, it's exciting, too. I never would have thought that I'd do something like this, but now that I have, I am full of my own daring. I feel more in control of my life than I have in months.

In my journal that night I write with a flourish of neophyte brio, "I am working this business, it's not working me," not yet knowing that in this business *everyone* gets worked, at least a little bit.

The floor manager at Peepland is named Rita, a pale, thin woman with minuscule pupils and ropy tendons bulging from her forearms and neck. She always has a Newport dangling from her lip and calls everyone "baby." Rita put me on my guard, with her stringy brown ponytail and utterly transparent supply-side nurturing. She always had some wobbly, rash-ridden girl tucked next to her, calling her "Mom." Then she and the general manager, Lennie, a dead-eyed white guy with a gray Jheri curl, disappear one fine day. Nobody knows where they went, but then, nobody cares. I certainly don't. Rita didn't like me very much, either, because one day I caught her on the way to the bathroom with a syringe tucked behind her ear like a pencil. She never said anything to me about it, but I am just as glad to have her gone.

Rita gives way to Lisi, a chunky Italian lady with thick ash-blonde highlights and boggy black roots who constantly powders her feet, leaving white talcum footprints all over backstage. Lisi plays sugar mommy to Jody, a tall, skinny, hideously plain girl. Lisi is always prattling on about how gorgeous and thin Jody is, and how she's going to get her portfolio done and make Jody a famous model. We all roll our eyes at one another because everybody knows damn well that Jody ain't gonna be no model. But we keep our mouths shut—you don't want to get on the wrong side of Lisi.

And Lisi gives way to K.D., a stylish, high-yellow shrike with a weave so big you could pack a lunch in it. K.D., short for Kandine, makes no bones about playing favorites, going so far as to draw un-flattering caricatures of women she doesn't like and hanging them on the dressing room wall. Broad-beamed women with orangutan faces, emaciated women covered in tattoos, women with mouthfuls of gold teeth. Ugliness is the ultimate sin in K.D.'s book, and those who deign to fall short of her standards are quick to feel her wrath.

You have to kiss ass with the managers, no matter what you really think of them, because they control the schedule. If a lot of girls want to work, who gets sent home is up to the manager's discretion. That means being told to come back another day, usually one nobody wants because it's slow.

Friday nights are unpopular. The money is great, but the girls either want to be home with their families or out partying. I like Fridays, though, because Mick buys everyone dinner. The bouncers come down to the basement, their hairy, gorilla-thick arms laden with boxes from Pizza King up the street, or Mick hires a kindly old guy to set up a buffet in the office and he fixes plates of sandwiches and pasta salad that we eat in the dressing room. I sit on the bench eating my turkey sandwich, watching the girls from the day shift get dressed up to go out. I admire how assured and sophisticated they are, done up with their gold—fingernails, name plate necklaces, bamboo earrings, bracelets, rings, and nugget watches, and their smart denim outfits and Fendi bags. They count their money, laughing and joking among themselves. To them, Peepland is just a means to an end, and the men milling around out there are fools. Their fools.

I am young, but I am far from the youngest girl working at Peepland. Some of the girls told me they had started there when they were thirteen. Depressing, for sure, but if you're on your own, where else would you go? "Back home" isn't an option. Some of the young ones are too rough to get close to, like Sophie, a skinny-ass white girl whose preferred form of greeting is a half-joking round-house kick aimed at your head, but most of them are eager to make a new friend, or at least have someone their age to talk to. I like Siobhan a lot, despite the fact that she is a compulsive liar. One day she'll claim she is a Brooklyn Jew and lives out on Ocean Parkway, even though she has a pronounced Southern accent. The next day she'll go on about how she is a dancer and is going to audition for work on a cruise ship, although you can see she is bow-legged and can barely walk straight, let alone dance. She attempts a pirouette, bungles it completely, then changes the subject. One of the few true beauties in our midst, with black hair, pale skin, small buds for breasts and a thick lower body, she'd look at herself in the mirror and crow, "I got juicy thighs, and a juicy ass!" Somebody else must've been taken with her great looks, too, because she wears a full-length black mink to work every day.

"What, are you kidding?" Laureen says to me when I present Siobhan's Brooklyn story as we share a Newport backstage. Laureen, my age, is five months pregnant with twins, and she still has braces on her teeth. "There's no way Siobhan's living in Brooklyn. She stays in the same hotel I do." One of the fleabag affairs down the street where for fifty dollars a night you could rent a room with graffiti-marked furniture, ashtrays spilling over with empty crack vials, and shit smeared on the walls.

It's no great achievement to get hired at Peepland—all you need is lingerie and a pulse. There are chunky girls, skinny girls, downright fat girls. Girls with saggy tits, small tits, freakishly large tits, surgically mangled tits. Cellulite, scars, stretch marks, bad tattoos. Girls who are quite stunning and some who are, charitably put, unconventionally pretty. They come from everywhere—Dominican Republic, Puerto Rico, Haiti, Jamaica, Trinidad, West Indies, New Zealand, Russia, France, England, Eastern Europe, and all parts of the United States. Some come for a day or two, others have been there for years.

With so many women coming and going, I am only able to remember them in small sketches. Ginger, with her gentle face kissed by freckles and her fine, red Andrew Wyeth hair tucked behind her ears. Every day she sits in the dressing room reading *The Wall Street Journal*, with her perfect teacher's pet posture. I couldn't imagine what brought her to Peepland, then Rachel told me she'd confided that a boyfriend left her after he'd gotten her pregnant. She had the abortion and vowed that if men were going to treat her poorly, she was at least going to get paid for it.

Patsy, a loud but very kind, long-haired Irish Bronx girl, discussing her upcoming Easter dinner and complaining loudly about her mother because, unlike Patsy, she uses frozen broccoli, not fresh, in her broccoli-and-cheese casserole.

Beautiful Marisol, with a short, bouncing ponytail and a light coat of brown fur all over her legs. She'd baby oil herself—fur and all—to a light, supple sheen and rake in tons of money. A rapper who was quite popular at the time used to come in looking for her, popping his neck and yelling over the music, "Where da hairy one at? Where da hairy one at?"

The women I get to know are aspiring models and actresses, single moms, illegal immigrants, druggies, rocker chicks, runaways, party girls, artists, secretaries, and security guards who drop in on weekends for extra cash, hookers who want a break from the streets, world travelers who want to finance their next adventure. Some women I only know by sight, as they clack by on their cheap heels on their way into the toilet stalls to smoke crack, the burning plastic smell filling the dressing room.

For the year I spend working there, Peepland is the most stable thing in my life. When all else fails, I can put on my sunglasses, hide my hair under a scarf, and take the train to Times Square. By dropping down into the rank, tacky basement, I am transformed. Instead of being this gaseous ball of potential, I'm an elemental force of nature, navigating the world by my own body, by a very simple set of instincts. Me, but not quite me. Anesthetized. Shrewder. Better.

There is nothing about working at Peepland that I find erotic—such as I know from erotic at my age. I'm no innocent, but I just can't understand the attraction of such a place, it's so filthy and pathetic. I know why the women are here: Money. We need the money for kids, clothes, trips, dreams, drugs, the time to build a life or something resembling one. We'll overlook the scuzz to get the job done. But what's the draw for the men? I'm mystified—I squint at them contemptuously and try to puzzle it out. Sometimes, if the tips aren't coming fast enough, I corner them: "What are you doing here?" "Is that a wedding ring? Why aren't you home with your wife?" When I'm not paving over foreboding with pimpy swagger, I wonder how I got here, how I fell so far so fast. I know there's a purpose here—this dip downward will fund my climb up, but this is not what I had planned. Not at all.

To live so close to the edge is terrifying in some ways, but curiously relaxing in others. I'm sort of glad to have a reprieve from rabid self-actualization. Nothing I do at Peepland counts toward anything, I'm just making money and marking time. While other people my age are taking calculated steps toward building a future, I am in manic free fall. They are safe and predictable, I gloat inwardly, while I am authentic and fierce.

I really don't know what the hell I am doing.

I take a drama class here, a voice lesson there, enough to keep up my cover. Out of a sense of duty, I still go to auditions but I care about acting less and less. I fear what people will think of me if they discover where I am working—shit, I know what a job like this *means*—but I also know that Times Square is a world apart from the East Village, and light-years away from New Jersey. If I don't tell anybody, nobody will find out. Peepland is a complete non sequitur to my "real" life, my own secret vice.

I don't have a career, a plan, or a goal. But I have my rage and I cling to it. I'm no longer mad at anything in particular, but I hang on to the feeling out of habit, as anger has kept the pieces of me together for so long.

Because I am a bitter little shit, the brutality and coarseness of Peepland suit me perfectly. Had I attempted stripping in one of the down-at-the-mouth topless bars where other East Village girls danced—Billy's Topless in Chelsea, the Baby Doll Lounge down by Canal Street—I would have exploded. I am not ready to withstand scrutiny or the demands of polite conversation. I'm better off where all the clientele wants is to grunt, gape, and paw.

They are losers, the customers at Peepland—Eliot's hollow men, headpiece filled with porn and fists full of tokens, shuttling dumbly from booth to booth. Intuition tells me to pretend I am older than eighteen—any vulnerability, particularly the vulnerability of youth, seems ill-advised, and in my cheap 14th Street wig and heavy makeup, I can pass for twenty-two. I'm sure advertising my age would make a lot of men drool—there's a girl here who looks sixteen, a delicate, dirty-blonde thing with a gravelly, waif-of-Dickens voice and a cleanly shaved pubis that gives her genitals the appearance of tender fruit. Men line the halls waiting for her. They slaver for youth, purity they can leave their sooty psychic fingerprints on. But I don't want someone going after that part of me, worrying my defenses the way a dog gnaws a bone to get at the marrow.

I get my share of special cases—customers with silk teddies under their business suits, or carrying a lunch box with a dildo clipped in where the thermos would be. More than these men want to look at me, they want me to look back. They furtively dart into my booth, obtain witness, then skid out on their pall of shame and perversion.

While I perform I silently taunt the men, revolted by their hostile neediness. Their bodies don't bother me—I only see what I want to, the scuff on a shoe, the loop of a jowl, the sweep of a raincoat. It's the talking I can't stand. I don't want access to their interior life in any way—and I certainly don't want them in mine. When they try to get to know me, who I am, what I'm really like, they are immediately rebuffed. No sale. I suppose I should feel "degraded" when they prefer to see me naked, but I am relieved to be just a body. I am safe hiding behind this flesh, this husk.

After several moves around the Lower East Side, I finally get a passable place to live—a run-down one-bedroom on East 11th Street. Deb, who let me stay in her apartment when I first got to town, was evicted after she came back from tour, so when my fifth roommate runs off to Florida on a coke bender, she moves in with me. A tiny person with brown saucer eyes and curiously intelligent hands, she sits on the steps of the loft over the living room that I sleep in and we talk for hours about the lives that we're trying to carve out, though I'm floundering more than carving. I guess I'm finding myself, if finding one's self means traveling with bands, dating stupidly, club-hopping, crafting bad performance projects, sleeping late, and shopping nonstop. Deb, seven years my senior, is much more together. She has a bachelor's degree in economics and a master's in journalism from Columbia, so when she isn't playing guitar in front of a roiling mosh pit, she writes financial columns for *Barron's* and *Investor's Daily*. After several months of living with me, she develops an extra-curricular interest in nudging me toward a goal.

She comes home late at night from band practice, wrestling her guitar case down the hall and into the apartment, yawning, "I have to be awake at 3 a.m. when the London bond market opens." Then she sees yet another heap of hot pink Betsey Johnson shopping bags on the living room floor and is scarcely able to conceal her alarm. Being much too sweet to come right out and tell me to get a life, she sighs deeply and says, with hesitation, "You know, maybe you should think about investing some of that money you're making."

Much of my earnings come from Calvin, who frequently visits me at Peepland. He stood out right away. Unlike the other customers, he doesn't simper or bark out commands. He leans against the glass and fixes his wistful gaze on me, then drifts away into whatever fantasy he's got working. He is not an attractive man, short and stoop-shouldered, his hair a weird orange frizz sticking out from under a tan fedora, but he is polite, almost reverential. He never fails to ask me how I'm doing, so eventually we begin talking. He tells me he is a former pianist who now hosts a popular radio show on the big jazz station. At first I don't believe him, because here I've heard all manner of lies, including a man who said he was a certain noted psychiatrist, passing his business card through the slot and saying, "Call me! I can help you!" while he shuddered violently. But I tuned in one day and heard Calvin's voice. It was true.

"So why don't you play anymore?" I asked.

"Too slow," he said, holding up his hands, which are thick-knuckled and stiff. "Arthritis."

Recently divorced after twenty-one years of marriage and living alone near Lincoln Center, Calvin doesn't appear to have much besides work (and Peepland), so I try to make him happy. I am almost moved to defend him when I hear two girls backstage snickering over his affection for garter belts.

If I focus my eyes a certain way, I can see both my own reflection in the glass and Calvin on the other side. When I do this, our disparate selves merge—lost angry girl and lost lonely man. His body becomes mine, the unholiest transubstantiation. And though I don't want it to happen, he will stay a part of me, as immutable a memory as my first kiss or my last day at home. In years to come, his face will come to me whenever I hear the sad reedy wail of jazz saxophone, or brushes whispering on a snare drum. What gets under my skin is what I can't understand—how could someone with that much accomplishment feel that empty?

The weight of the pathos is too much for my teenage self to bear and after a while, I begin to hate him. At first I was flattered by the attention, but I grow repulsed by this man drooping his way into my booth three, four times a week. What did he want from me? He is one of the most famous voices in New York radio, and I am just some dumb naked girl in a peep show. Didn't he have someone else to dump his troubles on?

He comes to see me one afternoon and instead of listening

patiently to his workaday miseries, I light into him. "What's your fucking problem? Don't you ever have any *good* news?"

His face freezes in a rictus of shock and agony, like he's just been shanked.

When I see his expression, I know I've done something needlessly cruel. I want to take it back. I can't take it back. When the window goes down, I hear the door slam and I am sure I won't see him again. Oh, well. Shrug. Too bad.

I step out of the booth. A squatty black man in a bus driver uniform is lurking, pretending to inspect a display of European bondage videos. I call over to him, "Are you ready for me now?"

My mother's eyes are a dark, mercurial hazel—by turns the color of moss agate and thunderheads. She has a withering stare, handed down and refined through centuries of Puritan reproach, that when turned on you is like having your foot nailed to the floor. I have done much as a teenager to earn that excruciating look—the all-nighters at CBGBs, the nose ring, the second nose ring, the college applications left unfinished on the dining room table. But now I am out on my own and she is away at school working toward another master's, and the only tether that connects me to her is her voice on the phone. When we speak, I do what I have to to keep that voice even, appeased. I am shaky out here, so I don't dare court her rejection. I need her love too much.

Do I intend to tell her about Peepland? No. Never. I would go to the ends of the earth to spare my parents the truth. When they ask me what I'm doing for work, I make something up. I am a maid, a waitress, a clerk. I will be anything but what I fear most: a disappointment. But I am much too young to understand the frailty of *never* or the true meaning of what it is to disappoint.

EIGHT

Bad Night in El Paso, Texas

Meanwhile, back in the present and back on the road, I'm lugging around the *Exotic Dancer Directory* as my preferred reading material. I just can't put it down—not because of the pictures of the dancers, or the handy listing of clubs by city, state, and type. It's the club names. The names kill me.

Late at night when I'm by myself in my motel room trying to come down from the molar-rattling adrenaline high that keeps me up a good three or four hours after a shift, I'll mentally index the names. There seem to be a few distinct categories.

Cats-n-horses: Jaguar Club, Feline Cathouse, Cheetah's, Pussy-cat Lounge, Crazy Horse, Wild Horse, Pink Pony, Foxy Filly, that type of thing.

Dolls: The Doll House, Satin Dolls, New York Dolls, Regina's House of Dolls, and the like.

Precious metals: Solid Gold, Pure Platinum, Gold Club, Gold Fingers, Platinum Club, etc., etc.

Body parts and movements: Hipps, Legs, Bunns, Cheeques, Shakers, Lookers, Jiggles, Wiggles, Knockers, and Beavers (which would be a little over the top were it not in Oregon, the Beaver State).

And a category so rife with stealth and guilt, we'll call it Sexual Rorschach: Cheaters, Obsession, Teasers, Anticipation Lounge, Tattle-tales, Antics, Secrets, Scandals, Sinners, Titillations, Forbidden Fruit, Skin Games, Peepers, Dangerous Curves.

I like the "Lounge" names. They're cozy, not a feeling this busi-ness often engenders: Glo Worm Lounge, Shark Lounge, Peek-A-Boo Lounge, Foxy Lady Lounge, Bigfoot Lounge.

The namesake clubs make me curious—I wouldn't mind know-ing who exactly they're named after. The owner, in tribute to his or her dream come true of owning a strip club? A child? A friend? Big Earl's Goldmine, Juicy Lucie's, Frank's Chicken House, Big Frank's Hen House, BookEm Dano's, Wild Bill's Pink Cadillac, Cadillac Carl's Cabaret, Brad's Brass Flamingo, Trixie's Gold Room, Nicole's Fuzzy Grape, Coz's Eight Ball Lounge, Phyllis' Angels. The austere and dignified Club Fred.

There are a handful of establishments that were named with some actual wit: Double Dribble Tavern, George's Dancin' Bare, Pop-a-Top Pub. And a couple that are clever, but maybe they shouldn't have bothered: 19th Hole Lounge, Up Your Glass.

• • •

In no particular order, some club names that I am taken with:

World Famous Boobie Bungalow
Sharky's Tiki Hut
Jumbo's Clown Room
Boom Boom Room
Stir Crazy Lounge
Gaslight
Booby Trap
Neon Cowboy
Chills & Thrills
Cherry Club
Golden Banana
Brass Ass Lounge
Stud's Pub
Witches Inn
Mud Puppy Inn
Billy Budd's
Valley of the Dolls
Sugar Shack
Weasel's Sportsman's Rendezvous

Prince Machiavelli's is perhaps the best name for a strip club that I've come across thus far. But that's the only good thing I can say about the night I spend working at this El Paso hole-in-the-wall.

A brief summary of what goes wrong:

1. A man I'm dancing for puts his hands on my hips and pulls me toward him. "C'mere so I can do a line off of your tits," he breathes, a slimy operator like Eric Roberts

in *Star 80*. When I refuse, he shields himself from the bouncer's view and uses a Visa card to chop several fat lines of coke on the sticky, wood-look laminate cocktail table and snorts them up through a hollowed-out ball-point pen.

2. Half of the customers are from Juárez, just across the border, and have trouble speaking English. And I have trouble speaking Spanish. (Why French in high school? *Why?*) A moment of levity between a Chihuahuan and me when I ask him "What's Spanish for . . . [*holding my hands out indicating huge fake breasts*]." "*Tetas falsas,*" he says and we both laugh.

3. The ringleader of a preppy bachelor party flags me down to dance for the groom-to-be. "Let me see your tits first!" the bachelor snarls, a bitter pill in a khaki wrapper. "Gee, how'd your fiancée nab a catch like you?" I snarl back, balling up the twenty and throwing it at him before I walk away.

4. Cocaine Guy follows me around the club sweating bullets and offering to give me a new Corvette in exchange for having sex with his wife and girlfriend while he watches. Please, like I'd be caught dead in a new Corvette anyhow.

5. Crawling around on stages in thigh-high boots for a week straight has abraded my knees so badly they look like massive popped blisters—red, skinned, and oozing. I show the manager my knees and he mercifully lets me leave at midnight. I have him escort me out the back door to my car because Cocaine Guy is hovering near the front entrance.

6. I'm hungry. Understandable craving for Mexican food. By the time I leave Prince Machiavelli's, it's too late for a real restaurant so the only "Mexican" I can find is Taco Bell. I

get a bag of *grande* burritos and eat in my motel room watching the lights twinkle over in the brown haze of Juárez.

Home suddenly feels very far away. I reach for the phone.

It's high noon at the Cruise Control Café and I am headed toward Wyoming with my lunch nestled in my lap. I've discovered the perfect configuration for eating a combo meal while driving: burger in the left hand, fries clasped between my knees, the right hand free to reach for the soda in the cup holder. And to steer.

I know a lot of people consider fast-food chains a modern blight and drive-throughs a decline of civilization, but I am truly grateful for them. They are a mercy of convenience, rescue for lonely travelers like me who just can't stand the thought of another meal in a restaurant alone. Telling the hostess, "Just one, please," then hiding behind a newspaper while gulping down a pot roast special so I don't have to make eye contact with other diners.

I am near Trinidad, Colorado, about six hours from home. El Paso to Cheyenne is two grueling days—a long while alone under the endless ice-blue spring sky, rolling along listening to the radio. After ten days spent largely in darkness, my eyes sting. I'm thrilled to finally see sunlight, but does there have to be so much of the stuff?

I flip between stations looking for the perfect country song. I've come to love country-and-western. I used to hate it, but now, between the deft storytelling and open-heartedness, I'm hooked. I like the trendoid-sanctioned artists just fine—Patsy Cline, Johnny Cash, Merle Haggard—but my favorites are the more pop-inflicted acts: Brooks and Dunn, Alan Jackson, George Strait. I'm not entirely sold on the yeasty sincerity of Garth Brooks, but his song "Much Too Young to Feel This Damn Old" is one I sure can relate to today.

I am tired, with a bone-deep fatigue I haven't felt in years. I turn the dial, trawling for sad songs. I need the formula for conveying heartache that country does best. A world-weary voice, stark and plaintive against the weeping of the fiddle, a steel guitar coming in to address the grievances of the strings, and then a crescendo that brings the three together, pulsing with emotion and blood—taste and restraint be damned.

The heartrending emotionality is pretty excessive, but I don't mind, for these are buttons that desperately need to be pushed. After days and nights of listening to couched offers, half-sincere compliments, and flat-out lies, both giving and receiving, I am desperate to hear something wholly-felt and true.

Colin Raye's "Little Rock" starts playing. I am singing along when my voice breaks, and before I know what is happening, I am sobbing uncontrollably. Not because what I'm feeling is so bad, but because it is so much. I am flooded with memories. The cold proposition that first night in Pueblo, the skin-peeled-off shame in Las Vegas, the sweet deaf couple looking at me so urgently in Dallas. That creepy, coked-out man trailing after me in El Paso. Desires and demands rushing toward my naked skin like greedy fingers. And the rest of it—the horrible car wreck, too many bad meals and not enough sleep, wrong turns and missed exits, the searing twang of pain in my thigh muscles from squatting over rest stop toilets, and the remnants of those desperate days at Peepland, which, whenever dredged up, always seem better off buried. I went through it all without any defense but emotional defense—and that's no kind of reliable armor.

When this was the only way I knew to survive, I had one focus: making money. I made myself slick and efficient. Anything else that crossed my mind seemed superfluous, almost irrelevant. If something disturbed me, or touched me too deeply, I would push it away or float up into the ozone of my own head and keep right on going.

But now I can't pull back, I can't callus over. I have worked too goddamn hard to slough away the bullshit posturing, the knee-jerk emotional withdrawal. I am dogged by ghosts of opinion, phantoms of need, but I am not able to shake them off. I can't just pull over to the side of the road, open the door, and say, "Everybody out!" This is cargo I'll have with me for a while.

Stripping takes out of me things that I didn't even realize I had. The near-nudity isn't the problem, or the physical vulnerability, or working well outside the margins of acceptable female behavior. It's the damn neediness: Angry men scowling at me like they can buy me for a dollar, lonely men professing love after a ten-minute chat with the specter of femininity that wafts before them, and confused and desperate men convinced that if only they could get a girl to do what they ask, however outlandish, things will be better somehow. These men don't just hunger for a glimpse of skin, because they could stay home and look at Miss August were that the case. They want some kind of connection, to tap the life in a live, nude girl. And no amount of professional distance on my part can keep that leeching feeling at bay. I've nothing left but exhausted tears, choked out silently, running in fat rills to my chin. I drive along crying and mopping my face with wadded-up Burger King napkins.

Randy answers his cell phone, the sound of hammers and a saw blade whining high and sweet through soft wood in the background. When I phoned him last night, he insisted on a three-calls-a-day schedule: when I wake up in the morning (or, more likely, afternoon), before I leave for the club or my next appointed town, and immediately after I get into my room at night. I'll be in Cheyenne soon enough, but I need him right now.

"Hi-ii." Oh God, I sound like shit.

"Baby! What are you doing? Are you okay?"

"I'm okay," I sniffle deeply, clearing my snot-clogged sinuses.

"I'm just so fried," I start, tears rolling again. "You have no idea."

"Where are you? Can you make it home?"

"I don't know where I am. Somewhere in Colorado," I say, eyes roving the landscape on either side of the highway. "I think I'm in Castle Rock." I feel better for having heard his voice. I'm coming back down now, almost on terra firma. "Yeah, there's the rock. Hey, it really *does* look like a castle!"

"That's only four hours away. You can make it. Just hurry, 'cause I miss you!"

I manage a faint, phlegmy squeak.

For a long time, I swore that stripping couldn't affect me deeply because I was working "with my body, not my soul." How ever did I get the idea that the two functioned separately? The muddle in my brain is exacerbating my physical weariness, and I'm bleary-eyed with fatigue.

This is what I was after, this clarity, and I'm overwhelmed. I know now why I tuned out so much, why I focused on the bottom line: Had I paid attention to every single thing that happened around me when I danced, and taken it all in, I would have gone absolutely out of my mind.

If part of my motivation for getting back into stripping was nostalgia, Lord, that notion is blown to bits now. What's that expression? "Happiness isn't found by looking back?" Making a tourist destination of the past is always a dicey proposition—you might be sorely disappointed that things were more boring or shallow than you recall. Or, in my case, you might find they were more complex and difficult than you originally thought. Sentimentality has been soundly trounced by reality. This is way harder than I'd remembered.

How the hell did I do this for six years? Well, I didn't work straight through nonstop. I took a lot of time off—weeks, even months. Sometimes almost an entire year. I needed plenty of breaks. And I need one now.

NINE

The Girl on the Other Side
of the Wall

It's nearly impossible to get a decent bikini wax in Cheyenne. I can't tell whether this is due to timidity on the part of the local salon staffers or some weird stripe of homophobia, but finding someone who will wax me, much less wax me well, has been a challenge. In New York, I went to a stern Russian beautician who approached the task with admirable stoicism. She'd march into the room when I was ready, pull off the sheet I'd wrapped about my hips, dust me down with baby powder, scoop the runny amber wax out of the pot with a Popsicle stick and spread it thickly over whatever hair showed around the thong's edges, press the muslin strip down on the wax, and after a series of perfunctory yanks—*voilà*! Then she'd tweeze out the strays, wipe off any waxy residue with a cotton ball soaked in baby oil, and with a grim duck of her head leave me to get dressed. Efficiency personified.

I found a woman in town who will do the job, but I can tell she'd rather not. She comes into the waxing room like a patient at the dentist's. I try to distract her with conversation—How's your husband? Seen any good movies lately?—but it's hard dredging up small talk while having your most tender flesh paved with sticky goo. I feel more exposed having this done than I do onstage, which makes no sense, really. And she clearly fears something about me, which makes even less sense. Is there any way I can hurt her in my compromised position, pants around my ankles, knees splayed to the sides? She is, after all, the one with immediate access to a large supply of scalding hot wax.

This is my monthly maintenance day, so after the wax, I'm off to get my nails done. I'm very fussy about my fingernails—I don't like them too long or artificial-looking, and I've followed my manicurist, Suzette, as she changed salons four times. She does them just right.

After filing, filling, shaping, and buffing, Suzette starts polishing, her lower lip tucked in concentration. Behold the French manicure—pink tint on the nail bed, and a big, clean swipe of white across the entire width of the free edge. French manicures haven't been fashionable in years, but ambitious, ornamental women— dancers, porn queens, trophy wives, rich divorcees—insist on them still, and for good reason: Nothing signals femininity engaged as a survival mechanism like those prim, "nice girl" colors painted on in doxy detail.

"Hey," I say with a laugh, lifting up the polish bottles to read the names, "there's a color called I'm Not Really a Waitress!" A glittery harlot red. I wish I could tell Suzette why I find this funny, let her in on the joke, but I can't. She knows I write, but the rest of my résumé is a mystery. I learned early on that I would often have to lie— outright or by omission—that I would have to cut friends carefully from the judgmental herd, to spin and twist in the face of bureau-cracy. Tell the wrong people and they'll never treat you the same again. You're stained: Slut. Idiot. Damaged goods. As with everyone I meet, I ran Suzette through my filter—cool or not cool?—and she just didn't scan right.

"Yep," she says, brushing quick-dry top coat on my nails, her smooth, white fingers moving deftly, "a lot of women want that color, but only on their toes for some reason."

By the end of the afternoon, I have spent three hours on my hair, an hour and a half on my nails, an hour at the gym, and another hour for tan and wax. I don't mourn this expenditure of time. Like suiting up for battle, getting my glamour on has a galvanizing effect. After a day of being ministered to by capable hands, I feel ready to take on the world, buffed to a high gloss and impervious to hurt.

When I get home late in the afternoon, I have to address the dinner question. I rustle in the meat drawer and pull out a plastic-wrapped package of ground beef. In my New York days, the most I could hope to find when I opened the refrigerator was a shriveled old turkey burger nested on a lettuce leaf in a take-out container, condiment packets, bottles of vitamins, and maybe a splash of green-furred orange juice at the bottom of a month-old cardboard carton. I do all the grocery shopping, yet I'm still surprised when I look in the fridge these days and find it stocked. "Hey, there's milk in here. Right *on!*"

I set the oven to 350 and ease into a nice rhythm kneading ingredients together for a meatloaf. I'm so relieved to be home for the next month, with nothing more stressful to do than tend to domestic detail or peck out an article. I don't have to cater to any-body's whim or force charm. For now I'm free from the stresses of stripping—anticipating desires, plumping up egos, presenting the most flattering angles, the strain of the charade. God, it's wearying.

I insist on helping with meals, even though Randy is a far better cook. I've never before had a kitchen big enough to stand in with my arms akimbo, let alone comfortably prepare a meal, so I am excited by the opportunity to learn some basic culinary skills. Should I be surprised that I enjoy futzing around in the kitchen and various other acts that indicate maturity? Outsider-fixated, I spent so much time kicking against domesticity that when I "settled down" in Wyoming, I almost had to fetishize home life, approaching it as either a weird experiment or a role-playing game. Like, "I'm buying something out of the Pottery Barn catalog! How camp," or "Look at me, I'm sassy and conscientious, hauling things to the recycling place." Having come to this late, I sometimes feel like an impostor, other times like a little kid clunking around in Mommy's shoes.

But inside the irony and winsome "How do I do this?" wonder is a little silvery burble of joy at the realization that I can be fully adult and still be me. I'm learning that what seemed like an ongoing struggle between freedom and domesticity was really just a style conflict, and I'm better off having a solid home base than living untethered and spastic in the vain pursuit of edge. I know it's heresy for a hipster to say so, but I think being a grown-up pretty much rocks.

I've got my freshly touched-up hair pulled back in a loose ponytail, my face scrubbed, and I'm wearing a black Porn Star tank top and a pair of old baggy gray sweatpants as I crash around the kitchen getting dinner together. Understand, I don't just make a good meatloaf, I *invented* the meatloaf. All manner of things go into the mix—breadcrumbs, corn, celery chunks, and finely diced onions. I spend an inordinate amount of time patting and shaping until it's a perfectly formed pink mottled hillock, an extra loafy meatloaf. I open the oven door as it cooks, like a mother looking in on a sleeping infant. I sing to it, "Search and Destroy," "Raw Power," maybe "I Need Somebody." Then, forty-five minutes later, this masterpiece is taken from the oven, basted in ketchup and Iggy Pop.

• • •

"Let's go look at the ladies."

I say this to Randy as he stacks the dinner wreckage—purple plastic cups, mismatched stainless cutlery, soiled paper napkins crumpled atop black china plates. He carries the stack to the sink, turns on the faucet, and yells over the running water, "Really? Okay."

Usually when we go out on a Friday night, we choose between the Outlaw Saloon and the Cowboy Bar. But I don't want to go to either because some tipsy cowgirl, ranch raised or store bought, always tries to corner me in the bathroom or stare me down on the dance floor. I don't take it personally, as there's not much else to do around here. When the selection of men is poor, the tough girls swagger around in Ropers, bun-hugging Rockies, and button-down tops—too tight but neatly pressed—spoiling for something that will make a good story at work on Monday. I know drinking and fighting are two of the sanctioned local pastimes—and I don't have much objection to either, although I rarely participate—but I don't need the aggravation right now.

Wyoming, the country's ninth largest and least populated state, has only six strip clubs. Not the least, by far: Montana has five, Vermont two, and New Hampshire only one. In Cheyenne, you've got two choices. There's the Green Door on Lincolnway, which is a tiny joint tucked in the back of a drive-through liquor mart. The sign atop of the building is missing a few letters. "DANERS 8–2 AM" it reads on one side, on the other, "DARS 8–2." Inside there's a smoky pool room where you can shoot a few, and in the barroom is a small, square linoleum platform tucked in a mirrored corner where the girls dance. They punch up their songs on the jukebox before they get onstage, and the men lean forward, creaking in their wooden chairs, dollar tips between their teeth. A fun place, but not tonight.

We're going to the Clown's Den. Astride our Harley, we're headed southbound at a blatting, gravel-spitting forty miles an hour.

We pass a handful of stripmalls, a flea market in a building shaped like a teepee, the VFW hall with bingo three nights a week, Big Country Estates trailer park, and a stock car track. In the opposite lane, livestock trucks carry sheep and cattle up from the feedlots in Greeley. We leave city limits and ratchet up to a world-blurring seventy-five. In the evening sun, the plains are golden fire.

The wind is raking my hair straight back, and I'm afraid my fall is about to fly right off. Two hundred dollars' worth of fake hair blowing down South Greeley Highway like a bleach-blonde tumble-weed? I don't think so.

I scream toward Randy's ear, "You've gotta pull over!"

He slows the bike and stops on the shoulder. A semi hauling sheep roars past. Little muzzles poke out of the air holes in the cargo trailer.

I bend at the waist and unhitch the combs that hold the fall to my scalp. A hank of my own hair has tangled into a series of knots around the crown, making it hard to pull the fall free of my head. I tug, tearing the blasted thing off, and a good bit of my real hair, too.

A pronghorn buck looks on from behind a fence. Curious by nature, antelope won't scatter like deer when they know you see them. He stands unmoving, his wide, dark eyes possessed of calm that a human couldn't hope to know.

"What are you staring at?" I call through the bent and rusting wires.

He lowers his black-antlered head and grazes on.

I roll up the fall and drop it in the studded leather saddlebag.

The Clown's Den squats eight miles south of town, in an odd sort of vice encampment situated right on the state line between Wyoming and Colorado. The club, a long and low roadhouse of dark logs, hunkers at the back of a gravel parking lot, with the club's name spelled out in spindly pink neon letters across the front. Behind the lot is a trailer home and a grocery that sells Colorado State Lottery tickets, and out in front is a fireworks store.

On a slow night, the Den is the most depressing thing you've ever seen. I've been in when no dancers showed up—none—and men sat along the tipping rail staring at an empty stage. I've seen nights when there weren't any customers, just dancers sitting in a row on a vinyl banquette along the wall—a party of only party dolls. But on a good night, it's the best. A circus.

Our friend Carmen slithers onstage, hips swiveling in sync with a heavy drum track. An ominous Germanic voice drones out Depeche Mode over the beats. An expert crowd-pleaser, Carmen plucks a man's cowboy hat from his head and squeezes it over her breasts so it stays put while she dances around. Another man stands close to slide a dollar under the side of her white velvet thong and she turns abruptly and hip checks him, to his great pleasure. She reaches down for a pitcher of beer that's next to the stage, and pulls an innocent-looking guy to his feet. His upturned face is pressed to her side. She steps over the tipping rail and pours the beer between her breasts, down her stomach and into the guy's mouth. He parts his lips to the sudsy flow as if it were manna from heaven.

Randy and I sit down at the tipping rail and order drinks. The girls come by and say hello. Here's Honey. Jessie. Monique. Pepper. Dee. The men smile to see me, a civilian female amidst the ranks. But I'm not the only woman in the crowd. At the far end of the tipping rail slouches a young, good-looking Mexican couple who are obviously deep in their cups—in front of them are several empty beer bottles, and a few dollars on the rail. With so many men vying for her attention, Carmen takes a while in getting to the two of them, slumped there at the end of the line. Finally, her second song over, Carmen kneels in front of the man, places the dollar bills between his teeth, and grabs them with her hands cupping her breasts.

Seeing this, the woman's lips all but disappear. Her pretty face hardens, her eyes go black as pitch, her chin pushes forth and her tongue works over her teeth with a hostile motion. When Carmen turns away and begins gathering up her bills, the woman says, quite loudly, "Aw, honey, I had no idea you liked them that cheap."

Everyone at the rail turns to her and stares. It was such a mean thing to say. Mean to her boyfriend, certainly, but meaner to the dancers. Meaner to us.

Her boyfriend doesn't know what to do—he tries to touch her arm but she jerks away. She grabs her purse and storms off to the ladies' room, her tall, sprayed bangs quivering with each angry step.

An old Allman Brothers song starts and Dee comes up to dance. Carmen heads back to stage two, unruffled, her tan skin glistening with sweat. She's twisted her crimped blonde hair up off of her neck to keep cool, and as she saunters through the club, she fans herself with her money. I think she rather enjoys getting a rise out of other women. I wish I could say the same for me. I feel like I've been socked right in the stomach.

I've become so expert at self-protection—deftly pruning disapproving people out of my life, avoiding humiliating scenes, monitoring my disclosure—that I forget how vulnerable I really am. How one thoughtless remark can cut me to the core. I could be smug, console myself with the notion that this woman is a small-minded prude and I'm not. That I am, in fact, the height of sophistication. But it wouldn't help. No matter what I tell myself—that she's probably just jealous, that I'm a bigger person than she is, that no one can make me feel bad unless I let them—that special brand of hatred will always hurt.

I look toward the ladies' room. She's in there, just on the other side of that wall. I could go in and say something to her. But what?

Did she come grudgingly at her boyfriend's behest? If so, I would tell her I give her credit for showing up. She can't be blamed for getting more than she bargained for.

Maybe she just doesn't want to see strange tits shoved in her boyfriend's face.

Maybe she's just had too much beer.

Does she resent the ease of access? How for a little money, women will dance around her man, press their breasts up against him, flatter and serve him? He can come here anytime and leave everything behind. Her complaints, her bothersome children, her tedious headaches, toothaches, backaches, cancers. He can step into a parallel world where flesh is supple and abundant, and Man Is King. The land of No Demands. His weightiest care is the price of a drink or a table dance that leaves him high and dry.

Maybe she hates the idea that dancers are getting away with something—cheating the Madonna/whore system by exploiting it baldly. If that's what she thinks, then I'd tell her that no woman escapes the system. Everything costs—her side, our side, either side of the wall exacts its own price.

Eventually, the girl emerges from the bathroom, still angry, still drunk, and leads her boyfriend out of the club by the snout. I watch them as they leave—her shoulders pulled back stiffly as though starched in place, his curled forward. There's no way I could say anything to her now unless I ran after her, which would be too much drama. Ah, well. I can't help everybody. Alas, and damn.

When Honey takes the stage for her set, she pulls me up with her. She lays me flat on my back so she can dance over top of me, the master to my slave, and I overhear one of the guys who smiled at me earlier say something to his friend about how I must "have no self-respect."

Now don't *you* start, buddy.

• • •

"Uh oh," I say to Randy, quickly pivoting to turn my back to the crowded restaurant, "customers."

Randy visually patrols every room he enters. He's a genius at it, really. But this time I spot potential trouble before he does. "Where?" His eyes scan the crowd at the Village Inn.

"Directly across from us in the smoking section. A whole tableful. They were at the Clown's Den earlier. They recognize me. Can you see them? They're looking right at us."

"Oh yeah. Okay," he says. He puts a sheltering arm around my shoulders and turns me back around to face front. The hostess comes over. "Nonsmoking, please," Randy tells her.

At 2 a.m. when the bars close, everyone's jammed into the all-night restaurants together—strippers, customers, the bar crowd, the bar bands, the bouncers. The only place where you *might* get some privacy is the Flying J truck stop out on I-25. Not here, though, right in the center of town.

We're seated at a booth along the wall, far from the table of customers, and blocked from their view by a large pie case. Randy goes to the men's room. When the waitress comes, I get pancakes for myself and recite his order from memory: chicken fried steak, hash browns, white toast, eggs scrambled with Cheddar cheese, and coffee.

Randy returns, and I gesture with my head to draw his attention to the next table over. A man is loudly mocking a dancer from the Green Door. We eavesdrop in silence while awaiting our food. As he talks, his mouth moves with comic elasticity—how drunk is this guy, anyway? "I wouldn't fuck her with somebody else's dick!" he howls to his friends, men and women in party clothes. Fake pearls and third-markdown trousers. Randy and I both know the girl he is talking about. She's a sour little moppet, purply lips ever fixed in a dolorous downward turn. She doesn't like me much, and the feeling is mutual. Still, I don't like hearing her dissed.

Our order is set down, the hash browns crisp at the edges, butter pats sliding off the pancakes. Randy picks up a fork and a wood-handled serrated knife and saws angrily into his chicken fried steak. "Who's he kidding?" he snorts, "Like she'd give him the time of day anyhow."

"Yeah, no shit," I grumble, reaching for the syrup pitcher. "A stripper gets hit on eighty times a night and if she's interested in hooking up with a customer in the first place—highly dubious—she's gonna pick *him*."

"I know *all* the strippers in Cheyenne," the pickled lout bleats on.

"See, that's why I don't work out at the Den," I say to Randy, skewering a bite of his steak and dredging up some white gravy with my fork. "This town is so small a guy with a mouth like that could be a huge problem."

Randy shakes his head and snarls into his coffee cup. "Guy just needs to get his ass beat. That's the only problem I can see."

TEN

Exotic World Museum
Helendale, California

Stripping is an outlaw profession, with but one prevailing philosophy: Take the money and run. As a result, the long and colorful history of exotic dance is overlooked and underrecorded. I've been content with that so far. The lack of known lineage meant I could craft my stripper self as I went along, without pressure to conform to what should be or the influence of what has been. In a business obsessed with novelty, one that maps the sexual mores of an age by pushing two steps beyond them, how can there be room for tradition?

But that lack of connection to the past has been bothering me lately. Becoming a stripper was a step I took with another woman, but one that left me feeling very much alone. I wish I knew someone who could lend historical insight, a little background. I frequently talk with my ex-dancer friends, but my contemporaries and I are in the same boat—still trying to sort out the recent past. We're newly minted alumni, moved to deliberate and process in that "Girl, let me tell you all about it" way. We sift without the perspective that only time can bring.

In stripping, there is no sense of continuity. Women take their stories with them when they go. Some don't want to remember, so they blot out that chapter of their lives like a fugitive erasing her tracks in the snow. Others simply don't care to be inconvenienced by a blemished past made public record. And others who might share their story are stymied by lack of time and skill to create, or by arbiters of culture who wouldn't deign to "take the subject seriously." The feminist in me is angered by the deafening silence—this is women's history, after all. But the listener in me isn't so much angry as disappointed. So many delicious stories, gone!

People look for themselves in books and movies. They count on those touchstones, not so much for gospel as affirmation that others have walked the same path. But for strippers, there is no *Giovanni's Room*, no *Easy Rider*, no *Basketball Diaries*, no *Well of Loneliness*. Perhaps if there were an intellectual tradition, a *floozerati* that inspired a body of work to consult and a philosophy to impart, I'd feel less marooned. There was the writing of Colette, then of Gypsy Rose Lee, and then almost nothing, unless you count *Showgirls*. Which I don't. I'd like to know my history. Even outlaws need a sense of belonging.

I'm increasingly curious about strippers from days past. In what ways was their job similar to mine? And how was it different? How might I find out? I could prowl library stacks for obscure, out-of-print books, dig through microfilm of old magazine pieces. But whatever I'd find would likely be tainted by the author's opinion. I'd probably learn more about what the writer thinks than anything else. I don't want an outsider's version of what it is to be a stripper. I want the story straight from the source.

I research the stars of burlesque, to see who I can turn to for testimony. Ann Corio, dead. Sally Rand, dead. Lili St. Cyr, my role model, dead. Am I doomed to discover my heritage through the obituaries? If I'm to learn anything firsthand about the history of striptease, I'd better move fast.

The first link to my lineage resides in the middle of the Mojave Desert. The Exotic World Burlesque Museum is halfway between Los Angeles and Las Vegas, just off Route 66 in Helendale, California. The first weekend in June, museum director Dixie Evans, who performed in the fifties as the "Marilyn Monroe of Burlesque," hosts a reunion of burlesque dancers and the Miss Exotic World Pageant—where young dancers can bump-and-grind the old-fashioned way for cash and prizes.

I fly out for the event and rent a car at LAX for the three-hour drive to Helendale.

As I drive along Route 66 beyond Victorville, the two-lanes shoot me past railroad tracks, talc mines, abandoned whitewashed brick bungalows, and a defunct, one-room go-go bar called the Lost Hawg. The Hawg must've really been rockin' in its day—the front of the building is decorated with dancing shadow figures and silhouettes of reclining girls like you'd find on a trucker's mudflaps. There's a warped wood cutout of a pig on the front door, too. Now all that remains is the shell of the building, ringed by tumbleweed and creosote bush. Word is, someone plans to make it into a barbecue place. I pull over and snap a few pictures, with the gnawing feeling that I missed something good.

The pavement stops at the turnoff to Wild Road and the car bounces over ruts and gravel. Man, I am really in the boonies now. The sky is a ferocious summer blue, and the wind whips sand and pebbles along the desert floor. Roadrunners, the black combs on their heads rustling in the breeze, pip by on skinny legs. Just after a bend in the road, an enormous black-and-white iron filigree gate rises on the right-hand side. Arching over the driveway, it says, in big white letters: EXOTIC WORLD.

A whitewashed fence runs the length of the driveway. All along hang white wooden stars with the names of burlesque queens hand-painted on them in red: Little Egypt, who supposedly started it all by bringing her "hoochie koochie dance" to the Chicago World's Fair in 1893, Tanayo, Ricci Cortez, Sheila Rae, Linda Doll, Tempest Storm, Blaze Fury—names both familiar and forgotten.

I'm stopped at the top of the drive by an older man in slacks and a striped polo shirt. His thick glasses have skidded to the tip of his sweaty, large-pored nose. I hand him the twenty-five-dollar admission, and he adds the bills to a thick roll pulled from his pocket. He motions me toward a parking space.

In the middle of the dirt parking lot sprouts a small grass island with a dry fountain at the center and, to the side, a ceramic statue of a pig in a sheriff's uniform. An old white stretch limo with EXOTIC WORLD painted on the side in gold cursive sits next to a mobile home. Two gimpy-looking black horses drink from a trough in a lean-to out back. Sprinkled among the buildings is haphazardly positioned plaster statuary, a random chorus of goddesses listing in the Mojave wind.

The museum is housed in a converted farm, a series of run-down trailers and modular units cobbled together around a covered concrete lanai. The main, six-room building used to be a goat shed. The museum's founder, Jennie Lee, the "Bazoom Girl," was a burlesque dancer who retired to the area in the 1970s with her husband, Charlie Arroyo. Previously, Jennie had owned two topless clubs, the Blue Viking in San Pedro and the Sassy Lassie in San Diego. In the late 1980s, Jennie developed breast cancer and her friend Dixie moved in to help care for her. After Jennie's death in 1990, Dixie took over the operation.

The museum, a repository of tarty gewgaws and girly artifacts, looks the way one might imagine the attic of Barbie's Dream House. The walls are covered, floor-to-ceiling, in old burlesque posters, pinups, tabloid tearsheets, and promo stills. By scanning the articles, you can learn that the child star Shirley Jean, who appeared in the Little Rascals, grew up to become a stripper named "Gilda, Hollywood's Golden Girl." Or you can amble about admiring Gypsy Rose Lee's costume trunk, Mae West's cape (shredded and dry-rotting by now), Sally Rand's fans, and Jayne Mansfield's pink satin heart-shaped posing couch. But every so often in the va-va-voomery is something totally odd—among a collection of rhinestone jewelry in a case is a key chain from Myrtle Beach and a miniature bust of George Washington in blackface. In a grouping of dancer photographs from the 1960s hangs an autographed 8 x 10 glossy of baseball player Steve Sax. Those wishing to honor the memory of departed peeler Sherrie Champagne may do so—an urn containing her ashes stands in the middle of a makeshift shrine.

Dixie herself, now several decades past a believable Marilyn Monroe comparison, wanders the grounds in a low-cut black cocktail dress. Four former burlesque queens sit at a folding table, grinning behind stacks of old 8 x 10s they are eager to sign. One of them, her spotted scalp visible through scant wisps of black hair, sits slumped and staring off into the near distance, her flowered polyester muumu tented over her chest and rounded stomach. "Oh, you'll have to excuse Estelle," whinnies the tanned-to-orange blonde in a leopard-print pantsuit seated to her right, "she just had a mastectomy." Young women, half-dressed for the contest—hair set in glittering rows of pin-curls, sequined bras showing through their thin cotton bathrobes—dart to and from the dressing room. A formidably muscled woman named Pillow, wearing a black turban and a black sleeveless unitard that shows off her remarkably developed arms, is running around trying to corral camera crews and photographers.

The show is about to begin.

The dilapidated stage—a wooden runway with two stone lions keeping guard at either end—has a white trellis behind it, with crooked wooden letters spelling out EXOTIC WORLD ranging across. Badly frayed and faded American flags whip themselves in the strong wind. Old Glory on the skids. Rows of folding chairs line either side of a rather neglected-looking rectangular swimming pool, and people are filing in. A group of senior citizens just off the tour bus lays claim to the shady seats.

I grab a seat in front of the tour group and crane my neck to examine the crowd. A mix of old-timers, hip kids with fancy tattoos and dark glasses, and a bunch of bikers with their hands folded in front of them, like schoolkids.

The event starts with the emcee introducing Dixie. She makes an entrance from the lanai in her slinky black dress and a black feather boa. Throwing her arms over her head, she struts around the pool's perimeter and minces up the steps to the stage. She greets the crowd, welcomes the media, and promises a grand time to all.

The old burlesque performers come out, one by one. Cynthiana in a black cocktail dress, Daisy Delite in a red feather headpiece that the wind bats like a cat toy, Dee Milo in a red fishtail gown. Cynthiana, stout and beehived, strips down to her black fishnets and tassled pasties and comes our way. She points to her breasts. "They used to go this way," motioning around and around, "but now," she points to the ground, "they go this way." All the old-timers in the row behind me laugh.

To see so much seasoned flesh on parade—stomachs protruding, upper arms jiggling, crow's-feet creasing and deepening as the women smile in the desert sun—makes me a little uneasy. Stripping is a young girl's game—I distinctly remember feeling "too old" to strip when I turned twenty-five. And here are women drawing up on three times that age out there shimmying and shaking. In a way, it's refreshing. Who says a woman can't flaunt her sex appeal well into her later years? But in another way, it's embarrassing. Mixed in with the audience's admiration is a slap of novelty, and maybe some ridicule. Sexy-matron-as-shtick. Am I being oversensitive? Why does this seem farcical? I suppress the feeling because I know how much I dislike people fashioning armchair critique about me when I dance. I'm not the one performing, so my sense of what's appropriate is not germane. I don't get to make that call.

The Miss Exotic World contest that follows charms me completely. A belly dancer, her hips a mad, whirling fury, balances swords on her head, one girl wears a bright blue sequined bustier with a peacock feather tail attached that she flips up behind her and fans out as she spins around, another girl, in the tradition of Kitty West, emerges from an oyster shell, and several others gyrate frantically to the stylings of the jazz combo. Watching the contestants move in the old, slow, hip-waving fashion, I remark at how much the style of striptease has changed. Stripping today is more athletic—less subtle and more high energy. We're an accelerated culture now. Who's got ten minutes to spend taking off a glove?

The real highlight of the show, the moment everyone has been waiting for, is the appearance of burlesque legend Tempest Storm. She is seventy-two years old and still performing! Not just for special events like this one, either. Mitchell Brothers in San Francisco recently booked her to commemorate their thirtieth anniversary and she packed the house for four nights straight.

After much fanfare, Tempest struts haughtily into the late afternoon sun wearing a beautiful purple sequined gown and a white and purple feather boa, both of which set off her long, preternaturally titian bouffant hairdo quite nicely. Tempest, born Annie Blanche Banks in Eastman, Georgia, is the only stripper to have performed at Carnegie Hall. A true star. Decades later, she maintains a diva's carriage and poise.

As she slowly disrobes, people murmur about her impressive figure. Five foot six and about 116 toned-and-taut pounds. In her auto-
biography, *The Lady Is a Vamp*, she reports that she dropped down to
this weight after a Las Vegas tryst with Elvis in the sixties during
which he surveyed her then-135-pound form and called her "fat ass."

The sax player goes crazy, splatting, honking, and wailing as
Tempest peels off layer after layer. How'd she fit so much clothing
under that skintight gown? Somehow her confidence and expertise
have transcended the novelty aspect, and she has the audience completely enthralled. When she gets down to her rhinestone-studded
fishnets, g-string, and net bra, she twirls her boa and commands the
audience to, "Eat your hearts out."

And we do. Yes, we absolutely do.

As the unofficial keeper of burlesque history, Dixie Evans has
many stories to tell, but the one I'm most interested in is her own.
"Burlesque was my mother, my father, my bread, my butter, my life,"
says Dixie. "In my industry, there were thousands of girls who could
sing and dance—neither of which I could do. So when I went back
East and met Mister Minsky, he said, 'You look like Marilyn Monroe.'
I didn't particularly want to do Marilyn, I wanted to do myself. But,"
she says, shifting into a breathy, Monroe-esque voice, "I deliberately
walked and talked and did a whole act just like Marilyn, you see. So
then I became the Marilyn Monroe of Burlesque. It gave me a gimmick, you see what I mean . . ." She continues in her regular voice,
"Because if you don't have a gimmick, you're not going to be a star."

Dixie started working after her father, a California oilman, was
killed on an oil derrick in 1939 just before her thirteenth birthday,
and she, her sister, and her mother were plunged into poverty. "My
mother kept saying, 'God will take care of us, God will take care of
us.' She sat in a blue chenille bathrobe for years with cold cream

crusted on her face and neck, and she looked like she was eighty or ninety though she was only in her thirties. I finally had to say, 'Hey, enough of this.' "

Dixie began as a chorus girl and page in the supper clubs. She thought she had it made when she was hired as a page for a show in a big San Francisco supper club, but after she got there, the show went broke within two weeks.

"When the show closed I went down to a strip joint, " she says, "and here's this girl on the stage in white fur chaps and a white fur cowboy hat, and she's shooting off her cap guns, and bumping and all this stuff. I'm sitting at the bottom of the stairs, watching, and a big man comes up, punches me in the shoulder, and says, 'Hey, I want you to cut your act short this show and get out and mix a little more.' I said, 'But I don't work here!' " Frightened, Dixie ran up the stairs and out into the street.

"In San Francisco the clubs had men out front to duke you in—a tap dancer, or a clown, or a doorman, or something. So this fellow who had punched me runs up the stairs to the mime out front, saying, 'Chase that girl!' Well, that clown is chasing me and now I'm getting *really* scared! I'm gonna be drugged and sent to China. He caught up to me and told me to meet this guy, Bernie Goldstein, at a Chinese restaurant the next day. Well, I did, at two or three in the afternoon. Here he is, slurping noodles, shaking his fork, saying, 'You wanna make some money?' He offered me a job as a stripper and I said, 'I don't have any costumes,' and he took out his wallet. 'Here's ten dollars.'

"Oh jeez, ten dollars, I was tickled to death! I went to Greyson's, a very cheap place, and I got a pink nightgown and a pillow. I had a big old cheap alarm clock. And my act opened with the big alarm clock ringing and I'd wake up and run all around the stage, to 'Mister Sandman,' then I'd put on the nightgown and throw the big pillow up in the air."

The club, the Spanish Village, located at the corner of Mason and Eddy, wasn't the lowest rung on the ladder, but like most strip clubs at the time, it was a clip joint. In addition to performing, Dixie was expected to mix with the customers and pursuade them to spend money on drinks. Most of her income came from alcohol commissions.

"You're supposed to drink as much champagne as you can so the guy will keep buying. One night the owner came up to me and said, 'When you sit with those people and order the champagne, you don't spill a drop, do you?' and I said, 'No sir, I don't.' And he said, 'Then spill it! You're not supposed to drink it!' I was trying not to drink too much, so I took a hot water bottle and put it in my cleavage. I'd be talking to the guy and pouring the champagne down my dress. Then the guy would put his arm around me, and *bingo*, the champagne would fly up in my face. I always carried a long chiffon scarf, so I got a big old sponge and began carrying it in the scarf. And as I talked to the guy, I poured the champagne into the sponge, and later I squeezed it out."

Dixie was much more interested in perfecting her show than hustling bubbly. "The minute they opened the club in the afternoon," she tells me, "I'd be down there rehearsing an act. You'd have thought I was going to be in the Metropolitan Opera. I couldn't understand why the girls would just get up onstage, sling their stuff around, then go take a shower. They'd been there for a long time, they had children, husbands. They weren't much older than I, but they were settled. They'd say to me, 'You don't belong in joints like this where you're only as good as the liquor you can hold. You'd better go back East where they appreciate an act.'"

Unencumbered and hungry for a more professional venue, Dixie traveled to Newark, New Jersey, to the famous Minsky's Burlesque Theater, where she was christened with the Marilyn Monroe mantle. She got an agent and joined the union, AGVA, the American Guild of Variety Artists. ("Dues were five hundred annually. For that, I think you got a nail in your dressing room painted once a year," she cracks.) She began traveling the country, by Greyhound bus at first, because the depot in any given town was always in the same run-down neighborhood as the burlesque theater. She did the circuit: the Follies in Los Angeles, the Tropics in Denver, and the El Rey Theater in Oakland, as well as dates in Miami, Buffalo, Chicago, Dayton, Detroit, and St. Louis.

She developed acts based on many of Monroe's signature pieces, her roles in *The Prince and the Showgirl*, *Gentlemen Prefer Blondes*, *Bus Stop*, and the like. Soon, she was earning nearly five hundred dollars a week, and was booked two years in advance.

Of course, I want to know about the costumes that predated spandex and thongs. "In our era," Dixie says, "we had to wear what were called strip nets. They were flesh fishnets with a strip up the back and little patch over the crotch, and a net bra and pasties. Most of the time, you could take off your net bra at the end of your act, but you'd better have your pasties on. You could affix the pasties two ways. Spirit gum is one way, but I used to take regular Johnson's adhesive tape and just snip it—about five or six one-inch pieces that I'd roll into loops and stick on the back all around. Then you blow on them to heat up the adhesive and put your street bra on over the pasties, and go on with your makeup and hair or whatever you have to do. Then at the last minute you take off the street bra and the pasties stay."

"So did the tape work well enough to keep the pasties on all night?" I ask.

"It was all right," Dixie replies, "but pulling the pasties off at night—sometimes you're so drunk when you get home, you just fall asleep with the darn things on and you roll over on them in your sleep and oh, they hurt!

"A lot of the girls liked to use moleskin for pasties and put rouge on the end so it'd look like your real breasts. Sometimes we'd get a couple of hairnets, whatever color we were down there, wad them up and sew them on the outside of the g-string. It kept the cops on their toes. You see, you got to put a little schmaltz into it."

• • •

Being the Marilyn Monroe of Burlesque meant that not only did Dixie have to fashion her look and her performance around whatever Marilyn was doing, it also meant that in a strange way, her life was linked to Marilyn's, a phenomenon common among impersonators. "I always put my makeup on at seven, seven-thirty at night, while looking at the news on TV. I was watching the news when I was working in Miami, and all of a sudden, I see Marilyn Monroe on a stretcher going into the hospital in New York. My heart sank, I was just sick.

"I sent her a telegram and about six weeks later, I got a letter. I opened it up and it said, 'My Dear Dixie Evans: Of my many friends and acquaintances throughout the entire world, your telegram was the greatest comfort to me at this time. Signed, Marilyn Monroe Miller.'" Later, Monroe's attorney threatened Dixie with a lawsuit if she didn't stop her Marilyn act. No suit was ever filed, but the original cease-and-desist letter hangs in the museum.

At the time, nightclubs featuring burlesque acts were a draw for celebrities who liked to catch the shows and enjoy some undisturbed frivolity. Imagine Dixie's embarrassment when one evening at the Place Pigalle in Miami Beach, she was about to perform her act based on Marilyn's tempestuous relationship with Joe DiMaggio and she found out that DiMaggio himself was in the audience! "My God," she recalls, "I didn't even want to go on!"

Dixie describes the DiMaggio act: "I strolled onstage in a really tight pink satin gown and a number-five Yankee cap. I'd be holding a long handkerchief and I'd say, like I was crying,

Boo hoo, well, why shouldn't I go right ahead and cry?
After all, Joe, Joe just walked out and left me flat.
Well, he didn't want me anymore,
He left no doubt of that.
So now he's gone and I'm all alone.
Well, I'm sure glad he left his bat.
Oh, but life was beginning to drag and things were becoming a bore.
Well, between his baseball and his spaghetti and what's more,
I just hate a man in bed that keeps yelling, what's the score?
Oh, so, give him back his own liniment and his cold, cold showers
and don't worry, if I need him, he'll answer my calls.
Well, why would he answer my calls?
Well, that's very simple
because I've still got him by his New York Yankee base . . .

"I never said the word, but I'd reach in my pocket, pull out two baseballs, plant a kiss on each of them, and toss them into the crowd.

"I used real major league baseballs at first, but that got expensive, so after a while I got cheap rubber ones at the novelty store."

In keeping up with her heroine, when DiMaggio and Monroe reunited, Dixie changed the finale of her act from "Stormy Weather" to "This Could Be the Start of Something Big."

"So, did you do it?" I asked Dixie.

"Do what?" she looks puzzled.

"Your act. For DiMaggio."

"Oh! Well, yes! He begged me to. 'Please,' he said, 'I've come so far to see it!' "

He later took Dixie out to breakfast, and afterward she brought him home to meet her mother.

I can't help but notice that in recalling the basics of her history, Dixie struggles to maintain her focus, flubbing dates and names and places. But when it comes to her various acts, she recites every bit perfectly—from blocking to lighting to costumes to that breathy Monroe whisper.

DiMaggio wasn't the only celebrity who caught Dixie's act. She performed before Lena Horne, Debbie Reynolds and Eddie Fisher, and Frank Sinatra. Her very first celebrity encounter was with Bob Hope when she was sixteen.

"During the war, I danced in USO shows. Me and four other girls went up to Camp Pendleton, that's a big Marine base, you know, and we did some silly ol' soft-shoe act.

"We do our thing and get offstage and another girl goes on, she's about fourteen or fifteen, an acrobatic dancer. Now, she's standing on her head with her legs far apart, spinning around and around and around and Bob Hope walks out, points right between her legs, and says, 'That's what we're fighting for!'

"Well, the Marines threw their hats up into the air and screamed and hollered and tears start streaming down this girl's face. She ran off the stage. Her mother is furious. We're in the next dressing room, we don't know what's happening. We hear all these guys screaming and stomping, and in the little dressing room next to us, there's crying and the mother yelling, 'I want an apology right now' and so forth. Naturally, when we found out what happened, we sided with the girl. And we held that against Bob Hope for the rest of our lives."

Dixie was forty-one when she retired from performing full-time in 1967—a fact that startles me. These days, unless you're especially youthful-looking or possessed of singular talent, you only have until your mid-thirties before managers at the coveted clubs look at you, clear their throat, and delicately (or not) inform you that they usually "book a little younger." A thirty-two-year-old friend of mine was let go by a club manager who told her, "We have to make room for the eighteen-year-olds." They want the newest faces, the youngest body. Today, the average stripper is in her early twenties, and a generation in the adult business is about five years. Not back then, to hear Dixie tell it. "At that time in history, you built up a name. Age didn't really make that much difference because if you were Irma the Body or Tempest Storm or someone, you had a name, you were a headliner, and you put on a good show. Your audience grew up with you."

On that principle, Dixie could have kept dancing well into the sixties, but when Marilyn Monroe died in 1962, so did Dixie's burlesque career. "Marilyn's death brought my life to a sudden halt," she says. "I went into a horrible depression. Yet your rent goes on, your life goes on, you've got to pay your bills." So Dixie started doing a Marilyn-less act, performing for conventioneers and retirees at private corporate-sponsored club dates in New York City.

But she did revive Marilyn one last time. At her friend Shirley Day's urging, Dixie put together a show called "A Portrait of Marilyn" and did a brief run at Shirley's nightclub, the Orient, on Manhattan's Upper East Side.

"I came onstage and did a little bit of every one of her acts. I had a big fake diamond and I said, 'Oh, diamond, you've brought me so much and yet so little.' Then, at the very end, I donned a black negligee while the band played 'The Blue Prelude.' Oh boy, the drummers can really go on that song. I'd turn my back to the audience and then lift one arm over my head and drop a fake pill into a champagne glass. Then the trumpet, he would scream out real good and I would scream and fall to the ground. I had a little blue telephone that I grabbed off of a table as I fell, knocking it off the hook."

When Dixie finished her first performance of "Portrait," the audience rose silently to its feet and many wept. Afterward, people came up to Dixie and thanked her for bringing Marilyn back, if only onstage, if only for a little while. Walter Winchell gave her tribute to Marilyn a better mention than he gave Arthur Miller's *After the Fall*, a play based on his relationship with Monroe, which was on Broadway at the same time. Her show ran for six months.

I can't imagine yoking your professional identity to someone else's, only to watch it collapse when that person passes away. Part of you dies, too. "Oh God, it was horrible," Dixie says. But she wasn't the only one with that particular misfortune. "There was a fella, Vaughn Meader. He impersonated President Kennedy, and in the early sixties, he was at the top of his career. He was on Ed Sullivan. He was making big money. Then, after Kennedy was shot, I saw him in New York at the B & G Coffee Shop. He was in this big black cashmere overcoat, you know, and the tears, oh, he had big, big, dark eyes. He just stood there outside, with the rain pouring down. His life was over. His career was over. People were only concerned about the dead president. They didn't say, 'Gee how's that poor guy Meader ever gonna pay his rent?' Oh, he was in very bad shape for a long time and so was I. Because of the guilt—the horrible guilt. The guilt alone was bad enough without not working on top of it," Dixie grimaces.

I'm chagrined to dredge up these painful memories. I don't want to drag her down on a day like today when she should be having fun, hobnobbing with the pageant contestants and TV crews. I pause for a beat so she can regain her composure, then change the subject and ask how she decided to start the contest.

Initially, the event was just a burlesque reunion, a chance for the older performers to get together, catch up, and relive their former glory. But the occasion was somewhat lacking, so Dixie decided that new blood would make the event more fun, and give a sense of continuity to the dying art of burlesque. Dixie gives a tinkly little Marilyn laugh. "I said, I think I'll have a Miss Exotic World Pageant and get some younger people. And we did. The young girls come 'cause they like to pay respect to the bygone era." Dixie takes her role as burlesque preservationist very seriously, bless her heart, even if the nutty, caravan-car quality of the museum doesn't have the historical *gravitas* of the Met. Burly-Q, bally girls, carnival strippers, tassel twirlers, and cooch dancers may be a thing of the past, but as long as Dixie's out here, sparkling like a desert gem, the Exotic World Burlesque Museum and Miss Exotic World contest will honor their existence—fringe, feathers, baubles, and all. I'm very glad about that, and I bet future generations of stripteasers, wondering from whence they came, will be, too.

Onstage, the world's worst Elvis impersonator is wrapping up his act after having scared away half the audience, and the contestants are gathered on the stage for the announcement of the winners. The sword-balancing belly dancer, a twenty-two-year-old from Los Angeles named Kina, who looks surprisingly like the fifties bur-lesque queen Yvette Dare (famous in her day for her "Dance of the Sacred Parrot," in which the trained bird took off pieces of her cos-tume with its beak), takes first place. Photographers crowd the stage to get a shot of the winner.

"The girls today are trying to do gimmicks again, to put together an act of some sort," Dixie says happily. "I know that they've got to get down and make their money, because they don't have the theater structure that we had. But I think the girls are trying to do something fun when they work—if that pole doesn't get too much in the way."

ELEVEN

The Eros of Tigger

The landscape as you drive north on I-25, then farther north still on I-90, changes a million times between Cheyenne and Billings, Montana. Certain areas, like the green-black mottled peaks of the Bighorn Mountains that rise to the west near Buffalo or the moon-cratered valley near Ayres Bridge, have a divine beauty. You can't believe there's so much unspoiled land, that nature could assume so many breathtaking forms. Other parts—miles of parched grassland interrupted only by craggy beige bluffs—look accidental and sorry, like God's stubbed toe.

ZZ Top blasts from the truck speakers as I press toward the Montana border at a steady eighty-five miles an hour. Randy naps in the passenger seat, head lolling against the shoulder strap, his black cowboy hat tipped down low to cover his eyes.

Driving to Billings was a spontaneous decision, as was Randy's coming along. There's a reason I'm not traveling by myself this time—we both wanted it that way. We have no protocol for these things—we can only follow the dictates of need, of jealousy, of protectiveness on a site-by-site basis. We're flying on instinct. When the prospect of Montana came up—tough-as-nails, fully nude Montana—we were of the same mind. Even though I wasn't going to work while there, I would not go alone.

As the trip to Alaska is imminent, I thought it might be a good idea to reacquaint myself with nude clubs, observing at first to get comfortable. I'd asked a dancer in Cheyenne for a suggestion, and she insisted that I had to visit Billings.

"What's so special about Billings?"

"Oh," she said, her lips curling into a smile wicked as a joker's, "you'll see."

After an eight-hour drive, I pull into Billings, passing the tall sandstone rimrocks that flank the Yellowstone River like twin guard walls. I wonder what I'm in for, exactly. And I wonder if I shouldn't just blow the whole thing off. I start each journey with a burst of excitement, gassing up the truck and cleaning the windshield, consulting the atlas, totting up travel times, and loading CDs and bags into the cargo area, just so. Then as I approach wherever I'm headed, my heart shrinks against my ribs, pressing in as if trying to make itself smaller in my chest. Anxiety threatens to topple curiosity and I want to turn back. Every time. I've never been an anxious traveler before—I've scaled rocks in England in the wind and pouring rain, wearing a sundress and slippery-soled boots, and sped down Thai highways riding in the bed of a pickup truck with questionable shocks. Never had a second thought about much, but now I'm seized by apprehension. I'm not afraid of physical harm. Though I do have that fear, it shows up at different times, in different forms—like when I'm alone at night in a motel room or passing a group of men in a dark parking lot. This anxiousness is more vague and more constant. It has something to do with fear of failure. I'm afraid of wasting my time—that I'm going to end up pissed-off or bored or agitated by something I can't sort out. Anything less than clarity is a wash and, joys of the open road aside, I'm on a desperate search. It wouldn't be too much of a cop-out to just check in to the motel and watch cable all night, would it?

ZZ Top reminds me, *"I'm bad. I'm nationwide."*

Shotgun Willie's isn't in Billings proper. It's a ways west, twelve miles down the highway in East Laurel. I turn into the parking lot of the Pelican truck stop, drive around back where there's a campground full of camper trailers and teepees, then pass a dozen parked semis positioned like sentries, blocking the club from view. Small and nondescript, the building is huddled in the back corner of the lot like it's got something to hide.

A long row of Harleys is parked out front, chrome gleaming under the lights hung in the eaves. Most of them are new, all of them are huge. Tricked out and fussed-over, they look menacing and elegant. I'm always happy to see bikes like these outside a club—they signify interesting times ahead.

The admission is three dollars for me, five for Randy. Stepping through the doors of the club, I smell beer right away—that's different. Pretty rare to find any sort of alcohol in a nudie club, anywhere. Opposite the entryway is a long bar. I head over to it immediately, taking a seat so I can wait for my eyes to adjust. The room is long and narrow, with a large thrust stage at one end. The ceiling is low, and the walls are painted a soft, dark red that makes the room welcoming. Almost womblike. A female deejay breaks in over the music, telling the customers, in a forced, breathy voice that sounds like porno and bullshit, to "keep your hands at your sides and your tongue in your mouth!"

I think I'd better have a beer.

I scan the room—pretty full, a blue-collar vibe for sure, with masculine goodwill and mayhem floating in the air thick as smoke. A few tables on the far side of the club are staked out by bikers in vests that read ROAD DOGS in big red letters. Along the right side of the stage are cowboys—or at least men in cowboy clothes. On the left side of the stage is a band of twenty-somethings, male and female alike, nudging each other, gawky, and embarrassed. Right in front of the stage, at a small cocktail table, sit two women who look like they're together. Behind them is a well-groomed middle-aged couple, she's wearing a little black dress and tasteful gold jewelry, he is in dress slacks and a button-down shirt. The rest of the club is full of local-yokelly looking men, and oh yes, dancers. A rowdy hotchpotch. Everyone is chattering happily, slapping each other in play, careening around, and hollering for more beer. Waitresses wheel through with full pitchers and a lone, bald-headed bouncer smiles in his watch over the club's jovial vulgar bounce.

A couple beers later and the door to the ladies' room doesn't lock. I search the club looking for a dancer or a barmaid who might show me to another bathroom—maybe one in the dressing room. The only dancer on the floor is sitting at the Road Dogs' table. I approach with caution.

"Hi, cutie," she says, looking me up and down with a glance that could either be read as "hello" or "fuck you," depending on what you wanted to make of it. She's got long, tawny curls and a full, real-girl body that looks like it's been through a lot but is suffused with a primitive grace that enables it to bounce back, no matter what. She's balancing a shot of whiskey on her knee.

"Well, hi." I smile. "I'm here visiting from out of town. The bathroom door doesn't seem to lock. Is there another one?"

As she shakes her head no, one of the Road Dogs pipes in. "There's rest rooms at the truck stop," he says, pivoting on his bar stool to face me, then pushing up his wire-framed eyeglasses with one thick finger. "If you'd care to hop on the back of one of our Harleys, one of us would be happy to take you over there."

It's a flirtation of sorts. And a dare.

I look at him, tidy and restrained despite his shaggy beard and considerable girth. His jeans and T-shirt look freshly washed. I picture him in an undershirt and boxer shorts, lumbering around a utility room, moving clothes from washer to dryer. Then I imagine him as a small boy, holding up a valentine to a schoolmate, handing his father a wrench as he bends under the hood of a car, pedaling a bicycle furiously down the sidewalk to test the limit of his strength.

"Don't listen to him, honey," the dancer says. Then she turns to the biker, "Would you *stop*?!" She lands a hard punch on his fleshy biceps.

"S'okay," I say to her, "you can't blame a guy for trying." Then I turn to the biker and bow a little. "Very nice of you to offer."

He cocks his head and leans over toward me, brows knit. "God, I'm sorry, honey, now what did you say?"

"I said, thanks anyway," bending in close to yell in his ear. He's a grizzled fellow, a fast-living forty, at least, and years of rock-n-roll and unbaffled pipes have probably left him hard of hearing. "But I don't think my Harley-riding husband would appreciate that very much!" I nod in Randy's direction. He's palming his beer bottle and looking my way, eyes round and careful. A girlfriend at a table full of bikers demands close watch, and he knows it.

The biker looks at Randy, looks at me, then leans back on his bar stool and raises his hands to say, "no problem." I squeeze the dancer's knee to say thank you as I walk away.

I risk the bathroom with the broken lock. No one comes in.

• • •

"Remember, gentlemen," once again the breathy-fake phone sex voice cuts in over the music, "keep your hands at your sides and your tongue in your mouth at all times." This may be the only club I've ever been in where hands-on and tongues-out is a continual hazard. Man after man flops onto his back on the stage, like trained whales in a marine park show. A big guy lands on the stage with such force his T-shirt slides up exposing his stomach, which rises rounded, hairy, and dough-white from the waistband of his jeans. He's got a bill tucked into his fly. A dollar in between his teeth.

With their hands clasped in wait over their bellies, or pressed flat to the floor, the men form an obscene, fleshy wreath around the perimeter of the stage. A naked girl with a blonde bob is dancing, her sinewy body twists and prances with an almost elastic quality. She steps over one man so she's facing away from him, and drops into a Russian split, landing with her bare crotch right on top of his head. Lying on her stomach now, her chin propped in her hands in an exaggerated gesture of carefree femininity, she bounces her knees on the stage, making her thighs and buttocks jiggle, messing up the guy's hair. Men all around the stage whistle and scream.

Quick as a flash, the dancer spins around on all fours and crawls over and down the length of his body until her nude crotch is maybe three inches from the man's mouth. Working her way down to his knees, she backs up, grabs the dollar that's in his fly with her teeth, and biting a little of his trouser fabric, she bobs her head up and down like she's giving him a blow job. Backing up farther, she pauses with her chest over his mouth and takes the dollar clamped in his teeth by squeezing it between her breasts with her hands. She ends up sitting on her knees, smiling into the man's face like she's a flower coming into bloom just for him. Then she moves on to the next guy and does the exact same thing all over again.

I'm stunned. I've never seen anything like it.

In every strip club I've been to, the stage is sacred space. Girls Only. Men can approach the side of the stage to tip, but that's it.

Dancers and customers may get scandalously close to each other on the floor, but the stage is the locus of female control and solely her domain. At one club, if a man so much as propped his feet on the stage, the deejay would shine a spotlight on him and say over the P.A.: "Get your feet off the stage!" Not in a brother-take-heed voice either, but in a tone that meant, "Move them, or lose your knee-caps." The sanctity of the stage is highly symbolic—like a woman's virtue, her bedroom, her sex—violate it and you violate her. And yet, here they are, breaking that basic rule.

There are no free tables near the stage, so the female couple invites us to sit with them. One of the women, fireplug stout with graying brown hair cut into a surfer mullet, sees my shocked expression and laughs a deep laugh, one that shakes her to her toes and back again. "What you're seeing here tonight? That's nothing," she says, waving her hand. "We were in here a couple weeks ago and the women weren't even using their hands to pick up the dollars from the guys' mouths."

"You mean . . . ?"

"Yep. They'd just squat down over a guy's face and pick them up, you know . . ."

"Down there?"

"Exactly!"

"Holy fucking shit," I sputter, before I even know what I am saying. I look at Randy. He says nothing.

One dancer stands out from the rest. Her hair is glossy black, layered, and teased full—like a guitar god from the 1980s. Her lower lip has a pronounced droop that gives her a look of sensual, exaggerated disappointment. What's remarkable about her is the way she dances—furious and agile, like a wild animal on attack. During her first song, she does a series of flips off the overhead bar, then crawls with impressive speed to the edge of the stage and lies down on her back. She spreads her legs wide, then—*Wham! Wham! Wham!*—she claps her thighs together like she's playing the cymbal part in *The Thieving Magpie.* When a man prostrates himself on the stage, she lies over top of him and, shaking her shoulders back and forth, she pummels him in the face with her breasts with comic aggression.

Her name is Stormy.

Stormy doesn't carry herself like an alpha-babe; in fact, she seems almost oblivious to her own magnetism, which only makes her more striking. She's obviously a crowd favorite—everyone swarms the stage when she performs, and afterward a steady stream of men whisk her off behind the gaudy tinsel curtains at the back of the club for a private, one-on-one nude couch dance. It's not that she's so lovely—although she is quite attractive—or so nice. Propelled by this amazing blast of carnal rage, she just naturally outshines everyone else.

"That girl is *scary*," says Kendall, the other of the two women who are sharing our table. "She could really hurt somebody." The deep, mournful hollows of Kendall's pale blue eyes indicate caution as a default position. With thin arms, she hugs her plaid flannel shirt around her as the air conditioner vent overhead spills out cold, sour air.

"One time when I was here," says her mullet-cut companion, who introduced herself as Darcy, "a girl was taking a dollar from my mouth with her teeth and she bit right through my lower lip." She pulls her lip down to illustrate. "I had to get two stitches. Another time, a girl stepped on my pinkie and broke the bone at the tip. It was an accident, though."

Now Stormy is grabbing onto the overhead bar that runs along the ceiling over the stage. She's got her legs over a man's shoulders with his head in a scissor lock between her knees. With a wild grin and a whoop, she presses her spike heels into the man's chest and pushes off into a back flip with cartoonish effect.

"You know she reminds me of Tigger, from Winnie the Pooh," I say to no one in particular.

"Okay, gentlemen," yells the deejay at the start of Stormy's second song. "It's time for a hostage dance!" A sheepish young man in khaki shorts and a red pullover sweatshirt is pushed toward the edge of the stage by his drunken buddies. The bouncer helps the man onto the stage, sits him down, then puts the victim's hands behind his back and handcuffs him to the go-go pole. The song starts and Stormy does a series of little torturous gyrations on and around him. His friends tuck singles behind his ears, in his pockets, in his mouth, down his shorts. Stormy works her way around his body, nipping the tips with her teeth, gathering them between her breasts, even taking up a bill between her butt cheeks. Occasionally she stops stripping the man of his money to grind lasciviously on his crotch, lap dancing in extremis. Then she grabs the pole right by the guy's ear and, throwing her legs up over his shoulders, repeatedly rams her crotch against his.

All the while a woman bleats over a bad disco track: "Lemme see your pussy! Show it to me! I wanna see your pussy! Show it to me!" The bouncer steps up to the stage and theatrically mops the guy's brow with a bar cloth.

At the end of the song, the bouncer trots over with a cup of ice water, which Stormy ceremoniously dumps down the man's shorts. Such indignity costs twenty dollars, and it's a very popular feature.

Every time I visit a new club, I do a little mental exercise, picturing what it might be like to work there. Would the money be good? Could I keep the customers interested? Would I have fun?

I'm having trouble here. I fix my gaze on Stormy, trying to imagine myself doing what she's doing and I can't. I just can't. I envision myself on all fours on the stage, sliding my knees around either side of a man's head and feeling his whiskers tickling my inner thighs. I shudder at the thought. Now *I'm* the girl on the other side of the wall. I can't see how a woman could work here. On a practical level, I understand perfectly well: You show up, you get into your costume, you take your costume off, you go through the motions, and you take home your cash. But viscerally, I don't get it at all. I can only wonder. I don't wonder about practical matters, like how you work when you've got your period. (You tuck in the tampon string. Or cut it.) Or how you stay "femininely fresh." (Good hygiene and bottle after bottle of cheap perfume.) I wonder about the intangibles: Is it frightening to have so many men get close to you at one time? What is it like to go home after spending the night bouncing your crotch over the faces of people you don't know? How long does it take to settle back into your body, because you'd have to go pretty far away in order to be that exposed for that long, wouldn't you?

Everything about Shotgun Willie's seems outrageous, like I'm watching stripping being spun by a tabloid news show: Can you believe *this*? There's a vague and off-putting savagery to this place. I'm not sure if it's due to the tensions between the different groups of men, the mix of alcohol and pussy, or the fact that the security staff looks so light. Would I expect anything different from Montana, a state notorious for the rawboned and unpredictable? This is a state with little use for speed limits. Like it or leave.

I get the feeling that if there *were* any trouble, the women here could give as bad as they get. No hothouse flowers, they. To them, this is just another day at work. Business as usual. For every impulse that I have to run into the dressing room yelling, "Stop! Don't do this! You can go somewhere where you don't have to take your bottoms off, or plant your face in some guy's crotch!" I know that my missionary zeal probably wouldn't yield more than a dancer shrugging, "It's okay. I'm used to it," while generously spritzing body spray into her neatly trimmed pubic hair.

I know that nonchalance well. Years ago, when I was dancing at the Mitchell Brothers O'Farrell Theater in San Francisco, a man was heading down the long hallway toward the exit. His boyish face was flushed, as if his necktie were fastened too tight, and when he walked past me with his young-important-guy stride, he said to his friend, unaware that I could hear, "That is a hell of a way to make a living." I grumbled to myself, *Well, screw you, then*, bristling at the pronouncement, which, given the setting, seemed a little ungracious. And now here I am thinking just like him.

For all my discomfort, I don't want to be a bad sport. When Stormy leaps back onstage for another set, I push a five toward Randy. "You want to go tip her?"

He shakes his head no. "She's too much for me."

"Let's you and me go tip her," says Kendall, shaking my arm. "At the same time!"

Randy slides the five back toward me and drops another on top of it.

Kendall and I take our tips to the stage and find a clearing between two stretched-out Road Dogs, one of whom, according to his insignia patch, is named Peanut. Kendall stuffs her money in the waistband of her long madras shorts, and I lie down next to her with the two fives, each folded in half lengthwise, tucked into the top of my bra, waving out like antennae from under my shirt.

My hands are at my sides. My tongue is in my mouth.

Halfway through the first song, Stormy crawls over me and pulls the dollars out from under my shirt with her teeth. It tickles a little, so I smile. She smiles back, her eyes dark liquid in that tough, hungry face. She says, "Thanks, sweetie," then she tosses her shoulders back, and *whappity-whappity-whappity* blasts me in the face with her boobs. They're cool and moist from her sweat. It's a little like being beaten with soft rubber erasers. She moves on to the next willing victim.

Kendall and I sit back down. "Well, how did they feel?" my boyfriend and her girlfriend want to know.

"Kinda rubbery," I say. "A little cold."

By now the crowd has turned over a couple times. Clusters of young men and women have come in, probably winding up a night-long club crawl. An athletic blonde gal and a guy who looks like he could be her brother are dragging a shrieking, overweight girl toward the stage. She pulls back to resist them, but they grab her shirtsleeves. Strands of straight brown hair escape from her ponytail and swing in her face. She tries to pull her arms out of her shirt to escape, laughing and yelping in protest. Finally, she lies on the stage while her friends shower her body with bills. She's giggling helplessly. The dancer takes the money from her in a gingerly, sexless fashion and minces quickly away.

Retail vagina.

I'm standing at the sink in the motel room brushing my teeth when the words pop into my head. With a start, I look at my reflection in the mirror. My face is tinged green from the fluorescent overhead. I know it's the light, but I feel as if the roiling in the pit of my stomach is what has queered my complexion. Retail vagina. That's got to be what's at the core of my unease with working nude, at least at a "spread club" like Shotgun Willie's. Some nude clubs forbid dancers to show genitalia; you can't even bend at the waist. But in a "spread club," the pussy shot is standard practice. So in this environment, there's this part of you—this very private, personal part of you—that's the center of your livelihood. Literally. Unlike working topless, dancing nude isn't so much about tease and suggestion. It's more about the packaging of your vulva. The dancing is almost a formality. You can dance like Cyd Charisse, and still be upstaged by what rests between your legs. Guys want to see it. They can't wait to see it. They crane their necks to get a look at it. They fix their gaze on it like they're waiting for it to say something profound. And they talk about it: How it's shaved; how it's shaped; what it might feel like, smell like, taste like.

Perhaps part of the attraction for men is the beauty of the female flower, but I'm skeptical. Maybe it's more about the submission. The access. Seeing the unseeable. Regardless, whatever enabled me to comfortably work nude in the past is gone. I reflexively clasp my knees together at the very thought.

Randy lies in bed watching a movie about an older man married to a model many years his junior. They're in Alaska and a photographer hired to work with the model is trying to edge her husband out of the picture. The plot revolves around competing for the girl, macho posturing in the woods, and bear attacks. I climb into the bed beside him, curling up against his side.

"Did you have fun tonight?" he asks, stroking my hair and hooking his foot between my ankles.

"Man, it was really something else. I don't think I could ever work there."

"You know, I'm glad to hear you say that. Because that place is a fight just waiting to happen."

On the drive home, we stop for gas in Buffalo and decide to find something to eat. At the Hole in the Wall Cafe, we have chicken fingers and mashed potatoes with gluey white gravy served on paper plates. While I wait to pay the bill, I examine the hunting photos on the wall. In one photograph, a beaming hunter kneels beside a felled buck, holding the animal's testicles in his hand. There's a slash of red in the white fur between the buck's hind legs. The caption reads, "Number One Nut Buster."

As we leave the cafe and cross the street to get in the car, I say to Randy, "I still can't believe that Stormy girl, you know?"

"Yeah, me neither!" he shakes his head, digging in his front pocket for the car keys. "She wasn't really like Tigger, though," he says. "Tigger is cheerful and sort of crashes into things because he's excited. She's more like the Tasmanian devil. I mean, she was *violent*."

He's right, too. She really was.

TWELVE

Anchorage, Alaska

Forget it. Just forget it. If you think you know something about the beauty of nature and you haven't been to Alaska, then stop right now and admit that you know less than nothing.

I'm not talking about the formidable glaciers, the crystal-blue streams, the emerald-green mountains veined with snow, the elk, moose, whales, or eagles, though I've seen them and they're breath-taking.

I'm talking about the girl.

There's this girl, with an atomic red pixie bob, in the entrance to the club. She's leaning on a piece of furniture that looks like a lectern, sucking on a cherry Tootsie Pop and looking bored. I am astounded by the amazing natural architecture of her ass, which immediately commands my attention when I stroll into the building after Randy drops me off so I can inquire about work. Rather than have a conventional door, the front of the club is completely open—come one, come all—and shielded from the street by a partition.

The nine o'clock sun (nine o'clock! sun!) sneaks in behind the partition and gleams off of the girl's deeply tanned flank. Her upper body is rather petite—under her shiny red PVC teddy, she has no breasts to speak of, and her face is a little girl's, but her ankles are thick, her calves sturdy and her thighs firm and mighty. The stuff of R. Crumb's dreams, the inspiration for a thousand hiphop songs.

This girl is a masterpiece. Mother Nature's magnum opus.

Good thing I'm female or I'd get slapped and branded as sexist for even thinking these things.

Am I staring? I must be staring. I'm staring.

The girl looks right at me.

"Hey."

"Hey," I smile, not lecherously but nicely. "What's your name?"

"Trixie."

Trixie. That is beautiful.

I love her.

It took Herculean effort to get this far. Not the actual distance—though that was a bit of an ordeal, having to fly from Denver to Chicago to Anchorage, where Randy and I landed at 10 p.m. under a bright orange gibbous moon, traces of sunset still in the western sky. The bulk of the grunt work was the psychological preparation.

About a week before we left, I decided I needed to lose five pounds. Alaska would go a lot better, I was convinced, if I pared down a bit. A couple pounds less would lighten me up to do battle with my inhibitions. They don't call it "fighting trim" for nothing.

I bought a can of mocha-flavored SlimFast powder and tried making shakes with skim milk, as per the instructions on the label, but despite my diligent shaking and stirring, the powder never fully mixed. It separated into globules on the milk's surface, a gag-inducing chocolaty sludge.

But I knew there was a more palatable, less torturous diet short-cut. SlimFast makes meal bars, so I went on a recon mission.

A trip to Wal-Mart is enough to give anyone a panic attack. Squalling kids everywhere, yelling parents, a clerk calling for a price check over the PA system, someone crashing a cart into a towering display of sandwich cookies, two packs for two dollars, and long lines at every checkout.

People prowled through the school supplies. *Wow, is it back-to-school time already?* I wondered. I felt a brief vertigolike flash of cognitive dissonance from browsing for stripping-related products near hordes of children toting boxes of pencils and colored plastic files to their parents' shopping carts.

I found the SlimFast bars between the food section and the pharmacy. I loaded up my basket with several different flavors. Chocolate chip, chocolate peanut, oatmeal raisin, cinnamon spice, a dozen in all.

I drifted aimlessly though the lingerie department, for grins. I spotted a display of black-and-white snakeskin separates, including some rather saucy hot pants. I put a pair in my shopping basket and headed for the checkout.

Stop, I told myself sternly. *Put down the hot pants. Put back the SlimFast bars. You can't expect to successfully self-medicate your apprehension with the ditz prescriptive of retail therapy and weight reduction. You should just sublimate and press forth.*

Well, repression be damned, I bought the hot pants. Snakeskin. Six bucks! Xanax and couch time billed by the hour can't even come close.

On my way out the automatic door, a harried woman collared her wandering toddler, her voice an extended groan of maternal frustration. "What, I turn my back for one second and you decide you have to run off and join the circus?"

● ● ●

It's some sort of cosmic joke that the one place I'm working nude is called the Great Alaskan Bush Company. After I meet Trixie, the manager comes over—a skinny, dirty blond rocker-biker mix with shoulders stooped by the weight of his foul disposition— and invites me to see the show. I watch a few girls go on. Some of them doff their dresses and crank their legs wide open almost the minute they step onstage, others wait till their second song to get naked and keep their legs together the whole time, which seems doable. And the table dances are strictly no-contact and topless, not nude. Most doable.

A woman I know who has never stripped once wondered aloud if there was really that much difference between working topless and nude. "You're almost naked already when you're in a g-string," she said to me, "so how is it any different to go without?" Well, the difference is huge, psychically. Long before my time, going bottomless was called "working strong"—for good reason. When you're completely naked, you're out there, sans cuirass. Extra mettle is required. Dancing nude was never a problem for me before, as I was all about the barricades, but now I'm acutely aware that there's nothing to hide behind, literally or figuratively. Someone looking at me sees every last inch of me, and I don't really like that. I feel as if I don't get to keep any part of myself as mine alone. But if I'm to do this, to strip Alaskan-style, I have to go all or nothing.

The club is a vast single room with tables at the center near the stage and restaurant-type vinyl upholstered booths on platforms farther back. There is only one stage—a large horseshoe shape with chairs and a bar counter all around it and a padded tipping rail, affectionately referred to as the meat rack. Behind the stage ranges a mirrored wall with THE GREAT ALASKAN BUSH COMPANY frosted on it. I gather they're going for a frontier motif—everything looks very rough-hewn and outdoorsy. The room has a high ceiling and a wrap-around walkway that accesses the dressing room and office on the second floor. A staircase from the far side of the walkway connects the dressing room and the stage. In the corner directly opposite, up near the ceiling on a small loft, perches an ugly, life-size soft-sculpture tableau of a Yukon frontiersman pressing his foot into a saloon girl's back as he helps tie her corset.

I want to have a good time, be someone fun and breezy, so the ponderous Barbie Faust is temporarily sidelined. I pick the stage name "Daisy." I like having the opportunity to reinvent myself every few weeks. A new town, a new club, a new me. Each time I draw up a new character, I incorporate facets of my personality that I wish were more prevalent. If I want to be sweeter, or more patient, polite, understanding, fun-loving, or glamorous, I can draw that out. Like dress-up on a constitutional level. Some nights, my persona seems so far removed from who I really am I feel like a female impersonator.

A girl playing the role of girl.

I can only change so much, though. No matter what I do, or how well I play-act, I'm never pure femme. My aggressive streak comes through regardless, but at least it can be cut with some sugar. I have learned quite a bit from my multifarious personae—what works and what doesn't. The positive reaction I have gotten in response to my more patient, friendly work self has informed and improved my slightly crabby quotidian self. If profit motive was the impetus for that change, so be it. I'm glad to have gotten more from this job than just money.

As I stand in the dressing room, I wonder, *what would "Daisy" wear?* Nurse's uniform? No. Evening gown? No. Plaid schoolgirl skirt? No. Something plain and pretty. I rifle through my costume bag and pull out a melon-colored minidress and thong. I don't know how fast the finish on the stage is, so I wear a safe pair of shoes— white, ankle-strap stilettos. I can change into platforms when I get out on the floor to do table dances. I sit at the mirror in the dressing room digging in the makeup bag for my rhinestone choker and as the other dancers file past, they say hi, introduce themselves. They get a fresh crop of girls who come up every summer from the Lower Forty-Eight to work tourist season, so they're used to new faces this time of year.

I have quite a while until I'm up in the stage rotation so I slink downstairs to see if I can get a table dance or two started. Getting up here cost a freaking fortune—to say nothing of the cost of a hotel room at the height of tourist season—and I really need to make my money back. Sitting by himself at a table by the stage, a middle-aged man in a button-down shirt and jeans catches my eye. He wears new-looking hiking boots and his beard is neatly trimmed. I take him up to one of the booths where he'll be more comfortable.

I step into the space between his feet and nudge his knees apart. When the song starts, I run my hands along my body, facing him. Then I turn around and bend at the waist, rolling my hips in a slow wave. I untie the halter on the dress and slowly uncover my breasts, one at a time. I face him, with my hands covering my breasts, then, in time to the music, bring them down and place them on his shoulders. I lean forward and grab the back of the seat behind his left ear so I'm bending over his shoulder.

When the songs ends, I ask if he wants another. He does. Then he wants four more.

I run out of fresh moves, and as I turn away from him and roll my hips yet again, I think he must be bored out of his mind. But when I turn around to face him, he's still leaning back, smiling, happy as a biscuit. My favorite kind of customer—he just settles in, drifts away, and wants dance after dance. I wish I could see what he sees, what enraptures him so. I suspect the fascination is a testosterone thing. I recall reading an interview with a female-to-male transsexual who said that once she started taking the male hormones, she understood what men got out of looking at skin magazines. For the first time, she said, the pictures came alive as s/he looked at them. Maybe the intense visual stimulation is a male province. I'm sure I would enjoy a woman table dancing for me, but not enough to drop over a hundred bucks to have her do it again and again.

As the night wears on, the club fills to capacity. Burly packs of Harley dudes, hot-to-trot tourists on hunting and fishing vacations, and a curious assortment of fuzzy-faced loners (you know what they say about Alaskan men: The odds are good, but the goods are odd). When men walk through the entrance, they're greeted by a guy stationed at the door—really good policy. There's also no dress code, which is another sound policy. I understand wanting to maintain a sophisticated air in a very upscale club, but I never have a very good time dancing in a place where a man can't enter unless he's wearing a tie. Bush Company is more friendly and casual than that. And they'd have to be—this is Alaska, home of renegades and nature men, guys who make it a point to live their entire adult life without even *owning* a tie.

But there's something else that's great about this club—a certain playfulness. The dancers put a lot of effort into their stage shows, some performing extended theme routines, which the men at the meat rack reward generously. There's free-floating lust perfuming the air in a fine mist. A benevolent swirl of orgone. Not a goal-oriented, predatory sexual energy like in Montana. It doesn't seem to want to go anywhere, you can just enjoy the vibe. When I'm not table dancing, I sit down with a customer and watch the girls. As they twitch their bottoms and roll languidly around onstage, there's no comparison between myself and them, no competition, no jealousy. Just admiration. I think back to what a customer said to me once as he fixed his eyes on the stage, dreamily, "The most beautiful creature in the animal kingdom is the human female."

Where do you draw the line, I wonder, between objectification and admiration? Is it a matter of manners? Intent? Money? I can pass off a casual leer as maintaining my competitive edge, so I don't need to worry about what anyone thinks of my girl-watching. Maybe it's a matter of time and place, of when it's appropriate. Or maybe it's just a matter of respect, of knowing that there's a complicated girl behind the glassy façade that's caught your eye, one whose wishes and desires may have nothing to do with yours.

Here it is, my turn onstage. I'm less intimidated than I was at the outset, because this is a fun place. A secure place. I chose my music carefully. The first song is "Brick House," an homage to women who butter their potatoes. This is not a song for a sylph. A diminutive dancer I know played it one night and was humiliated when a man in the audience shouted out, "But you're flat!" No, this is for someone healthy like me. As I come out onstage, the men cheer loudly. Wildly. I feel good. Strong. I'm not self-conscious about having shoulders like a Viking oarsman or quads that mean business.

I need to enjoy this feeling while I can, because it never lasts.

I strut the stage, smiling at the men, one by one. I am archetypal and fab.

Song two. The moment of truth. I lie back, press my feet on the stage and push up onto my toes as I wind my torso and work my thong down. I roll over onto my side and straighten my legs, sending the thong flying. The lights are hot on my skin. Here I am, bare-assed at the last frontier. I start to float away from myself a little because I'm nervous. But I'm pretty much okay.

I stand up and try to stay in character. Daisy rising. I am not a reformed nerd from New Jersey walking around with no underpants on, I remind myself. I am a goddess clothed in my own power.

I lean back, lift my arms over my head, then sway my hips slowly to the left as I bring a hand down to gently sweep my long hair over my right shoulder, concealing my breast—one of those tiny, feminine moves that can paralyze a man. Like the swarthy one in the last seat on the right side of the meat rack. I turn to him, a devastating butch confection, buzz-cut and wide-eyed—mook and boyish charmer all at once. I smile softly into his upturned face and he beams back. Beautiful. My heavens. Something other than nerves is making my legs shake. Why is it so much harder to dance for the cute ones?

I drop down in front of him, knees together, and motion for him to come close. He leans over the bar, right up against the tipping rail, hands clasped under his chin like an altar boy.

Can't touch. Won't.

"Are you in the military?" I ask over the breathless teenage chorus of my second song.

"Yes, ma'am."

"Ma'am?" I tease, hands on my hips, feigning offense.

"Sorry. Officer's manners." His ears are turning red. "What gave me away?"

"You look so capable. That, and the haircut."

Kneeling now, I hold his gaze. I blink slowly. He blinks back, his lashes thick black fringe. Easy, girl. Nice deep breath. Go figure—here's this blue-collar Adonis looking at me like I hung the moon, and all I want to do is cover up and run. But I stay right where I am. What did the Pure Talent class manual say? "You have to fully understand why men come to a club to begin with . . . *They want you to pay attention to them.*" I'm not looking away until I see that slow burning fire come up in his eyes. After giving him a shy, lingering "stripper you take home to meet Mom" look, I see it happen, the change I'm working for. A sign of life. His expression shifts from curious to grateful, something alit deep within. I want to shout for joy. I rise back up on my feet, savoring this feeling so rich and rare. I'm not thinking about money. Or rules. Or my body. Or the handsome man in front of me. For one small moment, I am naked and completely unafraid.

Dollars line the railing in front of every man at the meat rack. No one is doing that laser-beam-on-the-cootch stare. I haven't yet seen any motions for me to "spread 'em." Not that every guy is a crotch-watcher, anyway. Randy's friend Todd, a well-intentioned, timid fella, went to a nudie club in Denver once and when a dancer dropped down in front of him to give him a big old gap shot, he was so embarrassed he just sat there staring into his beer. The girl got really offended and said, loud enough for everyone in the bar to hear, *"Well you could at least look at it!"*

Randy walks up to the stage and tosses me a handful of bills. We're pretending we don't know each other, in case the manager gets uptight about boyfriends coming in while dancers work. I check his expression. Is he jealous? Freaking out? No, he's smiling. He fans himself like he's overheating. He rules.

When I get back on the floor to work the room for table dances, Randy comes up behind me, his breath humid warmth in my ear. "These men love you, baby."

"You think?" I say, reaching back to pull his arms around my waist. "Well, then, I guess it's tough noogies for them that I only love you."

That's true, too. It takes a certain kind of man to not only abide his stripper girl, but to celebrate her. They're rarer than one in a million. What he has to contend with: Knowing that foreign eyes are boring holes in his lover's body. Having to fight the "Hey, that's *mine!*" territorial reflex. My fatigue. Fear that some clown might hassle me in a way that I can't handle. The suggestion that no "real man" would "let" his woman do "that kind" of work.

Jesus, it's huge.

Not that Randy doesn't get jealous or territorial—anyone who's ever seen a guy try to talk to me when we're out together can testify to that. But he knows the customers aren't a significant threat—

they're more marks than men in my professional estimation. And his attitude may change, his limits might shift. But for now, I trust that he'll love me when I'm onstage, and guard me like a pit bull when I'm off. I daresay he's got a bit of a crush on Barbie Faust—and Daisy, my persona *du jour*. I've never put up with a man who couldn't accept my decision to strip, but I never dreamed that I'd find someone who treats me with such admiration, protection, and honor.

I stand over my costume bag in the dressing room, deliberating over which dress to wear next. A heavily freckled dancer crouches in front of the open locker next to mine. As she shifts her weight, her white leather thigh-high boots creak. Her long chestnut hair gives off the strong, hot waft of gardenia. She smells like she's wilting.

I'm halfway into my pink polka-dot bikini when she pivots on her boot heels and starts talking to me. "Is that your man that you had your arms around downstairs?" Her braces are a twinkling accompaniment to her voice.

"Yep." I tie the triangle top behind my neck.

"It's cool you've got a man who supports you doing this."

"Why? Yours doesn't?" I peek inside her locker. There's a Sears portrait of her in a red blazer and skirt, holding a fat, grinning baby girl in her lap. Next to the photo is a purple glittered sticker that reads SKINNY LITTLE BITCH.

"Oh, he likes the money just fine," she says with a derisive snort, "but other than that . . ." Her voice trails off. She shuts her locker door and spins the combination lock. "Anyway, you're lucky."

She's wrong.

I'm beyond lucky. I'm blessed.

• • •

My next night at the Bush Company, I'm up first in the rotation, just after the club opens at 4:30. There are only two men at the tipping rail, both young, and they don't look very impressed. As I walk offstage after my set, I hear one say to the other, "Oh, well. At least she has nice hair." (Ha! If he only knew!)

Did he think I wouldn't hear him?

In comedian Norm McDonald's "Weekend Update" segment on "Saturday Night Live," he reported in jest that a Virginia dancer stabbed a man for telling her she was too fat to strip.

In moments like this, I can see how that could happen.

There's no way to tell whether or not a customer is going to find me attractive. I can't tell by looking. Appearances aren't that instructive. I could analyze consumption patterns (body type, hair color, age, attitude) and figure averages (number of dances purchased, tip) but really, I've no set rule. All I know for certain is that the idea of "every man's fantasy" is a lie.

Later on, I'm leaning over the back of the booths just in front of the bar when I strike up a conversation with a Cadillac cowboy from Houston. He's just returned from one of those deep-sea-fishing expeditions where they promise you'll go home with a big fat fish on ice—a halibut or salmon—whether you caught it yourself or not.

We're making small talk, how long I've been up in Anchorage, how long I've been dancing, what I think of it.

He says, with clinical calm, as if he were sitting next to me while I'm lying on a couch and he's got a notepad balanced on his knee, "You must really get off on the power you have over men."

My jaw tightens. I'm well-acquainted with my pathologies. Well enough to have nicknames for them, so it's not his presumption of deficiency that rankles. It's more his delivery, like, if he can pin me on my power trip, get my fatal flaw down, *he'll* feel more powerful.

I hate that "I've got your number" crap. Does he really think that to know someone's pathologies is to know *them*?

I want to flail my arms and yell, "I'm a self-loathing misanthrope with body dysmorphia, intimacy issues, borderline manic depression, and situational exhibitionist tendencies. If you're going to analyze me, you nosy creep, get it right!"

I can't blame anyone who tries to figure out this stripping thing—the dancers or the dance itself. Some maintain that deconstruction is an act of coldness, but I don't think so. I've never considered curiosity cold. Why *not* try to drill down to the bedrock? On the face of it, there's really nothing particularly compelling about a girl taking off her clothes to music so she can make some money. But there's something about the *permission*. And the imagination. A guy will never get the girl, but he'll shell out an entire paycheck's worth of singles for the suggestion that he might.

Around midnight, I'm standing next to Randy by the entrance. We've dropped our cover, and the doorman knows we're a couple. He even offered to help Randy find work should we choose to relocate to Anchorage. But we're not interested in pondering a move just this minute. We're rendered slack-jawed and stupid by the dancer onstage. She entered in corporate drag—short black skirt, fitted pinstripe jacket, hair up, glasses. All business. Then she slowly came undone, taking down her long, blonde hair, stripping out of her uptight clothes, piece by piece. Now she's nothing but lean, tan limbs and glory. For her last song, she rolls an inflatable kiddie pool onstage, steps into it nude, and begins soaping herself with a sponge. The music in the background is a spare, shameless track of a woman moaning over a bass line. The tempo slows and speeds up and slows down again—the pace of sex. And she's lathering herself and sliding around in the pool, head thrown back. She is the ultimate Hitchcock blonde—an ice queen with a smoldering core. Men can scarcely stop staring long enough to put bills on the rail. We're held captive as she turns her back to the audience and squeezes the sponge over her head. A perfect white rivulet of suds runs down the center of her back, and as if trained, splits at the small of her back and covers her buttocks. She bounces a little, and the motion of her butt muscles makes the bubbles quiver. No one in the room is breathing.

We watch this woman, entranced. There is nothing in the club that can compete with what's happening onstage. A bomb could drop in the parking lot and no one would move a muscle. She has single-handedly brought the entire audience to its knees, this common genius, this protean hottie. And here is the heart of striptease: You can analyze and deconstruct the act all you want—you will never totally demystify it. You can't break the spell. Nothing can fully explain why some people take to strip clubs—sometimes to the point of addiction, why some find the very idea offensive, and why others just don't get it and shrug. What I like best about stripping is this, the arbitrariness. The mystery. The fact that you can't definitively state what makes one woman stand out from the next. That some tiny part of every dancer's soul spills out when she performs, whether she means it to or not. That you can see a woman totally nude before you, and there's still so much about her that you don't, and can't, know. And that you can never predict that singular instance, like right now, when the world falls away and the only thing that matters is the light falling on the stage and the dancer unfurling herself against the music the way a singer wraps her breath around a note.

THIRTEEN

Pillow

PJ's Showclub is in Spenard—a seedy neighborhood in southwest Anchorage that's full of auto body shops, cheap motels, and dive bars. PJ's is at the opposite end of the spectrum from the Bush Company: a humble hangout that takes all comers and dazzles none. Tourists, if they know about the place, tend to avoid it. But word rarely travels far about PJ's these days. It saw its heyday over twenty years ago when oil money and the Pipeline ushered in the state's second gold rush.

One gathers that money isn't so great at PJ's anymore. Customers are sparse, and one of the cocktail waitresses, a heavyset blonde with dark roots and scuffed white leather hi-top sneakers, wears a dress fashioned out of an oversize T-shirt that reads, in big black letters, WHAT PART OF TIP DON'T YOU UNDERSTAND?

Randy and I drop in there on one of my nights off from the Bush Company. On the wall across from the entrance hangs a dartboard and a list of several years' worth of Anchorage champion darts players. Tacked up about the bar are babes-in-bikinis alcohol posters. Neon beer signs color the smoke and dust in the air. We take seats at a cocktail table two rows back from the stage and a waitress comes over to take our drink order. She's an androgynous-looking woman, with silver-framed glasses and headful of long, wavy red hair that's flying off in several directions. A sexy mad scientist in a little black dress. She deals two napkins like a seasoned card sharp, collects our drink order, and zips off to fetch from the bar.

She look very familiar. I'm certain I've seen her before. But where? After she comes back with our drinks—a beer for Randy and the customary Diet Coke for me, I sit chewing on my straw for a while, and then it comes to me. "Hey," I say to Randy, "I think that's Pillow."

"Who?"

"Pillow! This bodybuilder lady who was helping out at Exotic World."

I had completely forgotten about her. We flag her down, and lo and behold, it *is* Pillow! This is a total coincidence—a happy accident.

Pillow is her real name, and she's worked at PJ's for twenty-one years. Growing up, she never had grandiose dreams of stripping, she just kind of, as she says, "slid into it sideways." She moved to San Francisco in 1975 after dropping out of high school in her native Santa Fe at the age of seventeen. One of the men she knew from the gay scene worked up on Broadway at a strip club called the El Cid. "He would make twenty bucks a night sitting in a booth for seven hours flipping switches. He ended up being less than responsible so I took over his job." Watching the four nightly acts go up while manning the switches, Pillow got the idea to strip. "The acts were making twenty-five dollars a night, so I thought, *hmm, I could make an extra five bucks a night, and I'd only have to get onstage for fifteen minutes out of every hour instead of working for seven hours straight."*

An extra five dollars per night might not seem like much, even in those days, but to cash-strapped Pillow, any raise was better than none. "Back then," she says, "I was staying in a hotel up on Columbus Avenue in a room that was $125 a month. It had a sink with a plug in it, and the bathroom and pay phones were down the hall. I made coffee in a mayonnaise jar, using a paper towel attached with a rubber band over the mouth of the jar as a filter. We'd steal ice and make an ersatz fridge in the sink. My boyfriend used to get food stamps, so we'd pay the rent with them, shoplift our groceries, and what little money I got, he spent on booze. Because of hanging out with drag queens, I knew quite a bit about making costumes—how to set elastic, how to make a bra out of shoulder pads, etcetera. I used to shoplift lingerie from the Goodwill, then sew on beads and lace and sell the costumes."

Pillow's stint at the El Cid was cut short when management learned that she was underage. "I had a bad fake I.D. and my boss figured it out. I was horrified." Pillow reluctantly shuffled across the street to the Erotic Theater, a dingy porno house that had no liquor license, and therefore could employ women under twenty-one. "It was just awful," she recalls. "They would run movie loops and play reel-to-reel music in the background. The guy that worked behind the counter was the projectionist, the barker, and the bouncer. We'd sit on a stool in the window while the guy barked and enticed men to come in off the street to watch the movie. Once he gathered enough customers, he'd start the film. Toward the end of the reel, dancers had to go through the audience to hustle quarters: 'Hi, I'm going to be dancing, but I need some money for the jukebox.'

"The worst part was working the crowd to get private dances

after the movie. They had this room in the back with a platform, which was a massage table with the legs cut in half and a carpeted top, and a bean bag chair for the customer to sit on. In 1976, it was thirty dollars for a half-hour show and fifty for the hour." These long and up-close shows were quite a switch from what Pillow was used to at the El Cid, where a girl took fifteen minutes to strip down to a g-string, and she had to be six feet away from the customer when she was topless.

Trying to successfully work the stage was a grave concern at the Erotic Theater, Pillow explains. "The Erotic Theater used to be a music club called the Barbary Coast and the stage was built to resemble a wooden ship, so there was this big sail sticking out from behind the corner of the screen, and this five-foot sloping pol- ished wood stage. The boom of the sail stuck out so you had to be careful not to hit your head. I tried as best I could to dance," Pillow says, but she gave up soon enough. "That's when I discovered floor work."

Pillow tired of the Erotic Theater but given her age, her employment options were limited. Pillow pocketed her fake I.D. and checked out another club, an old burlesque house called the Follies on the corner of 16th Street and Mission. "They had one of those big marquees with all the letters falling off," Pillow recalls. "You know, when they have to turn a letter upside down to make another letter—and they had some gnarly old porno posters hanging up, and eight-by-tens in glitter-covered frames in the window.

"I show up for the audition, and this short, pudgy old guy who talked around the stub of a cigar between his teeth looks me up and down like a customer would look at a chicken in a butcher shop, 'Yeah, let me see whatcha got, kid.' I go in the dressing room and there's all these tired-looking strippers back there smoking cigarettes with their feet up, they've got fifty pounds of makeup on—big fake lashes, old-fashioned showgirl makeup.

"The old guy says, 'Pick out a song.' I hand him my reel-to-reel tape and he goes, 'No, no, no, pick out a *song*,'—he wanted *sheet music*. So I had to pick something out of a fake book. I picked 'Hooray for Hollywood' because it was the only title I recognized. A man played it on a Wurlitzer while I performed. There was a couple of steps and a runway, and the surface was really uneven, plus, I wasn't wearing my glasses, so I'm up there wobbling around, and in my mind's eye I'm imagining all these old strippers rolling their eyes at this dumb, awkward kid with no tits. After I finish, I get down and the guy goes, 'Yeah, kid, come back when you got a better I.D. and I'll give you a job.' The guy knew I was underage all along, he just wanted to see me naked!"

The vulnerability that young Pillow felt because of her paucity of options became the ferment of her stubbornness today. Even though PJ's offers table dancing, Pillow abstains. While she will strip down to the buff onstage, she won't "show pink," i.e., expose her genitals. And she has special dispensation to excuse herself from the rotation of dancers, and instead has her own show times at 7, 9, 11, and 1 a.m. The rest of the time, she's cocktailing on the floor. "When I finally turned twenty-one and could work in a club where there were solid rules and a good stage, I vowed that I would never again stoop to the level of compromise that I had at the Erotic Theater," she says. "I would never let someone tell me that I had to do something I didn't want to do."

After turning twenty-one in 1977, she headed straight back to Broadway. She had a number of venues to choose from—the Hungry I, the Garden of Eden, the Off-Broadway. "I was one of the B-girls," she says, "as in Plan B." She even worked at the famous Condor Club, known for being the first topless place in the city, with Carol Doda performing sans brassiere atop a hydraulically-lifted piano. The same piano, incidentally, lifted all the way to the ceiling one night and fatally crushed club manager Jimmy "the Beard" Ferrozzo, who was having sex with a dancer on top of the piano at the time. The dancer lived, but she was pinned below her dead consort until they were discovered by the janitor the next morning. Pillow remembers the incident well. "I felt sorry for the poor girl who got stuck against the ceiling, naked, with that dead guy," she says. "But he was an asshole. Talk about karma!"

After the Condor, Pillow headed down Broadway to the Hungry I, a nightclub-turned-strip joint where Lenny Bruce polished his act in the fifties. "I worked the love act at the Hungry I with my friend Max. It was just stylized moves that mimicked sex, nothing graphic. Max was short and had a bad back so we couldn't do any lifts—you know, where the guy picks up the girl and spins her around, so we got into character acting and props.

"Our favorite routine was our *Star Wars* act. In 1977 *Star Wars* was brand-new. I was Princess Leia with buns bobby-pinned to my ears that I'd made out of hairpieces, and he was Darth Vader. We had a robot that we made out of a fifty-gallon drum put on casters, and Max had this homemade Darth Vader costume—a big cape, footless tights, and a homemade light saber.

"We would play variations of the *Star Wars* theme, and I wore a g-string that had MAY THE FORCE BE WITH YOU embroidered on it in little tiny letters. Max would take his Darth Vader helmet off to this heavy-breathing sound effect and act like he was using the Force to make me strip, that I was being 'Forced' to do it. When he took off his helmet, he had one of those leather bondage hoods underneath so you couldn't see his face. Well, one night, the deejay started our music but we weren't ready. I had to keep my head cocked to one side because one of my buns was falling off, and he didn't have time to tighten the strings on the back of his hood, so it moved and his eyeholes slid over making him totally blind. Since he couldn't breathe or see, he's missing all his marks. I hear this *Mmph! Mmph!*, and I realize he's almost going off the stage! So I grabbed the edge of his cape, pulled him back, and we had to jerry-rig the rest of the act."

Around PJ's, there are hollers for more beer. Pillow excuses herself and takes off to tend to her rounds. I look over to see how Randy is doing. He nods that he's okay. Last night after we left the Bush Company we had a terrible fight. A dancer who didn't know he was my boyfriend started flirting with him, which pissed me off. Then I spent a lot of time talking with a customer for free, which made Randy furious. We sat in the car at a drive-through shrieking at each other: "I swear to God I almost pushed that girl down the stairs. You could've told her right away you were with me!"; "If you're not making money off of a guy, I don't want you sitting with him!" and on and on. We got so involved in our fight that we didn't even notice that Randy had missed the drive-through squawk box entirely and instead recited our order into a garbage can. We definitely needed this night off at PJ's. I look at him and mouth the words *garbage can*, and he cracks right up.

A dancer wearing square-toed engineer boots clomps onto the stage—she looks like a backstreet Bette Midler. After stripping out of her black halter top and denim cut-offs, she perches indifferently on a chair, spreading her legs to the near-empty room. That's a hell of a note—sitting on a stage, showing your cunt to the world, and no one gives a damn. Not so much as a dollar. There's no deejay, so girls don't get an introduction before they dance. You have no idea what their names are, and the CD player tends to skip, so the dancers have to hoist themselves up from the stage, duck back behind the curtain, and give the stereo a whack.

Still, a thirty-five-year-old gal who has recently started dancing again to help her college-bound daughter pay for school tells me,

"We're like a family here." I don't doubt it. All the girls collect a pay-check, the minimum wage going a ways to ease any competition. And there doesn't seem to be any dressing room diva attitude, either. Perhaps the girls just don't think it's worth the bother.

Pillow wound up in Anchorage by chance. In 1978, a recruiter from an Alaskan club came into the El Cid. He handed her a busi-ness card, then told her about Alaska over dinner. Pillow liked what she heard so she said, "Sounds good. Get me out of here."

"I flew up to Anchorage and worked one night at this club downtown called the Embers, then later at the Wild Cherry," she says. But Alaska wasn't the Shangri-la the recruiter had promised. "I'd talked to a bunch of the other girls who'd come up from Timbuktu on a one-way ticket and had to stay at least as long as it took to make the money to go back home.

"The downtown clubs were just terrible. The girls were disgust-ing, squatting down and showing themselves. There was a girl at the Embers who shot a hard-boiled egg out of her pussy. You had to sell champagne and drink with the guys and they'd try to grab you."

Her friend and mentor from San Francisco, Brandy, was also working up in Alaska, so Pillow called around to all the clubs until she found her at PJ's. "Brandy sent a couple biker friends of hers after me. These two great big scary-looking, long-haired bikers walk into the Wild Cherry shouting, 'Who's Pillow?'

"And I'm like, 'Uh, me . . . ?'

"They go, 'Where's your stuff?'

"I kind of pointed to the dressing room area behind the bar and they barged right in. The staff is yelling, 'You can't go in there,' and the bikers just give them this look like, 'What, you're going to stop us?'

"One of them tossed my trunk up onto his shoulder like it was nothing. They said, 'You're coming with us!', and I'm like, 'Oh, shit.' Then they finally told me, 'Brandy sent us.' "

Pillow walked into PJ's and saw that it was a clean club. "On amateur night, girls would come from clubs all around the city. If a girl bent over when she was bottomless, the MC would hold his hat over her snatch, and say, 'If you wanna do that, girlie, you can pick up your paycheck downtown,' or something like that. Either that, or the light and sound man would turn off the lights." Pillow asked for an audition. She was hired right away and has been working there since that night twenty-one years ago.

Pillow lives in a trailer next to PJ's. A run-down four-room affair that she shares with three other dancers (and one of the dancer's six ferrets), it's not exactly the Ritz, but for thirty bucks a week, you can't beat it. It's certainly more space than she had when she first moved in during the boom years, there were two girls in each room and girls on beds in the living room.

The cheap lodging is the work of Hallie McGinnis, the diffident manager/owner of PJ's. Hallie inherited the bar when founding owner Papa John (a.k.a. PJ) died in 1982. If you can imagine Garrison Keillor leaving Lake Wobegon behind to run an Alaskan strip club, you've got a pretty clear image of Hallie. A mellow guy noted for his soft touch, he tends to hire freely and winces when he has to cut back on girls when business is too slow to make payroll. Nobody who works for him has anything bad to say about him. He's the only club owner in town who doesn't exact hefty stage fees or tip-outs, and, on occasion, he'll even front a hurting girl a loan.

It's time for Pillow's eleven o'clock show. Pillow cues her music in the tape player backstage. In 1995, she won the Miss Exotic World title, and once she starts dancing, it's easy to see why. Her dance is perfectly choreographed classic burlesque. Where a more modern stripper might undulate and grind, Pillow struts and kicks. She grabs the edge of her cape and spins in dizzying circles around the perimeter of the stage, her cape billowing out like a sail in the breeze. The femininity of her movements starkly contrasts with her muscular, ultra-defined physique. She doesn't make much eye contact while she dances, she looks like she's off in her own dream world. She later tells me it's because she is almost legally blind. She literally works the stage from memory. "I can make out shapes and stuff," she says, "but I don't know how many times a guy held an unlit cigarette in his hand and I thought it was a dollar, or someone would have a dollar on top of his head and I'd have no idea that the money was there. A lot of times I'd end up with five or six ones and a twenty and not know who gave it to me!" She also wears ear plugs onstage. "It's the Helen Keller School of Dance," Pillow deadpans.

Pillow is committed to keeping the spirit of burlesque alive. As the business gets more lascivious, Pillow uses her antiquated gestures as a hedge against the encroaching lewdness. "It's a shtick," she tells me. "I'm trying to cut the prurient thing. You know, the guys who hold out a dollar, 'Hey, baby, come here, yeah, yeah!' It lets the guy know, hey, you're not going to buy my time.

"I try to do it nicely," she says. "But inside of me I'm screaming, 'Go the fuck away!'

"When a guy wants a table dance, I'll be like, 'Oh no, I don't do that, I'm the waitress.' Or 'Oh no, I'm shy.' Sometimes the guys will get belligerent, like, 'What's the matter, my money's not good enough for you or something?' One time, a guy wanted a table dance and he kept escalating his price. Did I want the money? Of course I wanted the money. But I wasn't about to do it. It's a matter of principle. So finally, I just said, 'Look, I'd rather suck your dog's dick than give you a table dance. Now go away.' He just stood there with his mouth open. I think I got the message across.

"Table dancing started here in 1989, and totally changed the atmosphere. You used to sit down, have a drink and chat with a customer. Then the girls started pestering the guys. It killed the conversation. There was a type of guy who would come in, kind of mousy, real shy, but generally okay. The girls would hustle them for table dances, but the guys would be real uncomfortable. They didn't want to spend the money, but they didn't have the ability to say no. Once they started getting worked, they stopped coming in.

"They were replaced by the guys who like to throw their money around. The atmosphere became more competitive, it became downright mean.

"The change has been real insidious," Pillow says. "It just sort of wends itself in. The older girls move on and new dancers come and they've never been exposed to any other stuff. For them, it's status quo. I left Alaska to start doing the bodybuilding thing, and I came back in 'eighty-five and they were showing pink. It was subtle by today's standards—a girl on her back doing slo-mo stuff, but it had never been done. It got more and more explicit—how much can you get away with? At first the girls are like, 'Did you see what so-and-so is doing? That's disgusting!' And then six months later, everybody is doing it."

The obvious question then is why does she bother dancing at all anymore. Clearly, she's got the brains and wherewithal to go into another line of work. She is a rabid crafter, making virtually all of her own costumes. She bodybuilds and is an active Klingon (she even treated Randy and me to a recitation of a three-minute long anthem in Klingon—a complicated language with some tricky glottal stops). How is it worth it to continue working in an environment where you're not comfortable with what goes on? Especially when she's so obviously capable of other things.

Pillow's answer is simple: The dancing itself makes it worthwhile. "I like the performance. It's not a sex thing, it's a power thing. With dancing, you have the endorphins of the movement. You're in the moment. And you have the sheer kinetic joy. I've always called it my Blue Bolt. Athletes call it 'the zone.' You don't get it all the time, but when it happens, it's like a suspension of time. Of pain. There's no telling when it will happen—it doesn't always if there are a lot of people or a lot of money. I always saw it as an energy circuit—you're projecting out into the audience and they're receptive and they send the energy back to you.

"I'm not technically a good dancer, but I've always aspired to what my mentor Brandy had, where you transcend yourself. Brandy was overly tall, she had saggy tits, she had a huge nose, her hair was kinda scraggly, and her voice was this honking, braying thing. But she'd put on her makeup and go onstage and it was magic! She would turn into anything she wanted. You couldn't put your finger on the technique, but it worked."

But Pillow's not sure how much longer she can stay at PJ's. She still loves the dancing, doesn't mind the cocktailing, and is glad to have a place to perform in the manner to which she is accustomed, but things change. They've changed since she's started, and they'll probably do so again—most likely toward the extreme. Pillow was once a passionate competitive bodybuilder—one of the first women to embrace the sport—but stopped, for ethical reasons, when anabolic steroid use went from taboo to more common practice. She sees an obvious parallel in stripping. "What was bad and unacceptable became good," she says. "It changed out from under me. It's déjà vu all over again."

I can't say which I think would be better—to stick to your limits in a club and try to hang on to your place, or to just say the hell with it and move on down the road. But regardless, I admire Pillow for the strength of her resolve. It isn't easy to stand your ground when what becomes standard exceeds your comfort level. Most women would just go with the flow.

The night is drawing to a close. There aren't many customers left in the bar, and most of the dancers are huddled at a corner table talking. Randy and I finish our drinks and get ready to head out as a heavyset black woman in a red lace teddy and red flat-soled boots gets onstage. She drops into a deep squat and begins cackling maniacally. The few men sitting at the meat rack flee. Pillow sits on a bar stool against the wall, head bent down in concentration, studying her Klingon book under the white neon light of the beer sign.

FOURTEEN

Philosophy and Flesh

There are five CDs that I bring with me to every club, my "can't miss" collection. If I'm allowed to choose my own music, I'll pick from them: Metallica's black album, Sade's *Diamond Life*, Nine Inch Nails' *Pretty Hate Machine* (Nine Inch Nails is so popular among strippers, lead singer Trent Reznor once snorted in an interview, "I think my next album is going to be called *Music for Titty Bars*"), Kid Rock's *Devil Without A Cause*, and Mötley Crüe's *Greatest Hits*.

Mötley Crüe's "Girls Girls Girls" is one hell of a Proustian trigger. When I hear the motorcycle *vroom* and the priapic thrust of guitar chords that kick off the song, I'm blasted back in time to San Francisco. I see, with visionary clarity, dancers twirling nude around brass poles with lissome vigor, walking across the stage in the golden halo of a single spotlight, waving and blowing kisses and snapping the sides of their thongs as they're introduced by an incorporeal deejay's voice, sharing lipstick and bottles of imitation designer perfume in front of glary dressing room mirrors. The song was already ancient history by the time I moved West, but it's one of the first to sing the praises of stripper mystique—an anthem to an era of my life that left a fiery, indelible mark. The five years I spent dancing in San Francisco still float in my memory as random bursts of vibrant jewel-tone colors, or the explosion of fireworks.

I'm tempted to say the murder made me flee New York for San Francisco when I was twenty, but really, it was lots of things—which, when they ground to a dumb halt, had the decency to do so more or less all at once.

I come back to the apartment on East 11th Street after a week-end in Provincetown with a couple of friends, and Deb is in the kitchen cooking big pots of quinoa and adzuki beans.

She wipes her hands on a dishtowel and vanishes into her bed-room. She reappears holding a bit of newsprint. "I was reading the paper while I was temping today and look what I found!"

She hands me a short article torn from the *Daily News*.

The story is about Rita, the stringy-haired manager from Peepland who the girls called "Mom." It reports that "Mom" and a young accomplice killed Lennie, the floor manager who had van-ished—apparently over a drug-related matter. Rita and her friend shot Lennie, then wrapped his body in a blanket and threw it in the Hudson River. They were apprehended and Rita was sentenced to prison. Her accomplice got a reduced sentence in exchange for testi-fying against her.

I don't know what to think. I want to be shocked, but I'm not. The story is so terrible, but at the same time, not surprising. Rita was obviously strung way out to hell and gone, and given how fucked up Peepland was, this outcome made sense. If there was any kind of logic to the place, it was that the hardcore, thuggy hustlers and users would come to one of two ends: Go home and clean up, or pitch headlong over the edge. Accepting this as simple fact is but another thread in the fucked-up fabric of my life.

By now, I have abandoned acting completely. I don't enjoy it, and I value being a punk more than I care about being "adaptable." I know, too, that few directors would cast me as Ophelia with a purple mohawk. The last straw came when I was in Herbert Berghof's class for young actors at HB Studios. During an improv exercise in which we enacted a party scene, another girl in the class, attempting dialogue, asked me, "So, how's that bladder infection? Is it getting better?"

A small voice deep in my gut said, plainly and definitively, *I quit.*

To a person without a plan, New York City is a dangerous place. After a year at Peepland, Rachel, my entrée to the business, leaves to become a high-school art teacher. I get a job at Life Café, a funky restaurant right down the street from my apartment. With nothing much else to do, I start eating. A lot. I graze ferociously to fill the void; stuffing down anything cheap and devilishly satisfying I can find. Bagfuls of twenty-five-cent bodega snacks: Bon Ton butter popcorn, mini ice cream sandwiches, Little Debbie snack cakes, Dipsy Doodles corn chips, and Cheez Puffs. Greasy slabs of pizza. Entire pints of ice cream. Peanut butter by the tablespoonful. And enormous Mexican dishes from the restaurant, followed by surreptitious shavings off the forbidden mud cake.

I grow huge and reasonably sated, but remain bored.

I write a report for the San Franciso–based punk fanzine *Maximum RocknRoll,* and Tim Yohannon, *MRR*'s driving editorial force and the king of the dogma punks, offers me a steady column. The gig doesn't pay, as per 'zine custom, but Tim grants me unlimited space—more than enough rope with which to hang myself. My topics range from alternative health to juvenile anti-parenting screeds to women's issues, but my tone is always total aggro. I can authentically say that I was a jaded GenX twit before it was cool. Although, of course, it was never cool. But writing, I quickly discover, is a lot more interesting to me than any thespian pursuit. I latch on to this new passion the way a drowning woman grabs at a raft.

I scrape together some money from my café earnings, buy a cheap plane ticket, and fly out to San Francisco to visit the *MRR* house—a tidy duplex in Noe Valley with bedrooms full of "shitworkers" given free board in exchange for working on the 'zine, a large living room on the main floor crammed with Macs and production tools, and a sprawling split-level den downstairs that has an entire wall lined with Tim's extensive record collection, thousands of punk vinyl 45s and LPs with covers edged in dark green electrical tape. The most excellent house I've ever seen.

Compared with San Francisco, New York seems unpredictably violent. Uptight. Expensive. And, in my case, pointless. A cluttered landscape of scatty, unfulfilled hopes. I gather all my girlfriends together one night and give away almost everything I own. Books, dishes, jewelry, and heaps and heaps of clothes—the spoils of all those Peepland-funded shopping sprees. I reduce my possessions to five boxes, which I ship West book rate. Flying out on an economy ticket, I arrive in San Francisco broke, just barely twenty, and, for the first time in years, hopeful.

San Francisco's Lusty Lady Theater is as close to a liberating force as a sex business can get. The classified ads for the woman-owned and -operated peep show that run on the back page of the *Bay Guardian* and the *SF Weekly* emphasize the "fun, friendly, feminist" work environment. On Kearney Street, just south of Broadway in North Beach, the Lusty building is wedged into a steep hill. Out front is a red neon sign of a naked lady. As the sign blinks, she looks like she's doing the Shimmy.

I am not sure I want to get back into the adult business, but my temporary job at a Haight Street record store ends and my friend from *MRR*, Stella, a Central American activist, extols the Lusty's virtues. She had worked there, dancing in nothing but her buzz cut and combat boots, and her description of the management intrigues me. They are former dancers themselves, and don't allow any drugs or alcohol on the premises. The only thing dancers have to do is dance naked on the stage behind glass. They earn an hourly wage, so there is no hustling for tips, and many of the dancers are artists, activists, and college students working their way through school.

The entryway to the Lusty Lady looks like the foyer of an old-fashioned Barbary Coast bordello. The walls are mirrored and thick red velvet drapes with scarf valances trimmed in gold tassels hang in the doorway. I ask the hippie guy behind the desk if they are hiring. He is wearing a T-shirt with a tongue-wagging smiley face on it that says HAVE AN EROTIC DAY—the official Lusty Lady logo. He smiles and hands me an application.

I can't imagine why I have to fill out an application. There certainly was no such thing at Peepland. The application is full of unusual questions: How do you feel about men's sexuality? How do you feel about your own? Are you comfortable with your body?

I'm impressed that they take things like this into consideration when they hire women.

When I'm done with the paperwork, the guy buzzes for the show director and after a minute or two she comes into the hallway. A brunette in her early thirties with thick calves, she shakes my hand and introduces herself as Kelly. She's wearing a long, off-white cable knit sweater and jeans tucked into cowboy boots. Her mouth is an almost lipless horizontal furrow that she wrenches back into a sad, tight little smile.

Kelly leads me through the dark hallway. The carpet squishes under my feet, and there are black shapes—men—moving around us as we head toward a row of doors with lights over the sills—red for *In Use*, green for *Open*. Kelly opens a corner door and we go into the booth together. There's a built-in bench that we sit on side-by-side.

"You ready to see the show?" Kelly asks.

"Ready!"

"Good attitude, I like that," she says, dropping a quarter into a red, illuminated slot.

The window rises and the first thing I see is pink. A bright pink carpet in a tiny room with mirrored walls. There are four nude women on the other side of the glass, dancing, leaning against the mirrors and posing, and sticking their butts in the windows while men drop quarters and watch excitedly. This is a girl aquarium!

A childishly plump dancer comes over to our window. In her black Vampira wig, she wears a big yellow polka dot bow. She sits down on the raised ledge beneath the window, holding her yellow-gloved hands over the soft pooching milk-white flesh of her belly. Then she blows us a kiss and with a kick of her black granny boots, she's up and away to another window.

"Customers aren't allowed to direct the show in any way," Kelly says as I watch the women crouch with their legs spread, cocking their heads coyly to one side or tossing them back in counterfeit ecstasy. "They can't motion you over or tell you how to move. We do ask that you smile, act sexy, and look like you're having fun."

I can do that.

I hadn't intended to audition today, but Kelly asks if I am interested in trying out, so I figure why not, since I'm already here? I don't have any costumes so Kelly just puts me onstage in my white leather high-top sneakers. "This is Polly, ladies," she says, sticking her head through the curtain in the doorway to the stage. "She's going to audition." Kelly disappears to watch me dance from one of the booths with one-way glass.

I step onto a stage full of smiling faces. I notice that the carpet is really red, not pink. A black girl with long silky dreads squats down in front of the window of the corner booth Kelly and I were in. The window only comes up about waist high, so she grabs onto the handlebars on either side of the window and spreads her legs, leaning her head back as she sways to the music. Oblivious to the man, only his torso visible, masturbating at the sight of her exposed crotch, she leans her head back farther to look at me, upside down. "Hello! I'm Shy."

News to me!

The stage is a modified rectangle, with three sides lined by windows. Two corner booths allow a customer to sit, but the rest of the booths have windows at eye-level, which is about waist-height on the stage side. Three of the windows have one-way glass so dancers can't see the customers. The girl in the Vampira wig is kneeling in front of the one-way window in the center, licking her fingers suggestively. The two other girls onstage flit from window to window, pinching their nipples, slapping their buttocks, or dancing to the music on the jukebox.

The crescent of glassed-in faces around the stage is startling—so many men seeing me all at once! But I remember what Kelly told me, "Customers aren't allowed to direct the show," and I feel relief. I scan the windows. A fat Chinese man with unexpressive features. A pasty, beak-nosed yuppie with his tie tossed over his shoulder standing back in the shadows to hide his face. A young, eager Filipino guy in a football jersey, his nose practically pressed against the glass, looking as if he's seeing naked women for the first time in his life. And three mirrored panes that reveal nothing but my own reflection blinking back at me—the mystery men. I'm not beholden to any of the onlookers, I only need to look like I'm having a good time.

I try to move sexily, but I'm completely new at this so I'm sure I appear foolish. The sneakers don't help. Looking at myself in the mirrors is hard, because I feel so big. Some of the weight is coming off, but I'm still thirty pounds heavier than I was eighteen months ago. I jump around in my sneakers for the length of a song, then Kelly's head pokes through the curtains again.

"Okay, come on out. You can get dressed."

I wave goodbye to the other dancers and follow Kelly down the carpeted steps to the damp basement office. The office is next to a locker room with a worn-out couch and payphone in it.

"That was great! You've got a terrific grin," she says, as she offers me a seat next to her desk. Was I grinning up there? I hadn't noticed. On the desktop is a huge schedule sheet laid out with names partially penciled in next to a half-empty coffee cup with an oily smear of russet lipstick on the rim.

When I first entered Peepland, I was frightened, and when I saw what working there was like, I became petrified. Then I just shut down completely. But here at the Lusty Lady, I am not even remotely scared. The stage feels self-contained and snug, like the inside of a snow globe. I feel the hinge of my jaw start to relax, just a tiny bit.

I get hired, and immediately the New York years I left behind just a few months before—the wayward, confused Peepland and Lower East Side years—get slammed in a drawer, and I won't think about them for a long time to come.

As if the audition wasn't indication enough, I know that working at the Lusty Lady will be different when I see the list of dancers' pseudonyms. Usually stage names are predictable—oh great, another redhead named Ginger. But here women call themselves Polyester, Chicklet, Euphrates, Arp Quasar, Cherriluv, Sacred Amnesia, Virginia Dentata, Squishy, Insertia, Velveeta, La Meme Fromage, Vixen Bliss, BamBam, Seldom, Rag Doll, Sistar Aqua Divina, and the chilling but brilliant Tralala.

After some deliberation, I choose the stage name Tawdry. I buy a huge wig of long, synthetic auburn curls at an overpriced shop in the Mission run by a grouchy Korean couple, and show up for my first day of work with a pair of pretty patent leather ankle boots and my wig in a plastic bag.

The shifts are thankfully short, only three-and-a-half to six hours. For ten minutes out of every hour, I am allowed a break. I lounge in the dressing room and drink tea, or chat with the show directors about what the Lusty was like when they were dancers. Kelly's stage name was Attila the Honey.

In her book, *The Lusty Lady*, photojournalist Erika Langley, who documented her years dancing at the Lusty's sister operation in Seattle, writes, "The Lusty Lady doesn't look like a comforting place, a place to find yourself or harness your power. It looks like a peep show, a funk-scented, creepy-dark hallway where men wait to stand in a booth, feed quarters, and watch naked dancers behind glass." But she found, as I found, that it *is* a comforting place, and that the finding of self and harnessing of power are pursuits that the Lusty could foster.

Because customers can't tell the dancers what to do, we learn a little something about controlling our sexuality. At no point is a customer allowed to point, beckon, or issue demands, which seems like a trivial detail, but isn't. When a guy taps on the glass, we tell him, "Cut it out, you aren't the boss here. We are!" or "Don't knock on the window, it scares the fish." Repeat offenders are asked to leave.

I love this aspect of working at the Lusty. I can be discriminating in who I perform for. I can walk away from a window whenever I want. And I can play. For the first time. If I didn't have anyone telling me what to do, and it were up to me, what kind of sexual role would I adopt? As long as my breasts and crotch are showing, costuming is up for grabs. I wear severe, thigh-high black suede boots and elbow-length black gloves. Plaid schoolgirl skirts. Lace corsets trimmed in maribou. And always the big red wig, which I don each day like a piece of armor. The ring through my upper lip goes over like a lead balloon with the management ("Tawdry, that looks awful," Kelly told me in the office, when the piercing was brand new and an ugly, angry red) but otherwise, my experiments are appreciated and encouraged. To be treated as if my sexual self-expression is important and unique makes a profound impression on me.

Dancing together, naked, side-by-side onstage, we Lusties grow very aware of the individual beauty of our bodies. Not having to compete with one another for tips, we become friends. We become agents of our own path. And, since we never have to hustle to make our money, we are never humbled by the word *no*.

For me, living in San Francisco is like attending a sex and gender institute, or an esoteric college. I am confronted with new ideas every day, with different ways of integrating politics and desire. I had always lived uncomfortably with the notion that making sex a significant area of inquiry meant you were a bimbo, a head case, or a person with no better bargaining chip. The implication was that a woman had to choose between her sexuality and her credibility—you couldn't have both. But this is San Francisco in the early 1990s and radical sex activists are challenging every assumption with unprecedented wit and style. What a fucking blast! I feast on the works of the local talent: Susie Bright. Gayle Rubin. Pat Califia. Geoff Mains. These are people struggling to save sex. Like every woman in this country, I came of age sexually bent under the weight of guilt and judgment. My sexuality was something I knew how to use for financial advantage, but enjoying it to the fullest was a foreign concept. I gave a lot of lip service to autonomy, but I had no idea how to attain it, really. By reading these authors I feel like I am learning to walk upright.

Every so often I call my former roommate Deb in New York to tell her what a great time I'm having, like the school geek calling home to report to Mom that she's become the princess of summer camp. "Wow, sounds like you've really found a home for yourself!" she says, approvingly.

These are the dawning days of sex-positive feminism—when the notion of female desire is being reevaluated and affirmed—and at the Lusty Lady, we snap up the idea of women's erotic empowerment and work it like a reflex. Unlike the sexually repressive, reactionary timbre of feminism's earlier era, this is a halcyon period of expansion. Catharine MacKinnon and Andrea Dworkin are dismissed as helplessly retro while Camille Paglia, the last of the Great American romantics, tosses verbal bouquets to strippers from her post in the Ivory Tower. We Lusties aren't sleazy, anti-feminist sellouts, we assure ourselves, we are gender warriors, reestablishing the parameters of enlightened female behavior. Spreading our legs for the men dropping quarters and thrusting out our breasts behind the peep-show glass, we are naked and militant. We are pretentious and sweet. We are, in our way, deliciously naïve—all impudent struts, cogent analyses, and queer shoulders to the wheel.

While it has certain humane attributes, the Lusty Lady is no utopia. I have to punch a clock at the beginning and end of every shift. The pay starts at eight dollars an hour and, after dollar-an-hour raises every two weeks if dancers are on time and comply with all the rules, maxes out at twenty-two dollars. You can make more if you work in the one-on-one Private Pleasures booth, but the house takes fifty percent of your tips. The theater opens at 9 a.m., so if you get the early shift, you have to be onstage, naked, and pretending to have fun, at an hour when most working folk are yawning at the office coffee maker. Talking among dancers onstage is forbidden.

The days of combat boots and buzz cuts are over. There is some latitude allowed in appearance, but the show directors want you to look as conventionally pretty as possible—you get sidelined for being too heavy or having too many piercings or tattoos. Only one dancer at a time is allowed to wear black onstage. Freaky hair like dreads or unusual colors has to be covered by a wig. If too many girls shave off all their pubic hair, word comes from on high to start growing it back.

And the place stinks—I mean, *stinks*—of mildewing carpet, ammonia, cleaning solution, dirty wigs, and sperm.

Then there's the parade of dicks. In the corner booths, they are clearly visible. You see so many ejaculations it's like a bad porn film, *Onan's Revenge*. Plus, men flicking their tongues, making the treading-water motion that means "spread your legs," putting scraps of paper with a dollar amount scribbled on it against the window. Men who look at you like you're a foreign object and men who drop a quarter to see you and then don't drop in any more, leaving you to feel like a repulsive hag.

In my mind, the customers exist more as a lurking, spewing visual distraction than as individuals. Some dancers make an effort to talk through the glass and get acquainted with the men, but to me they're a bunch of sexual components: demeanor, size, preference, gesture, potency, frequency. I do have a clear favorite, or I should say, there's one that I actually like. His name is David and he is perfect. Physically perfect. Big, white picket teeth, washboard abs, slender waist, and a thick shock of brown hair hanging in his bright blue eyes. He comes into the corner booth, takes off every stitch of clothing, and makes himself totally happy. I look at him and marvel, Why would somebody that cheerful and handsome come to a place like this? How could somebody be that horny, all the time? When he is about to leave the booth, he always says, "Tawdry, if you ever get lonely, call me!" I ask him what he does for a living and he says he can't tell me. What could it be? Model? Actor? Software developer? Trophy husband?

Every now and then David brings in a girlfriend. I've seen a few women in the booths with their boyfriends, looking scared and ill at ease, mouths shrunken into tense circlets. It was obvious who came up with the idea to come in. But not David's girls. They sit pressed up next to him, smiling, waving hi. Then hand goes to fly and they start doing something that leaves me totally scandalized.

Lusty customers love to show off. Businessmen cruise each other in the hallway and enter the booths in pairs to give each other blow jobs (customers are only allowed one to a booth, but if they're giving us a performance, we let them bend the rules). There is a guy who can suck his own cock. Another can stick his fist up his ass. The customers at Peepland struck me as wounded and retarded by their own desires, but here, I am shocked at this steady stream of perfectly chipper, seemingly well-adjusted people who cannot wait to have sex standing up, or masturbate wearing rubber dishwashing gloves, or squeeze out their wife's breast milk all over the window. It is as if by looking through that thin pane of Plexiglas I can see into the happy, perverted secret heart of America.

Minx Manx, the peep show persona of my friend Carol Queen, loves the Private Pleasures booth—*loves* it. The booth is at the end of the hallway opposite the stage, with PRIVATE PLEASURES spelled out in cursive pink neon over a curtained window. A dancer opens the drape and sits in the window looking comely, in hopes of attracting customers who want a private show. The booth is a carpeted four-by-four perch filled with throw pillows to lounge on. The customer's side is a linoleum-floored stall with a bench and a money slot in the wall. When money gets dropped in the slot—five dollars for three minutes, tips on top for specific acts—the dancer hits a counter on the wall that starts the timer and the intercom so the dancer and customer can negotiate whatever show he wants to buy.

Carol, and her alter-ego Minx, is the whore with the heart of gold and the brain of Krafft-Ebing, so she is thrilled to spelunk in the erotic depths, talking dirty, doing dildo shows, and being a perfect audience for her customers' antics. Because she is so sympathetic to sexual quirks, she attracts the kinkier guys—one who inserts a dildo almost the size of a fireplug up his butt, another who asks her to read a particular bit of scripture while he masturbates. They flock to her, our Saint Francis of Lusty. Even though I could never be that patient with an endless procession of sexual idiosyncrasies, I am deeply impressed by the fact that she can. Where she sees it as a grand adventure and a turn-on, I see it as a tax on my emotional health. Too much, too close. I'm not judgmental. If it's consensual, I honestly don't mind whatever your brand of perversion is. I just don't necessarily want to facilitate. Private Pleasures is too much like Peepland for me, and I don't welcome any reminder of the place.

Dancing at the Lusty Lady is a contradictory experience. While you're encouraged to express yourself, that expression is limited to the "shiny happy" variety. And on one hand, in the process of showing your body to strangers for money, you learn that your sexuality is priceless and uniquely your own. On the other, your precious sexuality must be expressed within the confines of acceptable age, size, shape, and style. Despite being a great draw in Private Pleasures, Minx is let go for accidentally missing a shift when she'd taken another job. Bottom line: The Lusty Lady is a tightly run business. Making money for the owners is the mission objective, and a small paycheck is your reward for helping achieve that end. Anything beyond that is a perk.

Being impolite to the customers is a punishable offense, but sometimes we're rude anyway, especially on those tedious late shifts when our feet hurt and we long to trade our pinchy heels and smelly wigs for pajamas. One night, around twelve-thirty or so, a heavily tattooed dancer named Maya sashays over to a booth where a man stands beating himself with a studded belt. As she turns to wag her high, mulishly strong rump in his window, she says, "*Somebody's* got some childhood trauma he needs to act out!" A comment that strikes me as rich, coming from a stripper.

For all the ups and downs, I like being at the Lusty—dancing in that sweaty, red-carpeted mirror box that smells like girl. Sometimes I get tired, feel ugly, exposed, burdened, bored, or annoyed, but often, when I'm surrounded by all these smart, aware, sexual women— young, fierce, and fighting back—I'm delirious with joy. That happy fireworks feeling.

Somewhere in this festival of personal growth, I decide to tell my parents how I have been supporting myself. I am afraid to tell them, terrified really, but I'm also quite enamored of the novelty of Not Hiding. Doesn't every San Franciscan long to come out about something?

This isn't going to be easy. My family is not emotionally well equipped for surprise revelations. When I think about our reticence, I see myself lit by a glaring spot on a stage in a pitch-black comedy club, pacing with a mike in one hand and gesticulating wildly with the other, saying, "I wouldn't say my family is *repressed*, but . . ." The joke doesn't have an ending, but it illustrates my knowledge that the repression is so extreme as to be comical. Or sad, depending. When I was a teenager, my mother confided in me that she hadn't cried since 1978, when my father had a heart attack.

Because we are, at the core, shy and rather reserved people, we tend to spring important things on each other in the car. That way there's no eye contact or sudden movements. Or means of escape. I employ this tactic when I tell my mother about the Lusty Lady after she picks me up at the train station during my first visit home after moving to California. Thanks to the blessing of selective memory I am unable to recall exactly what she said when I told her, but I distinctly remember her knuckles turning an alarming white as she gripped the steering wheel. She didn't yell. She did not cry. I didn't expect her to. We're WASP, we don't *do* hysteria. I try to imagine her thought process at the time: After the initial shock wears off, she thinks to herself, *How did it come to this? Where did we go wrong? Well, she's not a drug dealer. She is not a prostitute. She is a smart person, but why, why . . . ?* I feel her trying to temper pain with logic. What hurt her more—the truth or my keeping it from her? I want her to know, want her to be fully in my life, but to lay this on her leaves me seized with "rotten kid" remorse.

I suppose I decided to tell her now because the Lusty Lady seems relatively harmless—if she's to find out I'm a stripper, better I should be working at a politically progressive place. I have been operating under the assumption that honesty is the best policy, but when I see my mother's face, I wonder: What good am I doing by telling her this? Now I'm embarrassed and she feels like a failure—to say nothing about how she feels about me. Declaring your sexual independence to the world is one thing. Doing so to your mom is quite another.

She tells my father, who, as he drives me back to the train station at the end of the visit, says to me, sighing, "You have so many talents. It's a shame that you can't make a living using one of them." There is disappointment in his voice. And worry and hesitation, yes. But no anger. If nothing else, my parents are rational people—maybe to a fault. I do my best to assure them that where I'm working is safe. I'm not in any danger and I don't feel I'm doing anything distasteful (I sort of fudge that last part).

I only tell them about the Lusty, though. I don't mention Peepland. I am not ready to tell them about that.

From that day forward, we never address the subject head on. They'll ask if I'm still dancing. I'll say yes. We'll circle around, tensions crackling, Freud pacing the margins, then move quickly on to the next matter of discussion. I will wonder forever after if I shouldn't have just kept it to myself. The truth may have set me free, but what did it to do them?

For many women, the Lusty Lady is a portal club—an entry to the adult industry that leads to more challenging and lucrative venues. Lisa, a hyperactive, black-haired nymph I used to work with at Life Café, moved to San Francisco shortly after I did. One afternoon, we meet in North Beach for lunch. She tells me she has been working over at Mitchell Brothers. "Have you thought of auditioning there?" she asks.

The Mitchell Brothers O'Farrell Theater, located at the corner of Polk and O'Farrell Streets on the periphery of the run-down Tenderloin district, is the crown jewel of San Francisco strip clubs. The club has a daunting reputation for being the hardest to get into. Girls sometimes have to audition several times before they get hired. Others win the Monday night amateur contest and walk away with just the twenty-five-dollar prize, because taking first place doesn't mean you've got a job. You have to get The Card. Once the audition is over, the hopefuls gather backstage and Nellie, the personnel director, comes through and thanks the ones she isn't going to hire, and she hands out cards with her phone number to the ones she wants, saying, "We'd like to hire you, if you're interested. Please call me tomorrow to schedule an orientation." When I lose a few more pounds, I try out. After my audition, I stare in disbelief at the business card in my hand—baby blue with a dark blue star at the center.

I'm in.

Mitchell Brothers has the cachet of being the brainchild of bad-boy porn impresarios Jim and Artie Mitchell. The Mitchell Brothers have long enjoyed local celebrity status for their innovative triple-X films like *Behind the Green Door* and their hard-fought First Amendment battles. But in April, 1991, the Mitchell reputation is forever tarnished when Jim, heretofore considered the mellower of the two brothers, walks into Artie's house one night and fatally shoots him as he lies in bed.

I start working at the O'Farrell Theater in November of that year. On my first day there, I am excused from Mardi Gras, the dancer line-up and introduction that starts every shift, but I do have to lead the rotation of girls in New York Live. I hover nervously, inspecting myself in the mirror as the girls file past in their lingerie on their way to the stage. Some of them toss a quick "good luck" over their shoulder. When the introduction ends, I steal one last look at my reflection. I'm wearing my black suede thigh-high boots, a burgundy lace bra and panty set, and a shiny black cotton Victorian dress with a long, full skirt and leg-of-mutton sleeves. Not a slick ensemble—I look like bait for Jack the Ripper—but I am a beginner, after all. I pace behind the curtain taking deep breaths. The deejay introduces me, the curtains draw back, and I step out into the spotlight beam to the opening notes of "Hot Child in the City." The first word of the song is "Danger." I have arrived.

If the Lusty Lady is college—ideals, self-discovery, political consciousness, and all that—then Mitchell Brothers is the real world, a sophisticated venue that requires dedication and discipline. I love to sit in the front row in New York Live, the room with the big stage, and watch the show. Such range! Such talent! Dazzling, colt-leggedy gals who come out in beaded evening gowns and strut with such authority you'd think they were trained by Gypsy Rose Lee herself. Gymnasts able to do backbends so deep that they touch their chin to the floor behind them. Tiny, athletic girls who work the pole with ease, jumping all the way up to the top and swinging around for the entire length of a song.

Mitchell Brothers bills itself as "the Adult Disneyland," with enough fantasy tableaux to inspire E-ticket thrills in even the most jaded porn hound. When I'm not star-struck in New York Live or fumbling my way through my first lap dances (somehow I always end up poking a guy in the side or whacking him in the head with my elbow), I marvel at the shows in The Rooms. In the Ultra Room, latex- and leather-clad dancers flip from a trapeze and chase each other—crops and paddles in hand—up and down the length of the narrow mirrored stage while the customers watch through the glass of their private booths. The Kopenhagen Room girls, lit only by the flashlights that customers are given at the start of the show, writhe in unison in the red-carpeted pit between the deep-cushioned couches. The Green Door Room, a giant shower, hosts four-to-six bathing beauties at a time. The curtain draws up and the dancers sway together, limbs entwined, as colored lights caress their bodies. Their bare skin glows pink, then aqua, then sky blue, and back again under shimmering clouds of steam. They step from the shower and pair off for table-top shows, carrying baskets overflowing with feathers, lotions, powders, love beads, and other sensual paraphernelia. As I watch these women, each of whom exudes the supreme confidence of a sexual adventuress, I wonder, *will I ever ascend to that level? Do I dare attempt that extreme?*

Dancers are granted flexibility in their style, but the rules of conduct they impress upon me when I am hired are not open to interpretation. New girls are given an orientation by Nellie, an officious blonde who used to dance at the theater but has since plumped into the role of wife, mother, and personnel director. Seated at her desk in the office across the hall from the dressing room, she outlines the rules with tense, don't-fuck-with-me authority: Dancers are considered independent contractors and are required to pay a stage fee for every shift they work—twelve dollars during the day shift, seventeen at night. No quoting prices for lap dances, ever. When seated with a customer, you must face forward and he can't touch your breasts, crotch or buttocks, and you can't touch him anywhere below the waist. This is useful information; however, I learn the most important things from the other dancers. Nellie's suggested enticement when approaching a customer, "Would you like company?" is only marginally effective. I see that the girls are more successful with lines like, "Would you like to play?" or "Are you ready for me?" I learn to always carry a twenty-dollar bill on me so when a customer asks, "How much?" I can sort of, kinda, not really make it visible so he can get the hint, even though what comes out of my mouth is the required, "Whatever you wish. The bigger the present, the bigger the fun."

The dancers teach me how to swing upside down from the pole, spotting me as I grab the pole at chest height and kick my legs up and over my head, then slide down. I practice the trick so many times that the shape of my ribcage is permanently altered. I am strangely proud that the left side has flattened in the spot where my body makes contact with the pole, cherishing this mark of experience like a dueling scar.

And the dancers teach me how to manage the stress of hustling for tips. Sitting in the customers' laps isn't the hard part. That's easy enough to become accustomed to, as dissociation is old hat to me by now. But the rejection is hard to take. For every customer who says yes to a lap dance, five more will say no. That's a lot of *no* to hear—I never get used to it. When I feel discouraged, I do what the other dancers suggest: Go upstairs and hang out in the dressing room until you feel better. I sit under the vanity counter, my knees tucked under my chin, telling myself that I am reclaiming my sexuality in the public arena. But I'm really learning to tether my self-worth to how much I earn. On a good night, I'm a porno superstar. On a bad night, I'm a wretch.

Access to the feminine charms at the O'Farrell Theater requires more than a handful of quarters like at the Lusty Lady. Admission is thirty dollars, thereby ensuring a flush clientele. The customers come from everywhere. Busloads of Japanese tourists. Rock stars. Conventioneers on expense account. Silicon Valley computer scions. Eccentric Asian businessmen. A German chocolatier who always drops in with a huge box of truffles for the dancers to share in the dressing room. Someone once quoted Artie Mitchell as saying, "Don't bring the deed to the ranch, you might fall in love." That probably really happened once. Heaven knows there are some amazing tokens of affection presented.

These men don't just proffer large sums of money. They love to play Stage Door Johnnie, too, showering favorite dancers with lavish gifts. One girl's regular, a gravelly-voiced college rock icon, buys her a brand-new Harley Davidson. Another girl is given a Porsche by her regular, which she immediately sells to pay for medical school. An eighteen-thousand-dollar emerald ring is presented to a girl on-stage, insurance papers included. Some dancers talk shit, I'm sure, but a lot of the stories they tell about their trinkets are true. Rolexes don't lie—not the real ones, anyway. I prefer cash, as the presents possess weird energy. The man might not expect so much as a phone call from you saying when you'll be working next, but he'll want some kind of connection to you, some kind of exchange, so whatever he gives has its own gravity. The married girls with regulars have to hide the gifts from their husbands, or sell them. The husbands don't mind the cash, but the stuff sends them over the edge, as a gift is so much more personal. A signifier that the connection with the customer has crossed the line between transaction and relationship—even if the relationship is limited to an hour or two in the customer's lap every week or so, with him petting your hair as he tells you about his day.

Nellie, the skirt of her baggy flowered rayon dress whooshing when she walks, enters the dressing room one morning as a dancer is winding an Ace bandage over the top of her newly implanted breasts to get them to drop down faster.

"My God, it's like Cyborg World in here!" Nellie exclaims. Every time you turn around there's a new nose, a new set of breasts, surgically slimmed hips.

Dashing off for a new cosmetic surgery procedure is as common as breathing at the O'Farrell. One Los Angeles surgeon does so many boob jobs for the theater, he offers a bulk discount. If three dancers at a time come in, he takes twenty-five percent off his fee. That we are considered San Francisco's stripper elite, beneficiaries of the genetic crap shoot, doesn't stem the constant march toward physical perfection. Girls tell each other constantly, "Oh, you don't need anything," but that's akin to, "Of course you don't look fat." If you've already got the idea in your head, there's naught that will persuade you otherwise.

But wanting a better body isn't the only reason for so much surgery—what else is a girl to do with all that money? Indulging has as much appeal as investing. I luxuriate in some lifestyle enhancements myself. I spend a couple thousand bucks on fixing my teeth. I treat myself to a month in Thailand. I upgrade my fanzine from newsprint to glossy paper. After years of roommates, I move into my own apartment, a five-room, roach-riddled flat at the corner of

Fell and Gough Streets. Then I buy a BMW (how's *that* for punk fucking rock?).

Upon assessing my spending habits, my friend Len, a genteel Ivy League–educated butch dyke and former paramour, drills into my head that I need to stop squandering money on stereotypical stripper things and save some. Cars and travel are not investments. Dare to be radically solvent, she encourages. Don't end up broke like so many other dancers who cope with the stresses of stripping by shopping. "Think of it this way," she offers. "How many dancers do you know who have a closet full of Chanel bags and no savings account?" Plenty. And how many of them suddenly find themselves off the schedule at the O'Farrell with no warning?

Her point is not lost on me. I know there are dancers who are very serious about financial security. Some own several houses. Others invest in the stock market. Still others have a couple hundred grand buried in their backyard.

I knuckle down. Goodbye, piercings. Hello, gym membership. I color my hair Hollywood blonde and become the apotheosis of the yuppie stripper, hitting the Stairmaster each morning, then driving to the theater, where I work as hard as I can. To boost my profit margin, I cut back on dancing in New York Live in favor of working The Rooms. I am determined to save money. Eventually, I have enough put away to support myself for a year. Because I never know what might happen.

You can make a lot of money at Mitchell Brothers if you apply yourself—a thousand dollars a shift is not uncommon, though my average is considerably less. But that money comes at substantial cost. The club harbors a savage atmosphere of paranoia because you can be let go at any time, for any reason—being overweight, underweight, too old, frequent tardiness, and the absurdly cruel "overexposure." You have to keep on top of everything, especially your looks. We all feel the pressure. One night, I stand at the mirror in the bathroom between two women laboring over their makeup and one says to the other, "God, I can't wait to get married, have children, get fat, and just let myself go."

The management is capricious and tends to play favorites. Some girls stay forever because they're nasty in the audience and the guys love them. Other girls get fired for breaking a minor rule. There are girls who get sacked for rebuffing the advances of one of the owner's friends who gets fresh, while another suffers no repercussions for punching a rude customer right in the face and bloodying his nose. Now and then, they get rid of ten to twenty women at once, flushing out the ranks to make room for new faces. More than any other club I've seen, the O'Farrell Theater seems permanently cast with a pall of panic and doom. The sword of Damocles is forever overhead.

I can't lie—they cut me a lot of slack and treat me well. I have no idea why, as I am not one of their top girls. But still, for all the breaks I get, I'm just as afraid of getting pink-slipped as any other dancer.

When management asks the dancers to come up with last names to heighten our starlet appeal, I tell them to bill me as "Lily Burana," right out there. Here I am! Unashamed! Sex positive and proud! I had known the shelter of my own hard exterior at Peepland, and the shelter of sisterhood and managerial support at the Lusty. But this is the first time in the sex industry that I have known the shelter of status—and my own considerable hubris. For the first time, I start working without a wig. I don't have to hide anymore. I walk into the theater without a disguise. I figure, if someone thinks I'm a tramp, they know I'm a tramp of a certain pedigree.

Somewhere along the way, the nimbus of sexual fairy dust that hangs over San Francisco condenses into a stifling fog of political correctness. What began as a push for affirmation of alternative lifestyles morphs into an unspoken rule that you can never criticize any sexual minority, *ever*. And I am leading the charge. When I publish a fanzine created by and about people in the adult business, I write in the editorial, "There is absolutely nothing wrong with sex work except society's hypocritical attitude toward it." Sanctimony and condemnation are the bane of my existence, and I am ever poised to take on any offenders, wielding the damning term "sex negative" like a circus knife thrower. Dare to impugn dancing? On *my* watch? Taste the blade, sucker! I am quick to stress that stripping is legitimate work. Hard work. Undervalued work. And woe to the person who suggests that a stripper can't be a feminist. What is feminism about if not exercising your options? My body, my choice. Inwardly, my ambivalence about the work has deepened; however, my façade is becoming smoother and more politically astute, more vocal. My showmanship is improving on every level.

I have my financial safety net, and I'm starting to earn money as a writer, but there are other areas of instability cropping up. My self-worth continues to fluctuate based on how much money I make each night, on how many shifts I am granted per month. I am getting older (twenty-four!) in a business where aging is treated like a federal offense. For someone who considers herself a rebel, I sure seem to be living by the numbers.

Eventually, I tire of being braced against everything. Dancing was supposed to be a day job, but it has come to occupy an unreasonably large part of my life. Am I a sexually sophisticated feminist warrior woman, I wonder, or just another coasting 'ho? Like a spreading stain, the paranoia and hyper-vigilance I feel at work seep into my off hours—I try in vain to ward them off by intoning, "I am not my body, I am not my job." I can never relax.

I worry that I am developing stripper damage.

Stripper damage isn't something quantifiable. It's a state of being. In this job, there is no neutral territory. No repose. It's chaos.

You're managing the chaos, you're in control. Then, suddenly one day at work, you're not. That invisible thread that keeps you together just snaps and shit's flying everywhere.

Exhaustion. Men in the club sucking the life out of you and women outside the club sneering at you and bitchy management and bitchy coworkers and you feel fat and old and insignificant. And then the inner monologue begins . . .

. . . *If this is all I'm good for, then what good is my life? How much time do I have left, anyway? You'd think that for all I go through I'd make more money, but what if I can't ever find a job that'll pay me more than this?*

I am my body. This amazing machine, fierce with life, made up of eighty-five cents worth of chemicals (okay, a buck twenty-five, adjusted for inflation), capable of the miracles of pleasure and creation, is a money machine. Tens, twenties, fifties, hundreds. In the abstract, I am worth more than the sum of my parts, but marketing them as I have, my parts seem to be worth a lot more than the Magical Miraculous Total Me.

A boob lift. That's what I need. Yeah, that's it—a concentric mastoplexy with aureola reduction and symmetrical realignment. Lipo. Eye job. Collagen. Botox. Chemical peel. Better living through surgery, right?

And the motherfuckers know when you're out of it, too. You're radiating frailty and hate like the rays of a malignant sun and you can't make a goddamn dime.

Would you like company?

Wouldyoulikecompany?

I said, would you LIKE COMPANY?

I SAID WOULD YOU LIKE COMPANY?!

Now you're crying in the dressing room, girls putting their arms around you, patting you, daubing at the eyeliner that's run down to your chin.

It'll be okay.

It's okay.

No, you're really sobbing now, *it's not fucking okay.*

Then you're out on the floor looking at the pretty new girls through eyes narrowed to slits, thinking, "Oh, just you wait." Then you're canceling shifts, lying in bed all day watching movies and eating Mallomars. Better living through glucose.

I said if it really got to me, I'd quit, but now I can't quit. So now what? Hang on here till I'm kicked to the curb, then work my way down to the shittiest club in town? And after that, then what? I don't *even* want to go there.

The promise you made to yourself when you started that you'd work the business and not let the business work you seems like a joke now.

But you gotta do something, you just have to, because you've seen the girls with *serious* stripper damage and you don't want to end up like that. That permanently shell-shocked look. That inability to de-dramatize and get life on track. Another surgery every few months, a different hair color. Crazy boyfriend or girlfriend yelling or whining or hitting or cutting down and spending all the money. A life small as a mouse/insect/penny and self-hatred wide and deep as the sea.

Now, you ask yourself, how is this worth it?

You say, I should get out. Yes, I'll get out.

Then you think, maybe I just need a vacation.

I think I'll go to Hawaii.

I heard there's some good clubs there.

I can make the trip pay for itself.

I am about to turn twenty-five and I am helplessly addicted to *Dynasty* reruns. Every night I come home from Mitchell Brothers just in time to watch the show at 1 a.m. After dropping my costume bag on the bedroom floor, I retire to the living room and lie in front of the television on a folded-up blanket doing leg lifts while Krystle and Alexis battle each other against their luxurious Denver backdrop. Roaches crawl out from under the futon and skitter over and around my legs, but I flick them off and keep going. Lift, and hold. Lift, and hold.

In one episode, Alexis storms into Krystle's office in a perfumed snit. Wearing a chinchilla coat and matching toque, she leans over Krystle's desk and sneers an ominous threat into Krystle's quivering face. The hat, squat and ludicrous with its bulbous gray pelts, sits on Alexis's head at such an assertive angle, one gets the impression that the hat—not the woman—is backing Krystle into the corner. In another episode, after Alexis bankrupts her ex-husband, Blake, by masterminding a hostile takeover of his company, she buys the house in which Krystle and Blake live. In a turf-marking display, she stands on the staircase and begins throwing their possessions into the atrium hallway below. A crystal fox coat goes sailing over the balcony.

I believe the *Dynasty* reruns gave me the idea that the best twenty-fifth birthday present I could give myself would be a fur coat.

Ruth is one of San Francisco's middleweight madams. Not the kind who sets up girls on clandestine penthouse trysts with a movie producer or flies them off to Nice to meet a shipping magnate. Rather, she's the executor of connections between willing and able-bodied—if not scrupulously discriminating—young women, and attorneys, accountants, and dentists seeking reprieve from their stressful, lonely jobs, or the tedium of family life in Orinda. I guess her business falls under the rubric of "high-class escort service" but when the popular image of prostitution is streetwalking, what can't be classified as high-class by comparison? Of the few girls I know who do outcall, none of them can stand working for her, as she is notoriously petty, not particularly rigorous in screening her clients, and really more interested in volume than anything else. They'd rather work off referrals or run ads in the local adult paper and set up their own appointments. "If you need a lot of low-paying work in a hurry," they say, rolling their eyes, "you go to Ruth." But they do admit she is a very good shopping connection, and so when the issue of the fur coat came up, one of them made a phone call for me.

I call Ruth myself the day before my birthday and tell her that I'm so-and-so's friend, the one interested in getting a fur coat.

"Yes, of course," she says, "I was expecting your call." I hear a little girl's high, thready voice in the background. Ruth muffles the receiver with her hand but I can just make out her saying, "Quiet, Emily. Mommy's on the phone." There's the slight suctiony sound of her taking her hand off the mouthpiece. "I'm sorry," she says to me, "I have two daughters at home and the youngest is eight, and well, you know how it is. Anyway, why don't you come over tomorrow at two o' clock and we'll go to the Gift Center to look at some coats." She gives me the address and we hang up.

The next afternoon, I take the N Judah train from Van Ness station to her house in Cole Valley. I arrive just as a dark green Honda station wagon is pulling into the drive.

A slender, middle-aged woman gets out of the car. She's dressed in a baby-blue sweat suit and white Keds, and has big, red hair, like a post–*Gilligan's Island* Tina Louise. Or Stefanie Powers. A large pair of black sunglasses practically obscures her entire face. A small girl with the same brilliant red hair pulled back in gaily colored animal-shaped barrettes gets out of the passenger side. She must be Ruth's younger daughter.

"Are you Lily?" the woman asks, juggling McDonald's take-out bags and soda in either hand.

"I am. Are you Ruth?" I ask. Duh. Who else would she be? I'm a little nervous. I think I'm about to see the inside of a brothel. I stand there staring, shielding my eyes from the sun shining behind Ruth, illuminating her like a saint in a portrait.

The young girl comes around to her mother's side. Ruth hands her the bags and drinks and shoos her inside.

"Come in for a minute, okay?" Ruth says to me, heading up a red brick staircase that leads to an enclosed porch built over the garage. "I need to pack up my furs. I want to take them with so I can have them appraised."

Ruth's house is a gracious two-story Edwardian done up in advanced shabby chic. Baking smells waft through the rooms. Wildflower arrangements set in steel buckets sit on every table in the living room, and the overstuffed couch is a beautiful moss green paisley velvet. French doors separate the living room from the porch, which has been transformed into a Jacuzzi room. An extremely thin woman with long blonde corkscrew curls, twenty-ish, I think, is getting dressed beside the hot tub. Some thin women seem deprived and ravaged, but she looks futuristically sleek, like she was compressed for efficiency. She buttons up her fitted burgundy suit jacket, straightens her miniskirt, and slips her bare feet into a pair of expensive-looking black leather pumps with delicate heels. She balls up a wet silver maillot in a towel and walks through the living room and into the kitchen where I'm sitting at the table with another girl, also in a suit, who has introduced herself as "Alyssa from Maryland." Alyssa's heart-shaped face is framed in a lank, blonde pageboy tucked behind her ears, and her small chin comes to a shy point. She is eating a bowl of macaroni and cheese made from a box. As Ruth busies herself in the living room closet, Alyssa from Maryland tells her about her new boyfriend. ". . . And the best thing about it," she says, tipping up her little chin with pride, "is he's Jewish, too."

The long-haired blonde opens the oven door, looks inside, and inhales deeply. "Almost cookie time!" she says in a voice that surprises the hell out of me. This glossy creature has the raspy croak of a carnival barker. She closes the oven and sits down at the head of the table. "Hi," she honks, thrusting her hand forth, "I'm Elissa. Not *that* Alyssa," she says, pointing to Alyssa from Maryland, "I'm Elissa from Florida."

I shake her hand, not too hard. Her bony knuckles feel very fragile.

Ruth's voice singsongs into the kitchen. "Elissa, your wet bathing suit had better not be on my nineteenth-century farm table, dear!"

Elissa sweeps the damp bath towel ball under the table and whispers to me, "She's such a witch about her furniture. Once I left a glass on a nightstand without a coaster under it and she swore she'd make me pay for the refinishing."

I make some sympathetic noises, then I say, "I like your suit."

In her call girl chronicles, my friend and fellow Lusty alum Carol Queen writes, "A good hooker dresses up, not down." I imagined that meant evening gowns, but no, she goes on to explain, it means looking like an executive secretary. How boring! It's bad enough having to wear a suit to work in an office. Who'd want to wear a suit to work as a prostitute? I mean, if you're going to do it, you might as well go all out and do hooker-luxe. I'd rather work in the realm of the over-the-top elite escorts, sitting with a client at Le Dôme in an Azzedine Alaïa dress, fashioning my lipsticked mouth into a pout because I wanted a *princess*-cut diamond, not an *emerald*-cut.

Of course it's ridiculous for me to even consider what kind of call girl I'd prefer being. I've already established several times over that I'd be a complete failure in any adult trade besides stripping. I've tried various other gigs—from pinup girl, which wasn't too bad, to a two-week stint as a professional dominatrix in Manhattan, which was a disaster. I should've known pro domination was beyond my ken— I've always been touchy about the commercial nexus between sex and therapy. I don't have the stuff to make a living mucking around in someone's psychosexual ooze. The majority of the clients at the dom house were either Catholics or Hasidic Jews and I really couldn't cope with watching them thrash around so violently within their guilt. I felt the sting of their shame as acutely as a wound in my own flesh. I'd dutifully wield whip, crop, cane, and quirt, unsure whether I was helping the men exorcise their demons, or exercise them. When they'd leave as rumpled and stooped-over as they'd come in, I didn't feel that my ministrations were aiding them in any meaningful way. Quite the opposite, actually.

I did have one client I liked, a younger, golden-haired Hasid named Sammy. He specifically asked to be caned, and whenever I brought the rattan down to stripe his buttocks (so hairy there was a kiss curl at the top of the crack), he'd turn to me and say, brightly, "Tank you, my dahlink mistress." But Sammy, grinning in his undershirt and yarmulke, was unique. The slightly bruised disposition of the other men left me so shaken and disturbed, I had to quit. Everyone was very nice about my leaving, but all the other dominatrices I knew did look upon me a little pityingly after that.

It's said that everybody in the sex business has their niche, and I agree. There's a supposed hierarchy headed by "she who exerts the least effort for the most money," but really, more than anything, it just comes down to personal comfort. I'm not suited to anything too psychological (dominatrix or phone sex operator), too public (porn star), or too freighted (hooking)—I don't want any of the judgment or the baggage that comes with any of them. The stick bends the other way, too. The call girls I know couldn't be bothered with the complications of stripping and wouldn't for a minute consider working in such public places, where any old person can walk in and gawk at you with no obligation to shell out. Dominatrices are too independent to be bothered with club politics, and a porn actress wouldn't countenance making her money one dollar, ten dollars, twenty dollars at a time, and doing eight-hour shifts standing in too-tight shoes. I like the clubby feeling of being surrounded by the other dancers, and the amateur theatrics of the music, costumes, and lights. Most important of all, I like the premise of being unattainable. At the end of the day, I want to have something that's exclusively *mine*, something off-limits. So what if I'm not the baddest chick on the block? The fact remains that I need some space between myself and the edge.

While I'm sitting at the table chatting with Alyssa and Elissa, a door off the back of the kitchen opens and a woman I recognize comes out, says hello, grabs a few paper towels, and ducks back through the door. She's a friend of a friend, a long-time call girl with activist pretensions. I've been introduced to her several times, and she always gives the appearance of maintaining vigilant watch over every interior movement. Were her rigid self-control forced out with naïve bravado, she might have the charm of a petulant toddler, jutting out her chin and saying "Am *so* right!" Or, if she fused it with noblesse oblige and some panache, she could be a thoroughly modern Mame. But her inner patrol is pushed forth by sheer, steely force of will. Her mannered words, facial expressions, and measured emotional reach give her the reptilian poise of a politician's wife, but when I look at her closely, I intuit something clicking furiously inside. Everything she encounters is precisely examined, calibrated to her satisfaction, and then a response is fashioned and let out one bit at a time, like water through a series of channel locks.

I know she has the reputation of being well-read and politically conscious, but she gives me the creeps. She's the exact opposite of my posse. Fancying ourselves as smart girls in a dirty business, we're always hamming it up and bursting forth with rowdy, pedantic pronouncements. I love that know-it-all streak—even if we get cut down all the time as being delusional or self-indulgent, we try to cram some ascendance in there anyhow. But this gal shows none of that spirit. She's nothing but glacial calm. What seems to everyone else to be impeccable composure seems to me like complete absence of any detectable personality. I'm polite whenever I see her, but secretly I call her RoboWhore.

The oven timer dings and Ruth hollers, "Leslie!"

There's a thunder of running feet as Ruth's older daughter bounds down the stairs and into the kitchen. She puts on a pair of baking mitts and pulls a tray of oatmeal raisin cookies from the oven.

"Leslie," Ruth calls, "say hi to Lily!"

Leslie stands there holding the tray of cookies and sniffs dryly, then fixes me with a black, poisonous stare. I imagine Leslie lying on a therapist's couch ten years from now, waving her hands—still in baking mitts—in the air and saying, "All I wanted to do was bake some goddamn cookies and my *mother* was so busy running her *whorehouse* she couldn't be bothered!"

I walk quickly from the kitchen to see if Ruth is anywhere near ready to go.

Ruth has pulled the coats from the hall closet and is now stuffing them into black plastic garbage bags. I watch as they go in: A black fox jacket with silver fox diamonds on the sleeves, a rust-colored Mongolian lamb jacket, a sheared beaver coat dyed in a modernist pattern of primary colors, a black sheared beaver coat with silver chevrons on the collar and sleeves, and a full-length lynx-dyed fox— off-white with black spots.

These are the ugliest furs I have ever seen in my life.

I help hold open the last bag for Ruth. "Oh, I looove the Gift Center," she says, folding in the black beaver coat. "It's so pretty. And they have a café in there so you can have lunch when you shop and make a whole day of it. I'm there at least once a week because it's just so great." Grabbing her purse, she heads into the Jacuzzi room and opens the front door, leaving the bags on the floor in the hallway for me to carry out. "Besides," she says airily over her shoulder as she drifts out the door, "I'm a Jew. We always buy wholesale."

In that moment, I liked Ruth tremendously, this nice Jewish lady with her nice Jewish call girls. Without complaint, I pick up the trash bags bursting with furs and toddle after her.

"Zah way the coat moves when *you* move, zat is called zah 'sweep,' " Olga tells me. Olga is the proprietress of one of the three fur salons in the Gift Center. Her thick Russian accent, with its dense, drawn-out vowels and jumbled consonants landing solidly on the hard *K* sounds, makes me feel very glamorous.

I spin round and round in front of the mirror, wearing, according to the tag, a black ranched Canadian mink with a Norwegian fox tuxedo and sleeves. I hold the right side of the fox-fur tuxedo in my hand, admiring the way the hem flares out when I spin. I feel a bit guilty about the fox, but minks are vile little rodents, mean-spirited and no more endangered than the common sewer rat. I can't work up much remorse about wearing them. I'm too busy imagining myself as Julie Christie in *Doctor Zhivago.*

Ruth went off to another shop to get her coats appraised, down at the other side of the Gift Center. We're separated by dozens of storefronts, full of all kinds of luxury junk—precious gems, cheap cloisonné knickknacks, Chinese lacquerware, knock-off designer handbags, hair accessories, porcelain cats with ribbons tied around their necks, gilt picture frames, and desk accessories made of cut crystal.

"I'll take this one," I chirp happily to a smiling Olga, doing one last spin before the mirror. With its huge fox cap sleeves, the coat makes me almost as wide as I am tall. I look like a fuzzy little linebacker, but I'm so impressed with the fact that I'm standing there in a fur coat, a fur coat that I have the money to pay for myself, that I don't even mind. Soon Ruth will come along and purchase the coat for me using her resale license. I'll in turn buy it back from her at a markup of two hundred dollars, making my total cost twenty-two hundred. A steal.

"Yes, absolutely byoot-eeful," says Olga, slipping the coat off me and zipping it into a long canvas garment bag. "You look like princess."

Ruth drives away from the Gift Center on Division Street. The sun slants through the guardrails on the freeway overhead, casting bright oblong patches of light on the shadowy pavement.

I have unzipped the garment bag and sit quietly in the passenger seat, running my hand over the soft fox collar. To fill the silence, Ruth tells me about her business. I have the imprimatur of some of her former girls, so she trusts me, which is kind of neat. Even if I'm not anxious to participate, I'll happily listen to gossip from any corner. She brings in girls from all over the country, and many of them travel around the country on a circuit. Sort of like being a feature entertainer or a traveling house dancer, but hooking instead of dancing. They pay rent for a week, or a month, and split the money with her sixty-forty, in the girls' favor.

I remember her daughter staring me down in the kitchen. "How does your older daughter deal with it?" I ask.

"Oh, she's fine . . ."

Oh, really? I think to myself, remembering the flat rage in her face.

". . . and if she isn't, well, too bad. It's my house!"

I'm starting to see why Ruth is regarded as kind of a jerk.

"I did really well this past quarter," she bubbles. "I made fifty thousand dollars."

I nod, feigning approval. I think of Gina, a bikini model who dances at Mitchell Brothers, and how she had just bought a new house in the South Bay and, with the down payment and escrow due, had herself made fifty thousand dollars in the past three months. Dancing.

By the time we get to my house, I've had just about enough of

Ruth. I thank her for her time and generosity and hoist myself and my new coat out of the green Honda wagon, then stand on the curb in front of my apartment until she drives away.

That evening, I put on a nice black dress, heels, and my brand-new coat, and take the 8 Market bus to the Castro to meet Len for dinner. The Cove is just a basic diner-type place, where people go for quick, uncomplicated meals, so I'm wildly overdressed. Well, the hell with it, drag queens eat there all the time decked out in full regalia before heading out on the town, the fluorescent lights bouncing off their cheap wigs and limning the cracks in their foundation. Besides, I'm kind of bummed that I didn't make spectacular plans for this milestone birthday. I want to feel festive, even if the mood doesn't fit the environment.

Len is sitting at the corner table, in plain view of the entrance. When I come through the door, her eyes widen at the sight of the coat, which has taken on a regal sheen under the hard lights of the diner. When I get to the table, I try to cheer myself up by doing a voguish spin and grandly tossing the coat onto the booth seat.

"Oh, *purr*!" she says, grabbing a puffy fox sleeve and rubbing her bald head against it. "You are Venus in furs!"

Desmond, the waiter, who we both know from the leather scene as "Looking for Daddy Desmond," comes by to take our order. Len tells him it is my birthday and holds up my coat.

"Girl!" Desmond swoons, running his hand along the nap of the fur, as his eyes, always wide and needful, grow absolutely huge. "Oh, girrrrl!"

A few nights after my birthday, I am sitting on the futon couch with my mink draped over me like a blanket, a few roaches racing on nimble, filthy feet over the slick black pelts. Before *Dynasty* is a true-crime detective show—one that adheres to fact but embellishes every detail with a lewd camera angle or fraught commentary, interspersing titillation with a severe emotional yank. This episode is about a rash of prostitute murders in a Pacific Northwest city, and how the killer had evaded the police for years.

The chief investigator is talking about why the murders had never been solved—largely because none of the women were ever reported missing. He also says that when their bodies *were* found and identified, they were revealed to be prostitutes, lowering to nil the priority for bringing their killers to justice.

"We usually classify this type of crime as 'NHI,'" the detective says, his stubbled chins wobbling as if to defy his tersely held jaw. "No Humans Involved."

This knocks the wind right out of me. I have never heard anything so cold and awful in all of my life. I don't live in a bubble—I know that any foray into the sex business makes you less of a person in the eyes of many. But I didn't know that in the eyes of the law you cease to be a person at all. It's one thing to be considered cheap. It's another to be considered disposable.

Why should I care? That isn't my element. But I *do* care. I'm different from the faceless women on that show—yet not so different that if I met the same end, the reaction would be more "How could this have happened?" than "She asked for it." Far more chilling than any concerns about myself, though, is this realization, this sudden horrible awareness, that this country has an honest-to-God throw-away class. I have discovered a depth of indifference that I previously would have thought impossible, and I am ashamed that we could ever let it get so low.

I watch the night's *Dynasty* episode, but the hour floats right through my head like so much fluff. The detective show left me numb and profoundly uninterested in any syndicated escape. I switch off the television and walk the long hallway to my bedroom. The covers do nothing to warm me as I lie in bed, so I pull the coat over top of me and tuck it under my chin. I stare at the ceiling, watching the beams cast from the headlights of passing cars track from one end of the room to the other. Absently stroking the fur, I wonder if what I bought myself is anything more than a very expensive comforter. I certainly can't wear it to work—most of the girls are into animal rights and would give me an earful if they ever saw it. I'm not really sure what I'll do with the coat, but it is the most luxurious thing I've ever bought for myself, I know that. And I know that I am twenty-five, fully, unquestionably adult, and things are going to be different this year.

FIFTEEN

Opportunity Costs

You know a stripper is pissed when she calls somebody "honey." I'm more than halfway through my cross-country itinerary, and as I've traveled, I've heard a lot of "honey."

"Honey, we don't allow dirty dancing here," barks an irate dancer to a perma-tanned colleague at the Bush Company in Anchorage. The offender had bent forward and rubbed the top of her head on a customer's crotch during a table dance, i.e., done a "pecker check," and the other girl saw fit to set her straight on the rules.

In Dallas, at the Lodge, a haughty dancer swings her thin arm, smacking the hand of a greedily smiling man away from her firm, plum-shaped behind. "Listen, honey, if you touch me there again, I'm going to have the bouncer throw you out of here on your ass."

Me in the dressing room at Prince Machiavelli in El Paso, to the jittery Australian girl seated to my right at the vanity: "Excuse me, but you're stepping on the case for my Kenny Wayne Shepherd CD, honey."

• • •

I don't think strippers are inherently grouchier than the rest of the population, however, there are plenty of occupational irritants that can set a girl off. The first thing that really, truly pissed me off about stripping I encountered in 1991, when I signed on at Mitchell Brothers: stage fees.

When I start, the fee is twelve dollars for the day shift, seventeen for the night. Then, when dancers at a neighboring strip club organize against their similar stage-fee arrangement, the O'Farrell managers rescind the stage fees. Later, the fees are reinstated, at ten dollars per shift, payable at the beginning of the month when you pick up your schedule, and the fees are nonrefundable. If you cancel your shift, you don't get the money back.

I can't recall any dancer saying she likes paying the fees; in fact, I'd say the stage fees are generally viewed as a pain in the neck. After all, we see no return for our payment. If a bouncer walks us to our car at the end of a shift, we tip him separately. We tip the deejays ourselves. The fees serve no clear purpose—all we know is that we have no choice but to pay them.

My closest friend at the theater is a dancer named Phoenix. Like me, she's an artsy blonde from back East. But unlike me, she radiates a warm glow of sultriness and charisma. Someone once said, "She reminds you of smoky bars, black velvet, the blues." She takes to the stage like a diva supreme, but backstage she is helpful and friendly to the other dancers. When she works, Phoenix doesn't enter her own world, she engages herself in yours. Beneath her charming façade, however, is steely resolve. You do not want to do wrong by Phoenix.

Phoenix gets fired, after being at the theater for six years, and shortly thereafter we go for a walk in Golden Gate Park. The conversation takes a turn toward the stage fees, and the fact that dancers at the

Market Street Cinema, a neighboring Tenderloin theater, had filed suit against the management on the grounds that the stage fees they charged the dancers were illegal. This, Phoenix says, has inspired her.

"Did you know that before 1988, Mitchell Brothers dancers used to be paid by the theater?" she asks me.

No, I didn't know that.

"Oh, yeah. We were," she says. Apparently, dancers used to earn an hourly wage, in addition to whatever tips they could make. Then, in 1988, the theater gathered the dancers together for a meeting and told them it was "their choice" whether they wanted to remain employees or give up the paychecks and become independent contractors. Never mind that the actual rules of the theater didn't change—dancers weren't offered the latitude of true independent contractors, but it was still suggested as the better alternative. The dancers went for it, and they stopped getting paid and instead started paying to work.

Phoenix suggests that it's possible that the theater could be forced to stop charging stage fees and reimburse the dancers for the money they'd paid over the years. She wants to wage such a fight; however, she doesn't want to do it alone. Understandable, when you consider that Jim Mitchell had killed his own brother just a few years ago.

I give the idea close consideration. I am a feminist. Certainly concerned with the welfare and well-being of strippers. This seems like an honorable cause, a justifiable one. I'm happy with the luxurious atmosphere and great earning potential at Mitchell Brothers, but I know there's plenty of room for improvement. Phoenix was smart to approach me—she struck my activist chord. I tell her I'm up for the fight if she is, we make a pact, and we shake on it.

But what attorney would help us? We didn't have money to wage an expensive lawsuit, and besides, who would take the concerns of two strippers seriously?

Enter Beth Ross and Elliot Beckelman, two labor rights attorneys

Phoenix found through referral. A few weeks after our pivotal walk in the park, Phoenix and I sit down with them and talk it through. They help us determine that what we have, g-strings, girlie shows, and lap dances aside, is a clear-cut wage-and-hour case. We go down the list of what constitutes an employee versus an independent contractor:

"Can you make your own hours?" Beth asks.

No. We have to arrive at the theater at least an hour before whatever show we're in starts.

"Does management control the parameters of how you do your work?"

Yes. Phoenix and I tell them about the "drop top" rule, requiring dancers in New York Live to be topless by the end of their first song, and bottomless during the second. How Jim Mitchell would insist at times that the girls do daisy chains on the stage in the Green Door Room. And how, if a customer complains to management that he didn't like a show, occasionally the dancer has to give him his money back.

"Are you allowed to come and go as you please?"

No. In fact, we have to sign out every time we want to leave the building during our shift. Presumably for safety reasons, but still.

"Is your performance ancillary to the basic function of the theater?"

No. As Phoenix says, "Without the dancers, Mitchell Brothers is nothing but a snack bar. And not a very good one."

Regardless of the lip service given dancers about being "independent contractors," Beth and Elliot ascertain that dancers at Mitchell Brothers are employees. Not only are we entitled to an hourly wage, we most certainly should not have to pay for the privilege of gracing the O'Farrell Theater stage. Beth's firm agrees to take the case on contingency.

• • •

As the weeks pass, Phoenix (whose real name is Jennifer) and I brainstorm with Beth and Elliot. What do we really hope to accomplish? We don't want to be in it for ourselves—we'd like to file a class action lawsuit that will benefit all the dancers. We want every Mitchell Brothers dancer—past and present—to get restitution for stage fees and lost wages. We want true employee status, with everything that comes with it—wages, benefits, worker's comp, unemployment eligibility. And we want Mitchell Brothers to stop charging any kind of pay-to-work fee. Forever. What we want are basic workers' rights; however Phoenix and I feel like we are reaching for the moon. We know that dancers don't appreciate paying the stage fees, but will they stand behind us? The O'Farrell Theater is the best gig in town, and loyalty to Jim Mitchell is fierce, despite the sometimes stressful environment at the theater, despite his shooting Artie.

We can't talk much about the suit ahead of time, for obvious reasons. I have to be especially discreet, because if someone squealed and I got fired, *kaboom*, I could no longer be the class representative for the current dancers. Jennifer, now no longer in the business, agrees to represent the class of former dancers (although the statute of limitations limits the class to women who worked at the theater since 1991). We quietly start doing research.

We find that this type of suit has several precedents. Dancers in cities around the country—Anchorage, Minneapolis, San Diego, and Pittsburgh—have filed similar suits. And each and every one of them was resolved in the dancers' favor. We are shaky-kneed, but emboldened by this discovery. I am burned out on dancing, but this seemingly righteous pursuit stirs my blood. Things are going to change, for the better, I am certain. And I am going to be an agent of that change.

On a windy day in March 1994, Jennifer and I, in ladylike attire, minimal makeup, and upswept hair, stand between Beth and Elliot on the steps of San Francisco's City Hall and announce our class action lawsuit against Cinema Seven, the parent company of the

Mitchell Brothers O'Farrell Theater. Flashbulbs pop and reporters scribble furiously on their notepads as we answer questions from the media.

We tell them that we will no longer be silent about the unfair practices at the O'Farrell Theater. We stress that this is a lawsuit about fundamental labor rights. And that while we are scared, we are determined. We will not let the stigma surrounding exotic dancing prevent us from seeking our due.

After the press conference, Jennifer and I walk down Larkin Street, our lapels flapping in the cold spring wind. We grin, exhale with relief, and hug each other.

We have no idea what is going to happen next.

News of the lawsuit spreads quickly. We retreat to Beth's office to call some of our dancer friends at home to see how the suit is being received.

"Hallelujah!" screams one dancer.

"Right on! Thank *God* someone is finally standing up to those guys," effuses another.

The response is overwhelmingly positive.

But not for long.

The next morning, the theater management holds an emergency meeting. "This lawsuit is an *attack* on *your rights*!" Jim Mitchell, now out on $500,000 bail, gravely states from the stage. Of course, the lawsuit is no such thing—in fact, it's the exact opposite. But it's in the theater's best financial interest to drum up opposition. An attorney for the theater sits close by Jim's side.

Mitchell urges the dancers to sign a petition protesting the suit, and to agree to pay the theater's attorney (yes, pay the theater's attorney) to organize a countersuit. Dancers flock to the stage to sign up.

This is just the beginning.

The following Saturday, Jennifer and I host a meeting at her house to brief dancers, past and present, on the basic intentions of the lawsuit. With the intimidation tactics already in full effect, only a handful of women show up. One dancer arrives, eyes alert and cold, her perfectly made-up face a flimsy mask of support. She never says so, but she seems to be there to gather information to report to theater management. Of course we welcome her; we have nothing to hide.

Public reaction to the lawsuit is mixed. Some people see us as petulant brats, motivated by greed rather than priciple. You make so much money already, they argue, why should you get any more? Others scoff: You're strippers. You expect fair treatment? Just consider yourselves lucky that you're not a grim statistic or a laughing-stock. The local sex activists are confused. Jim Mitchell and his cohort operate a beautiful, long-running theater that raised the bar on quality in the industry. Jim was considered a comrade-in-arms, or at least an unassailable ally. To see him under attack by his own dancers casts him in a different light.

In the theater dressing room, a dancer posts a scripted "manifesto" against the lawsuit. She decries how the lawsuit presumes to speak for her. Dismisses it as condescending and patronizing. "You think you're kicking up dust," she writes, "but you're standing on a paved road." Oy. My own brand of activist rhetoric has cycled around and bitten me on my sequined behind.

Dancers are urged by management to opt out of the class to protest the suit. The majority of current dancers comply. Some assemble counter-organizations and counter-suits that are repeatedly thrown out of court. A counter-organization called "Save Our Strippers" plans a benefit at the Great American Music Hall, next to the theater. Dancers are told to sell the hundred-dollar tickets to the customers, or buy them themselves to resell later. When Jim Mitchell pressures a dancer named Mila to buy a ticket, she reacts by refusing flatly and joining Jennifer and me as a named plaintiff in the lawsuit. We are very happy to have another current dancer sign on.

Misinformation runs rampant among the dancers, despite the efforts that Jennifer and I exert. There is speculation that we filed the suit for publicity. (We receive countless offers to duke it out with the opposing side in the press, which we categorically decline.) That we filed the suit for revenge against Jim Mitchell. (This suit, we remind people gently, is political, not personal.) That the suit is a precursor to unionizing attempts. (I've always been against unionizing the sex industry. Union organization in a quasi-legit business seems like a nightmare in the making.) Most off the mark is the rumor we hope to close the theater by bankrupting it.

Shutting down the theater is not our goal. We don't want the dancers' livelihood to be threatened—not to mention, I still work there! I am not yet able to support myself solely as a writer. And besides, in order for the class action portion of the lawsuit to work, I have to continue dancing at the theater so the suit will have a representative for the current dancers.

My first day back at work is the scariest day of my life. A few weeks have passed since we filed the suit, and the tension has escalated. I am so frightened, I can barely bring myself to open the front door to the theater. Dancers stare silently at me as I pass. I sit alone in the smallest dressing room, wondering just how I am going to manage. I had anticipated returning to work a conquering hero. A naked Norma Rae. And now I am verging on pariah status. Another dancer comes in and sees me sitting at the mirror, slowly filling in my eyebrows with an unsteady hand. She immediately turns and walks out. I am blatantly shunned.

As the weeks pass, many of the dancers warm up to me. Quite a few approach with reassurances. "I want our working conditions to improve, too," they whisper. "But I don't want to lose my job."

No one is actively hostile toward me, except one little blonde pipsqueak who mutters under her breath about "kicking my ass," which, given that I have about six inches and thirty pounds on her, is an amusing proposition. I heard her in the audience one night when I walked onstage, saying to another dancer, "Let's throw pennies at her head!" I walked right to the edge of the stage in front of her, looked her in the eye, and shouted over the music, "I dare you to try it!"

She never says anything within earshot after that.

That's the worst of the aggro. There's a lot of hissing behind my back, but no confrontations. Neither Jim Mitchell nor any managers get in my face. I don't receive any threatening phone calls, disturbing mail, or unwelcome visits at home. Jennifer is always a source of tremendous strength, our attorney Beth, and her new partner on the case, Lynn Rossman Faris, work doggedly on our behalf, and despite all the pressure to oppose the suit, the number of named plaintiffs grows from two to nine.

I never adjust to the fact that what was initiated in hopes of advancing the status of dancers is viewed by some as a setback. Objectively, I know it's not my fault, but still I feel terrible that everything got turned around and crazy. Disappointment crabs me and makes my heart heavy. I open the paper and wince to read an article in which a dancer derides the lawsuit, declaring, "We love our daddy, Jim Mitchell."

Daddy? Come on!

Well, there *is* something of a family dynamic at play in every club at which I've worked long term. Nothing unifies like a shared arena of misbehavior. Cast out from the larger "family" of the straight world, we band together and seek support in one another. And any comment or action that suggests that the newfound family might be dysfunctional is met with squinty eyes and sharp tongues. How dare you?

How dare we, indeed.

Now I'm one of the family's bad seeds, which hurts. Throughout my three years at Mitchell Brothers, no matter how intense it got, no matter how fried, aggravated, or scared I was, I could count on the other women. I never felt that the sex industry was my family (*please!*), but the women with whom I worked were my tribe—and now I have been banished. I begin having terrible nightmares in which I stumble into the dressing room with a knife between my ribs and none of the dancers moves to help me. There were many things I'd hoped to accomplish with this lawsuit—developing a martyr complex was not among them.

In addition to dancing at the theater and pursuing the lawsuit, I take a job editing a small local magazine, a job I am neither good at nor particularly interested in. But it gives me a focus away from the O'Farrell drama, as well as a means of supporting myself that doesn't involve nudity. I'm stressed to the gills, yet pressing forth. After several weeks of being knocked off-balance, I am regaining some equilibrium. But oh, those nightmares . . .

Support for the lawsuit comes in fits and starts. Some dancers make it clear that while they appreciate our efforts, they can't work up the steam to get mad about the stage fees or lack of rightful employee status. They are making good enough money, they feel, and if forking out fees and forgoing benefits is the price they have to pay, literally, then so be it. Others cheer us on, but make useful mention that some of the opposition may be a reaction to our militant tone—a point well taken. We're aren't experienced activists. We have the strength of our convictions but not much finesse.

But we feel we are in the right, so we don't give up. And ultimately we prevail. We settle with the theater in the summer of 1998. From start to finish, the whole process takes over four years. In that time, I move from San Francisco to New York to Wyoming, Jennifer moves on to a dot-com job in Silicon Valley, and our attorney Beth gives birth to two children. As part of the settlement agreement, the theater agrees to make payment for the back stage fees and missed wages of over six hundred former and current dancers still in the class, 2.85 million dollars' worth. And while they don't have to admit any wrongdoing, they are legally required to classify the dancers as employees.

When I look back at this long, drawn-out resolution to the San Francisco years, I feel world-weary, inspired, but mostly extremely glad that chapter has closed.

Now as I travel the country, I have found fees are de rigueur—house fees, booking fees, stage fees. The terminology varies, but the hand in the till is the same. Compared with what women are being charged elsewhere, the ten bucks I used to pay at Mitchell Brothers seems like a bargain. When I dance, I pay fifty dollars here, seventy-five there. One club waives the thirty-dollar house fee on a girl's first day, but that's the extent of the breaks. I've yet to pay less than twenty-five dollars in fees and twenty dollars on top of that in tip-outs to bartenders and deejays. Clubs that classify the dancers as employees aren't any better, either. At one club, I got paid an hourly wage, but I had to pay back my own minimum wage at a rate of seven dollars an hour, plus the taxes on my table dances, and tip-outs and house fees, which totaled more than one hundred dollars for the night. So far on this journey, I've paid out almost a thousand dollars in miscellaneous fees and tip-outs. The tip-outs I don't mind so much, because I'm happy to slide some cash to a bartender or deejay who has done a good job (I did, however, mind the place that made me tip the managers). But the fees still chap my hide—up to one hundred dollars for being late, for chewing gum, even for not smiling onstage—as does the house taking a percentage of girls' table dances. In some cases, it's nickel-and-dime exploitation—maybe twenty-five dollars or so. But in busier, glitzier clubs, girls sometimes pay fees upwards of two hundred dollars a shift. Club owners get away with it because they know dancers won't protest. Either the dancers don't know that in most cases the fees are illegal, or they don't make a fuss because they don't want to jeopardize their job or draw attention to themselves. But such scams have become industry standard. Just as customers expect to pay to play, dancers now expect to pay to work.

When I left Mitchell Brothers, I couldn't believe dancers everywhere weren't up in arms about the fees and tip-outs, but traveling the country has mellowed me. Not everyone can tilt at windmills, and most dancers just want to make their money with as little fanfare and frustration as possible. My activist entreaty has gone from "shake the system" to "get educated, get solvent, and get out." I applaud any woman who attempts to right the wrongs of the adult entertainment business, but I'm not convinced they can be entirely overcome. If a woman can leave the industry with some money, some insight, and some dignity, that's radical enough for me.

Things have changed drastically since I left San Francisco. The business seems harder, and heavier—as the social opprobrium has lessened around stripping, the dancer ranks have swelled and you have to sweat more to make less. Finding clubs that don't allow customer contact has been difficult. And establishments that were once familiar to me have transformed dramatically—or vanished. Peepland burned down in a blaze of suspicion. The Lusty Lady became the first unionized strip club in the country, but as sex-positive feminism spread and the peep show gained greater notoriety, particularly in elite academic circles, some felt the renegade philosopher Lustygirl image grew stale. ("Oh great," groaned a stripper friend as she read the contributor list of a recently published feminist sex-worker anthology, "more Lusty Ladies and their precious thinky thoughts.") Even Mitchell Brothers has changed. I couldn't help but notice the staff of other clubs smirking when I said I'd worked there, so I contacted some friends who still danced in San Francisco. Throughout our conversations, the word *extras* (code for illegal sexual acts) came up. A lot. Apparently there are now rooms where dancers can be alone with the customers, and sometimes the privacy is put to good use. And now Mitchell Brothers dancers no longer have to pay twenty dollars a shift. Despite the employee classification, they are required to pay a "quota" of over two hundred dollars for the day shift, and three hundred for the night. Ah, progress.

I'm sure that the lawsuit and my increasing disillusionment with and departure from stripping is a huge factor in why I decided that I had to get on the road to reexamine the business and what it means to me. Yes, my upcoming nuptials play a large part as well—I want to be done with this by the time I get married, draw a clear line between past and future. But when I quit stripping, the stress of the lawsuit left me so badly shaken, I never bothered to figure it all out. I just ran away to a new life. Or rather, limped away.

One of the dancers who opposed the lawsuit from the start, a pedantic gal in a Louise Brooks wig, stood behind me the morning I went to pick up my monthly theater schedule after filing the suit. She turned to the dancer next to her and sneered, "Now *there's* a used-up old thing!" I just ignored her, but I thought to myself, first, *I wouldn't mind smashing her smug little face.* Then I thought, *But she's got a point.* I was twenty-five, and I felt about a hundred.

That curled-over, dried-up feeling dogged me for months to come, after I moved to New York and went from struggling journalist to dot-com editor kid, to contributing editor at two glossy magazines. I was through with stripping, but stripping wasn't through with me. I was old for a stripper (that I wasn't stripping any longer didn't do anything to dull my anguish over this realization). I was old, period. If my peak was in my teens and early twenties, I thought, why hang around, taking up critical space? With every day that passes, I'm depreciating. I would fantasize about dying a swift and painless death, not because I was self-destructive, but because I'd survived for years as a daring young thing and I didn't know how to grow up.

Feeling prematurely over the hill is part of the exit package for strippers. I know that now, but I didn't then. There's no stripper manual that tells you how hard it can be to move on, emotionally and logistically. My self-image changed. I missed the convenience. The flexibility. The money. And the attention. I began to view stripping not as a day job I wanted to leave but a habit I had to kick.

I wish I'd known at the beginning that getting into stripping is the easy part—it's getting out that's the bitch.

Facing the perils of stripping head-on is new for me. I can view stripping plainly now because I no longer have anything to prove—to myself or anyone else. I first started stripping at Peepland to prove I could survive on my own. Then at the Lusty Lady I stripped as a political statement. Then, at Mitchell Brothers, I stripped for financial security, and later, to advance the cause of improving working conditions. But now I'm just here to bear witness, no illusions, no agenda, no filter of idealism.

For me, what public face to wear is perhaps the most confusing thing about stripping. For all the roles I play when I strip—confessor, playmate, prop—the role outside the club is the one that taxes me the most. I get pulled in different directions by people's responses when they find out I've stripped, and what they expect of me as a result—iconoclasm, activism, contrition, bravado, a free emotional feel. I used to just play the Pollyanna Badgirl game—square my shoulders prettily in a stance of "no apologies, no regrets."

That has changed. I'm certainly not apologizing. But I do have certain regrets.

I regret hearing a woman at a dancers' meeting announce, "I thank God that I have this job. Otherwise, I'd still be at home getting raped by my dad."

I regret knowing that some club owners and managers (not exclusively men, I hasten to add) refer to the dancers who work for them, and fill their pockets, as "bitches" and "whores."

I regret that as I travel the country, I see women with bruises that clearly didn't come from a happy game of slap-ass, and cuts that weren't a kitchen accident.

I regret that one of the side effects of this work is selective vision.

And I regret that many times, when people expressed doubts about the soundness of my decision to strip, I mistook their legitimate concern for disapproval.

I wish stripping could be more humane, but then, stripping combines volatile elements: sex, money, and power. It is a business of many hungers. I suppose I became obsessed with stereotype-wrangling and politicking as a highfalutin form of pain management. Railing against stripping's outlaw status had a palliative effect. If I could blame the social stigma for all that is wrong and hurtful in stripping, I didn't have to face the hard truth that even in the most tolerant social climate, hunger isn't humane, sex will never be totally safe, and commerce isn't always kind.

I'd lie down in front of an oncoming train to defend a woman's right to strip for a living. But that doesn't mean I grant rubber-stamp approval to the business. I am a friend to strippers and an ally to the industry, but I'm no longer an apologist. Or a shill.

As I travel, I become more aware of the precarious balance that stripping demands. I know, and I've always known, that in the business of stripping the money is fast. What I've come to realize is that fast money doesn't equal easy money, and the difference between the two is not to be underestimated.

Still, a reflexive voice inside of me pops up from time to time. *No, don't acknowledge the bad stuff. Lie. Say that everything's great. That you're always in control. That the customers are always polite and respectful, the business has only helped you.* For as many people who disapprove of strippers, there are just as many who want to be supportive and compassionate. They trust my testimony, believing anything I say. I'm tempted at times to abuse that authority. *Do it*, the voice urges. *Spin it in your favor*.

My hesitation in publicly naming the ills of stripping is neither unreasonable nor uncommon. If there is one taboo in the sex industry, it's the V word—*victim*. We gripe freely among ourselves about the unsavory aspects of stripping. Hell, bitching is a bonding ritual like in any other in the workforce. But let an outsider in on it? No. "Sorry," we say as we draw the curtains. "There are no victims here."

It's not so much that I'm trying to protect my image as be pragmatic. Any negative information can, and will, be used against me. To shut down clubs, to shame dancers, to advance a conservative agenda. Anyone who thinks being sexually objectified is the ultimate degradation has never been politically objectified. It is maddening and, unfortunately, a constant threat.

The problem is that my self-protective instinct can lead down a treacherous path. Sure, I want to show the world that strippers can be capable, thinking, feeling people, able to set boundaries, to care for other people and ourselves. But taken too far, such emphasis on the positive casts me as Paglian caricature—all triumph and no clue. When I think of the times I huffed out, testily, "I've never felt degraded! I've never been exploited!" I wish I could reach back in time and put a hand over my own stupid mouth.

• • •

Now I can accept that having been a stripper means I may always be an easy target for ridicule. Act cheap, reap the cheap shot, right?

I'm less distracted by outsider derision and insider propaganda: The slut-baiting, the proselytizing, the rationalizations.

I'm learning to examine the chaos of my past yet remain in the present.

I'm learning to repress less and discriminate more.

Through this account-settling and inventory-taking, I may be "better." Less angry. Less defensive.

I'm more realistic about what can't be wished, or litigated, away—the burn rate, the danger, the market demand for novelty, youth, and beauty. And I'm more concerned with my quality of life than my shelf life.

I'm definitely more balanced.

But I'm nowhere near finished.

And I'm nowhere near Zen.

Honey.

SIXTEEN

Miss Topless Wyoming

A contest for the title of Miss Topless Wyoming? Why, I'd be a fool *not* to enter!

The event takes place in mid-October out at the Clown's Den, and is open to any woman who dares to enter. I'm not traveling anywhere until Thanksgiving, so I've got a couple of weeks to prepare for the four categories in which contestants will be judged— swimwear, interview, evening wear, and performance.

I've only ever done one stripping contest—besides the kind that act as a conceit for an audition, I mean. In 1993, while I was visiting my friend Sue and her roommate Julie in L.A., I entered the amateur night competition at a dinky, run-down club called Star Garden in the Valley. The Los Angeles area has a pretty advanced system of amateur-night contests—there's at least one being held somewhere on any given weeknight, whenever they need to goose the draw. Guys like seeing newcomers get up and shake it—even if they're only "newcomers" to that particular place—and the girls like the chance to scoop up a couple hundred bucks for two or three songs' worth of dancing. Some retired dancers supplement their incomes by working the circuit, taking their costumes out of the mothballs for a week every few months, going from club to club in search of first-place payout.

My night at the Star Garden was a fiasco. Ten women showed up to compete and we drew numbers to establish the order of our performance. I drew first.

After we handed the deejay our music selections, we were allowed to use the dancers' dressing room to change into our costumes two songs before we were due to perform. The dressing room was a tiny, curtained-off area, accessible only from the stage, so I had to scoot along the stage's edge while another woman was dancing.

The dancer up was a tall, nervous, Gidget-like blonde in prancy white go-go boots, doing a loosely fashioned Pony to the Monkees' "Stepping Stone." Her freckles glistened under a fine film of perspiration and her sun-streaked pageboy swung impishly as she danced.

When her set ended, she came huffing through the curtain, which was covered in lipstick smudges and unidentifiable crust, and flopped down on the floor, scattering her tips around the room.

She rummaged through a small, flower-print makeup bag to find her powder and started swiping at her sweaty, small-featured face with a tatty pink velour puff, muttering to herself angrily.

"These guys *hate* me. Once I get my nose done it'll be a lot better," she announced to the room, snapping her compact shut with a desperate resolve.

I burst through the curtain when my stage name—"Amy" that night—was called, attempting sexiness and professional command. The audience, metalheads downing pitchers of beer, rumpled construction workers with Carhartt jackets and split knuckles, and a couple of middle-aged Pakistanis in short-sleeved button-down shirts, was unimpressed. I could have come out doused in gasoline and set myself on fire, and they still wouldn't have batted an eye.

Three songs is an eternity when the audience considers you as entertaining as the wallpaper. Seductive glances yielded nothing. I couldn't impress them with pole tricks because they weren't allowed. The third song was the worst. Because of the laws in L.A. County, dancers can't be within six feet of a customer when they're topless, so for my last song—when I dropped my top—I had to stay within a triangle outlined in tape on the stage. If guys wanted to tip me, they couldn't give the money to me directly. So they'd ball up the money and toss it in my general direction. When you're on a stage wearing only panties and stuff is flying your way, the nature of the projectile, negotiable or non-, doesn't matter. It's just not very fun to have things thrown at you.

I finished to scant applause, with only twenty dollars or so in tips. Then I changed into my street clothes and sat down with Sue and Julie to watch the other contestants.

An emaciated girl from Las Vegas with snaggle teeth, lank brown hair, and a screech of a voice did a forty-five minute set of extended Ozzy Osbourne mixes. She came out dressed in a parochial school uniform and anklets, skipping—skipping!—to the merry-go-round musical intro to "Mister Tinkertrain," trying to appear coy and girlish, and succeeding only in looking like a speed-addled babysitter. At one point, she dropped down on her hands and knees and beckoned the crowd, grinning with those pointy, evil teeth, which prompted Julie to grab the back of my chair, whispering, "Hansel and Gretel, Hansel and Gretel!" under her breath with a mixture of panic and repressed laughter.

The snaggle-toothed girl did several pole tricks (against the rules) and later a dancer named Princess, a pert-breasted Latina who wore a pink feathered g-string, flashed her pubic hair at the audience (also against the rules). Subterfuge! No fair!

Neither of them ended up winning, but neither did I. I came in next to last, an honor that netted me a twenty-dollar prize. Any customer who might have clapped to help me win the applause vote was long gone by the time all ten girls danced. The contest started at seven and we didn't get out of there until midnight. I was there for five hours and made forty stinkin' bucks.

I spend my free nights preparing for the Miss Topless Wyoming contest. For the evening-wear portion, I buy a white spandex strapless gown and trim the hem and thigh-high slit with a white feather boa, affixed with several dozen well-concealed safety pins. I sit watching MTV, painstakingly gluing clear, star-shaped plastic gems to a pair of white mesh opera gloves, and trimming the tops with the remaining boa. I coordinate an outfit for the theme set and listen to the song for my routine for hours at a time, to get the choreography down.

I've decided to go with a cosmopolitan cowgirl motif. I will wear Randy's bull rider chaps—which are baby blue leather with silver metallic fringe, a shiny silver bikini underneath, a matching silver body-hugging cropped zip-front jacket, a beat-up straw Stetson with a silver sequined hat band, and silver stiletto heels. I practice unbuckling the legs of the chaps and stripping out of them in time to the music. Randy dremels the holes in the leg-straps so they're easier to undo, preventing any clumsy onstage buckling drama. I saunter around the house in the chaps, bow-legged, fringe swinging, bellowing in a Western drawl, "Giddout a the way, pardner, or I'm a-gonna hafta challenge yew for the title of Miss Topless Wahhhhhh-yoming."

I'm a fairly competitive person, but I can't take this contest too seriously. It's not like Miss Topless Wyoming first, Nobel Prize next. Still, why bother entering if you're not going to go to the limit? I agonize over every detail—hem length, hand gestures, what accessories will make me a more convincing cowgirl. I draw the line at spurs—they won't attach to the spike heels and, besides, I wouldn't want to get disqualified for scratching the surface of the stage.

• • •

The night of the contest, I get to the Clown's Den early, with my outfits in a garment bag and my props loaded into a plastic laundry basket. The dressing room is already full of contestants elbowing their way to the mirrors, lotioning their legs, struggling with curling irons, hot rollers, and hair spray. The atmosphere is pretty tense. Ashtrays harbor several smoke-spuming cigarettes and a few girls sit with a drink at their elbow. I'm the only contestant who doesn't work at the club.

The entrants, who range in age from twenty to about thirty-five, are very friendly, though. Nobody is bitchy or tries to psych out their competitors. I think we're all pretty realistic about the significance of this event. We offer assurances, zip each other into dresses, and wait for instructions from Sheila, the club owner.

Sheila comes into the dressing room and has us pick numbers out of a hat to establish the order of the line-up. Dammit, I drew first again. Another contestant kindly offers to swap with me for fourth place.

The evening-gown portion starts the show. We line up in order and the emcee leads us across the club from the dressing room to the stage. In the big contests for exotic dance titles, like Miss Nude World or Miss Nude Universe, there is great emphasis placed on "BQI," beauty queen image. The closer you get to mainstream pageant presentation, the better. Here, though, "evening wear" is a matter of interpretation. Girls wear anything from floor-length purple sequined sheaths to Snow White–style ball gowns.

The judges, local men hand-picked by Sheila, sit at the first row of tables in front of the stage, marking down our scores. No spectators are allowed to sit at the tipping rail to afford the judges an unobstructed view.

For the swimsuit segment, an escort walks us to the stage one by one, then helps us up the stage stairs so we can do a brief pageant walk-and-wave before we join the other girls in a line along the back wall. When I cross the stage wearing a black mirrored bikini Randy bought me, I beam extra wattage into my smile—as girly tradition dictates. Toothsome and irresistible, I am every babe hawking product at a trade show. I am Miss America. I am Esther Fucking Williams. My face is killing me.

The emcee isn't exactly Bob Barker. He's wearing baggy jeans and a beer logo T-shirt, and looks like he just rolled out of bed. The interview is just one generic question: What are your turn-ons? or Is this your first contest? or How long have you been a dancer? When it's my turn the emcee steps up to me, reading from my entry form. "This is Barbie." He stops to look me over. Up and down. "Forget it," he mutters into the mic, shaking his head, "it's too easy. So, Barbie. Tell us where you're from."

"Well," I say, smiling smiling smiling, happy, yes, smiling, "I was born in Sweden, but a year ago I moved to Cheyenne from New York City."

From the back of the room, a drunk yells out an incredulous, *"Why?"*

For the final leg of the contest, the theme set, we transform ourselves from bikini-clad contestants to a cop, a French maid, a cavewoman, a good-girl-gone-bad, a schoolgirl, an angel, a Celtic wench, a baseball player, a painter, a Brazilian Carnival princess, and two cowgirls.

When the escort walks me across the floor to the stage for my act, a beer-steeped roar goes up from the crowd. My fringe is flailing and the overhead spots are reflecting off the silver. This is why I chose these costumes—the white gown, the mirrored bikini, the shiny cowgirl drag—to take advantage of the light.

I stand on the stage with my back to the room, one hand on my cocked hip and the other tugging the brim of my cowboy hat. At the first strike of guitar chords, the audience goes ballistic. "Bad to the Bone" is one of those instantly recognizable, can't-fail guy songs. Like "Tom Sawyer" by Rush or AC/DC's "Shook Me All Night Long," its rhythm courses through the veins of every red-blooded American male born after 1950. It also boasts the raunchiest sax solo known to rock-n-roll.

Every second of my act is premeditated—from the grinds, to the spins, to the exact moment that I unhitch the buckle at the waist of the chaps and drop them to the floor. I pull the tie on my bikini top as slowly as possible, while the saxophone wails lustily. I turn my back to the audience once again, drawing the string out to its full length. I look over my shoulder. *You want this top to come off?*, my expression entreats the audience, *No problem. All you have to do is beg for it.*

When I get enough applause, I undo the clasp and bare my breasts as I spin around the stage, then I head to the corner where I've tucked a pink fuzzy blanket. I spread the blanket on the stage and start in on my best floor work. I check my reflection in the mirrored wall behind the stage to make sure the motion is right as I wind my torso in a backward crawl. When the last verse of the song starts, I grab a bottle of lotion and throw my head back as I pour it all down the front of my body. I watered down the lotion beforehand, so it's thin and runs everywhere, from between my breasts to between my legs. ("Do you know what that lotion looked like when you squirted it on yourself?" Randy will ask me later, with a devilish grin. Of course I knew!)

Underneath my thong is the world's tiniest g-string. It's so small I feel like I'm wearing a slingshot, but the discomfort proves worthwhile when in the last few moments of the song, I stand up, loosen the strings on the sides of the thong and, to the thunderous approval of the unsuspecting crowd, drop it to the floor. As the music ends, I'm standing on the stage, clothed in nothing but blue light and a brief scrap of silver.

While I take my bows, the judges mark their score cards. I cover up in a short, red satin robe and the escort meets me at the stage steps to walk me back to the dressing room. When we pass two young sporty guys sitting on a bench next to the hallway by the dressing room, one of them says, "Barbie, if you don't win, there is no justice." Right then, every minute I spent at the Pure Talent School honing my technique was worth it.

Tallying the scores takes hours. I mean *hours*. When they gather the contestants on the stage to crown the winner, it's almost one o'clock.

We're all standing in a row, clapping for each other as winners are announced in the categories of Best Interview, Best Face, Best Breasts, Best Legs, Best Buns, and Best Pole Work. These are certificate titles, and the women step forward to pick up their laminated awards.

Now it's time for the trophy titles. I'm trying to stay calm, but I am anxious despite myself.

"The next category is Best of Show. And the winner is . . . Barbie!"

Best of show! That's quite an honor. That means they liked my cowgirl routine. Excellent! I step up to accept the trophy and try to put out of my mind that they have the same category at the Westminster Dog Show.

I didn't take first place. I will not go down in history as the seventh Miss Topless Wyoming. I cannot use the title to garner tables at the chic eateries in New York ("Clear the DiCaprio party from the corner booth. Miss Topless Wyoming is coming for lunch."). But I made first-runner up, losing to the other cowgirl, and that's just fine. I got two honkin' big trophies, half a dozen roses, and $225—two hundred for first runner-up, and twenty-five for best of show.

• • •

Randy marches into the house brandishing my trophies like a proud papa after a Little League championship win. "Let's put these in the living room!" he crows, rearranging the framed photos atop the television armoire to clear a space.

I take the trophies from him, embarrassed. "That's goofy, honey. I'll put them in my office."

"No! Leave them here."

I framed his rodeo photos and hung them all over in the room, but I don't know, that seems different. I'm pleased that I won these trophies, but I doubt I'll want to see them every day.

Once I put away my costumes and props, and get the trophies settled on a shelf in my office, I trudge upstairs for a bath. I lucked out in the bathroom department when we got this house. I have one all to myself, set in a dormer on the second floor. When we first moved in, Randy set to renovating it right away, so now the walls are cornmeal yellow, the floor is pale maple, and the tub is an old iron clawfoot with brass fixtures and matching brass-tone feet. I fill the bathtub with the hottest water I can stand and slide in for a good, long victory soak.

Right now I'm elated, but normally when I dance, I careen between states of liberation and despair, of excitement and tedium, of serenity and self-hatred, lust, repulsion, sadness, inspiration, joy, and fatigue—often within the course of a single night. Everything used to end up entwined in a giant tangle of feelings, lodged in my guts like some vile emotional hairball. But now, after six months of careful consideration and diligent inner watch, things are falling into place. I feel like I'm gaining command of a wily, evasive force. So I'm not just enjoying the exhilaration of an unexpected win, but also the cumulative effect of forging order from chaos.

For so long, I felt like I was a total washout, just marking time until my (hopefully imminent) death. But now I've got a newfound sense of possibility—that time really is on my side. I'm not a decrepit old loser. In fact, I'm anything but, and I've got the trophies to prove it.

At the perimeter of my increased awareness and nascent optimism is an unexpected outcropping of stubbornness. Is stripping really so bad? I know I got out at a time when I desperately needed to prove to myself that I could do something else, but now that I've done that, why not keep on? I'm enjoying it. I'm good at it. And I don't miss my other, more cerebral life.

I haven't written anything since June. I don't have the mental energy to spare. My thoughts are absorbed in processing, organizing, evaluating what is happening to me, all that I'm seeing. I don't mind it being this way, exactly. In fact, it's kind of nice, like I've been given a break from adulthood. My mind has veered away from the demands of the straight world and has lapsed into a luxuriant, meditative dumbness, a lazy inward gaze. My perception is right on, my observations acute, but my intake is skewed. It's as if everything I see, hear, or touch is cushioned by a layer of cotton batting. Some knob has been twiddled, making the world appear to operate on a several second delay.

Not only have I not been writing, I haven't been reading, either. A stack of old issues of *The New Yorker* sits by the bathtub, untouched. The sight of them, piled haphazardly next to the pedestal sink, evokes a pang of tender guilt, the sort someone might feel if she had been ignoring someone whose friendship she'd worked especially hard to cultivate. Maybe I can at least page through and read the cartoons.

Sloughed-off body glitter floats on the surface of the water, then flitters down to the bottom of the tub, settling like festive colored silt.

I crack open an issue.

In one cartoon, a fussy poodle, shaved down to poufs over each paw and at the tip of its tail, minces on a leash past two onlooking mongrels. One mutt is saying to the other, "Something ought to be left to the imagination."

In another issue, a buxom young blonde jiggles her way across a college campus. "Good Lord, professor!" says one excited graybeard to the other. "There it goes—the theory of everything!"

If that's what it comes down to, I wonder, then why pretend otherwise?

A nefarious shadow self is rising up to mock my respectable self, calling me away from writing and back to stripping full time. Maybe, this shadowy being thinks, I am meant to navigate the world by instinct, doing indecent things. Even knowing full well the numerous downsides, I feel gutter glamour's addictive pull. I like living suspended in semidarkness. For all the attendant occupational hazards, it's the safer option, the low and easy road. The proper ambitions and ideals can easily be bundled up and stored away for future consideration.

And what of the business of being a writer? Those agonizing publishing parties, with Yalies creaking around in their leather pants, drinks in hand, going, "And what are *you* working on?" The chronic, embedded frustration because there are too many geniuses and no guarantees. That studied, "I'm not pleading" pleading look that comes over everyone when a person of greater influence enters a room. Editors who use the words *edgy* and *transgressive* with a straight face. The cash-flow hell. Why bother chasing paychecks around, hectoring magazine accounting departments, and cursing the empty mailbox for weeks, when I could get cash on the barrelhead each night?

Randy and I could go on the lam. Dancing is a highly portable means of employment. Have body, will travel. I'm in decent shape, don't have any visible tattoos, and have a bagful of long, blonde hair. I could go anywhere. Randy busts his ass every day. He's up and out the door at 7 a.m., and never home before dark. He could be my manager, keep my bookings and travel arrangements in check. I bet he'd love the change of pace.

Somewhere in a distant, scarcely accessible area of my consciousness is the memory of my friend Andy, a reporter, giving me a pep talk over French toast in a diner when I was depressed about my writing. "But journalism is forever," he said, the tone of his voice verging on panic.

Andy, you dear, you naif, you just don't get it.

I scrub my skin with a loofah, weighing the relative merits of either life. Right now the scales are tipping toward dancing, by a substantial measure. At its best, writing feels like a strike at posterity. But stripping, at its best, feels like cheating death. A blast of expansion. Staring down the litany of "shoulds" that defines a woman's lot. Do I want to resume the march of duty or stay on this thrill ride?

Is there any question?

I sink lower in the glitter-dappled tub until my eyes are just over the waterline like a croc in a primeval swamp.

I hover with the serene surety of an ancient, sharp-toothed creature that has weathered ice ages, great floods, poachers, hunters, belt-makers, and crowds of dumb humans wielding cameras and raw meat foisted on sharp sticks. A horn-hided beast that knows where its next meal is coming from, and that it will be taken, stealthily and quickly, in a series of violent gulps.

I've got plenty of time. Plenty of time.

SEVENTEEN

Scarlett

A stripper's story may end in any number of ways, but the beginning rarely varies: Young woman needs money. Young woman casts about wildly, weighs options, and, in some crazy moment, considers stripping. Young woman measures potential worst-case scenario against potential pot of cash. Young woman steels nerves and makes leap.

Miss Scarlett Fever jumped into the roiling chaos of Times Square, long before the family-friendly neon glare chased the darker elements from the area. You couldn't tell from looking at her today, with her sensible clothes, sturdy body, and wavy red hair cut into a stylish short cut, that she spent more than a decade working in the country's most notorious sex district. "I worked, on and off, from 1975 to 1986. It was insanity then," she tells me. "It wasn't a job, it was a lifestyle."

• • •

I've known Scarlett casually for a long time. When I lived in New York, I'd see her at parties, hear her name in conversation, run into her at a reading. That she'd been in the business was no secret and I found her candor interesting, but when I discovered that she'd worked in Times Square—my old stomping ground—I had to get to know her better. A few days before I headed to New Jersey for Thanksgiving with my folks, I set aside some time to meet Scarlett in the city and compare notes.

Learning more about the history of striptease has been the highlight of my year. Yeah, I've had a hell of a time at the different clubs—show me a colloquialism and you'll see a smile on my face. But the stories from way back then are what's rocking my little stripper world. To connect with these women and have them trust me enough to unspool their lives while I listen is awesome. There's honor in being an audience.

Raised in a middle-class Jewish household on Long Island, Scarlett started working at Robbie's Mardi Gras on Broadway right out of high school. "I had just turned seventeen and was still living at home," she says as we sit across the table from each other at Café Orlin on Saint Marks Place on a brisk November morning. "The first time I got onstage," she recalls, "I had to borrow a g-string from the manager—it was a tiny blue piece of scratchy, glittery fabric with a strip of elastic that ran between the cheeks of my ass. It was really tacky, it had somebody else's pussy stains on it. But it was my first g-string." Unskilled as she was, Scarlett considered the experience a revelation. "I felt so gorgeous. I felt wanted. It was like my bat mitzvah. It was like, I don't know, I'd become a woman.

"I was really awkward," she continues. "They told me to do floor work and I didn't know what they meant. The manager told me, 'Just pretend you're having sex and you're on top.'" But Scarlett had never been on top, so she started doing naked pushups on the stage.

Gimmicks weren't critical to the stage show like they were in Dixie Evans's day, but Scarlett developed her own nonetheless. "I had fabulous nipples," she says, "like little thumbs. I could hang my clothes off of them. I would sway back and forth with my dress hanging from one nipple, and that was it. A couple years later, someone taught me how to light my nipples on fire."

Of course, I can't resist asking: How *do* you light your nipples on fire? But I wait until the waitress puts my plate of eggs in front of me and serves Scarlett her pancakes with pumpkin butter and a side of bacon. "I love bacon. It's one of my weaknesses." Scarlett sighs happily, picking up a piece and folding it into her mouth.

"Now," she continues, "lighting your nipples on fire is actually pretty easy. You take a regular cardboard-stick match from a matchbook and split it slightly with your fingernail from the bottom up. Not too far—about a third or halfway up, depending on the size of the nipple. The match should look like an armless man with two short legs. The 'legs' fit over the nipple—it works better if the match sits at a slight upward angle so there's sort of a clamp action there." Then you use another match to light the matches once they're sitting securely on your nipples. " 'Course you can't keep them lit for long," Scarlett takes pains to point out. "The sexiest thing to do after lighting them is to have another dancer pull you close, light a cigarette off one of the flames, then quickly blow them out."

I make a mental note to try this as soon as possible. Good thing they don't have smoking sections in New York restaurants any longer or I'd corner her into doing a demo.

The seventies in Times Square were the days of Anything Goes, and Scarlett took advantage of the latitude, taking to the stage wearing cowboy boots and fishnets with the crotch torn out. "I did that to all my fishnets to cover up my legs because I thought I had too much cellulite."

The bosses weren't picky about appearances, as long as you were hustling champagne and the bar made their money. Mardi Gras dancers were real girls—short, fat, skinny, there was even a grand-mother. Scarlett marvels, "There was one girl, she had the biggest ass, thighs, tons of cellulite, really droopy tits—she was such a Long Island Five Towns JAP. And she made so much money because she could talk the talk." Another girl who worked there was a glue head. She didn't dance, she just worked the floor and hustled drinks, then sat in a corner sniffing glue out of a paper bag. Scarlett recalls the woman's broken nose, missing teeth, and scrappy, drug-ravaged body. And she, too, earned plenty.

Dancers were then compensated quite differently than they are today, when your take is usually what you hustle yourself—minus your house fees and tip-outs. "They used to pay seventy-five dollars a shift," she says. My mouth is agape. "I understand they have fees now for this, that, and everything," she continues. "There were no fees or fines then. I mean, there were things that you weren't sup-posed to do: You weren't allowed to touch yourself, but there were ways around that. No pubic hair was supposed to show, you weren't allowed to have customers touch you when you were onstage."

Working at the Mardi Gras, Scarlett says, was all about the champagne hustle. The champagne hustle is a total mystery to me. It sounds so old-school. And tipsy-making. Assuming you convinced customers to buy bottles of champagne to share with you, wouldn't you end up dead drunk at the end of every shift? Well, Scarlett explains, there was a way around that. Namely, the spit glass. "The spit glass is a frosted glass that sits by the side and the customer is supposed to think it's a chaser of club soda; it's filled about halfway with club soda. You'd take a sip of champagne, and then take a sip out of the spit glass and let the champagne dribble out of the corners of your mouth. That way you got through the customers quickly. You'd get the guys really drunk and get their money." The unpopular men got a little something extra. "We used to save the spit glasses for the customers we didn't like," Scarlett confesses. "We wouldn't wash them out and then serve them drinks in there."

"It was foul champagne," she says. "Really cheap and gave you a bad headache. Instead of getting the customers to buy me a twenty-dollar nip of champagne, I would get them to buy me a twenty-dollar shot of vodka. Then I could get through it. Otherwise I really couldn't."

I ask Scarlett, "Were you drinking so much because you were bored?"

No, she tells me, with a tart self-deprecation that sounds like the acid edge of peace long-since made, "I drank a lot 'cause I'm an alcoholic. That was one of the reasons I loved the job. The more I drank, the more money I made. I did a lot of *drugs* 'cause it was boring." Scarlett used cocaine—so much that after a certain point she couldn't snort it anymore because her nose was too damaged. "This was before crack and free-base. I was buying it in rock form," she says, "and I would just eat it."

One of the reasons I was interested in talking to Scarlett is that her tour of duty in Times Square ended just as mine began. I wanted to meet a woman who could tell me what it was like in the '70s and early '80s. When she talks, Scarlett uses the word *insanity* a lot, which strikes me as more apt than hyperbolic. It *was* insane—even when I was there. "Times Square was very, very different than it is today," she says, and I nod in agreement. I'd venture that it's not even the same neighborhood. The building Peepland was in is now an Applebee's, for Pete's sake.

Scarlett is a natural storyteller, unfurling her life with candor and ease—and a great Long Island accent. A young, Gap-clad couple strains to eavesdrop, eyes agog, whenever she speaks. They quickly redirect their focus to their cappuccinos when I fire them a scolding look.

Scarlett feels that for some women, the desire for familiarity and acceptance can obscure the hard realities of the sex business. "I think a lot of women who go into this don't feel like they have a family or like they have a place to be safe. I mean, I had a family, but I didn't feel like I did, and the sex industry is a very enclosed world. I was seeing the same people every day, so I thought it was okay." But nothing could be further from the truth. Scarlett was raped more than once. She saw a girl get stabbed onstage. And she claims to have been kidnapped. "This pimp who was trying to turn me out kidnapped me, locked me in a hotel room in Jersey, and I had to break out. He wound up killing two friends of mine a couple of months later." As Scarlett tells it, one of the girls who worked for him, Crystal, was trying to leave and he beat her up in an after-hours club one night when the two women were out partying together. Crystal kept her money in a condom in her vagina, in case she got mugged—a practice Scarlett says was a common preventative among the hookers she knew. He beat her up in the bathroom of the club, then reached inside her, and took all her money. Still, Crystal was determined to leave. Crystal's friend Angie was going to lend her money to go home to the Midwest. "Crystal was staying at Angie's," Scarlett says, "so he went there and killed the two of them. Literally sliced them up like roast beef, the cops said. Angie's kids were in the next room in a crib.

"We all knew who had done it," says Scarlett. "We told the police, and they didn't care. They did not care. As far as they were concerned, we were just clearing out our own. And we were part of the cops' lives. We partied with them—they'd sit in the bar drinking. I had cops drive me to work. So, you think you're protected . . ."

But you're not.

Scarlett sighs. "I tried to get straight. Once, I bought all these straight clothes—A-line wool skirts, low-heeled pumps, button-down shirts, good bras. I would get dressed in the dressing room, leaving work in all these clothes, and my friend looked at me and said, 'It doesn't matter what you wear, you still look like a whore.' She meant it with love, but I thought, 'You know, she's totally right.' "

Scarlett moved to Robbie's second location, which was where the Marriott Marquis, a large tourist hotel, stands today. Scarlett started doing favors for the bosses, "but not with customers," she says—a distinction that separated her from a number of her coworkers. Some girls tricked with the clientele, either in the back room or making appointments outside. One girl used to sell the key to her hotel room. She'd get the money up front—two or three hundred dollars—then give the man the key. Right at closing she'd say, "Meet me there. They can't see me leave with you, I'll get fired." But the key was bogus. "She looked so different when she left the bar," Scarlett says, "they'd never recognize her in a million years, and they'd be too mortified to come back and say that they'd been slammed.

"At the time I didn't think of what I was doing as tricking," Scarlett says, "because I figured I'd end up sleeping with the bosses anyway since they were the partners or the wise guys. What they were giving me wasn't money for sex, it was cab fare home. Three hundred dollars cab fare home from Midtown to the East Village? Right. A trick is a trick no matter what you tell yourself . . ."

• • •

That the business of topless dancing—and its profile in popular culture—has changed dramatically is not lost on Scarlett. "It's so different with the gentlemen's clubs where the women wear gowns. What I see people writing about now"—college girls stripping for tuition then moving on to the profession of their choice, experts extolling the divine power of the exotic dancer—"is so different from my experience.

"For instance," she goes on, "I worked with a girl who was fifteen. The most perfect body and little rosebud lips, like a Barbie doll. I remember when she got her first hundred-dollar tip, it was from a couple. She was so excited, she was jumping up and down onstage and we told her, 'No, no, calm down. If a couple wants you to come sit with them, this is not a good thing. These are not your parents. They aren't going to take you out and buy you clothes. You're fifteen, you don't want to go there yet.' " Within months the girl went from an innocent to a hard-core junkie, shooting heroin between her toes to conceal her habit. Her feet became so badly abscessed she could no longer put on her high heels. One day she sat crying in the dressing room because the managers wouldn't let her skip her stage show. Scarlett and her fellow dancers took turns spreading cocaine and lidocaine on the girl's feet just so she could get into her shoes.

For the first time since we sat down today, Scarlett seems self-conscious. "This is weird," she pauses. "I've never told this to anyone before."

But you know, it often ends up that way when two of our kind get together—the alliances are quick, the dish nonpareil. We share stories we won't tell anyone else because they might be used against us, taken away from us, lorded over us, or simply dismissed: "Well, it couldn't have been *that* bad." There's a million ways to hear this stuff, but we can be sure it'll get across the way we mean it—the way we lived it—when told to our own. When you've been through something that few other people are likely to understand, something that rearranges your soul and changes your position in the world and your view of it, anyone who's gone through the same thing connects right away. There's an almost palpable empathy—you've been there. You get it. Sometimes, like during this brunch with Scarlett, we trade war stories and gossip and make scathing indictments of the straight world. Other times we just say to each other without words, "Lean here."

"Stripping, even hooking, certainly has more respect now than it did then," Scarlett says. "There's this movement now to glorify it, to present it as legitimate."

I know what she means—it's the latest turnaround in popular perception. There are always market-driven half-truths coming and going like intellectual fashion. In the 1970s—"the golden age of porn"—there was a "self-discovery" angle to the sex industry: Me-Decade decadence and artistic experimentation with a First Amendment chaser. In the 1980s, the dominant theory was that everyone in the business was crushed under the thumb of the patriarchy and blinded by "false consciousness." Lately the slant is self-determination and a keen, if compromised, eye toward the bottom line—a savvy capitalist détente. But while the temper of the times may shift, the whole truth rarely changes.

Despite many shifts in feminism, Scarlett says, she doesn't think things have changed that much between the sexes. "My old boss said to me, 'More than anything, you've got to remember that the power of the pussy is golden. Men will do anything to get it. Not once they've got it, but to get it.' And women still trade on that, on all different levels. We want their money, so we give them 'everything but.'

"We know it's a game. They know it's a game. We don't want to hear that they just want to fantasize about us, and that it doesn't matter to them who we are or what we do, what our dreams are, or whether or not we have children, or whether or not we even like them. They have a scenario in their heads, and in the sex industry, our job is to figure out what that scenario is and give it to them."

She means, "*sell* it to them," I'm certain.

"Still"—she mellows a little—"I think women should be able to do this work. I don't think there should be such a stigma. I honestly don't have a problem provided it's a choice you make when you have a whole array of choices in front of you."

"Yeah, but how many women who start stripping have a whole array of choices, or believe they do?" I ask her. "Did you?"

"I had more choices than I thought," she replies. "I really didn't think I had anything else but my body. I was ready-made for this." Scarlett was molested as a child and raped as a teenager. Her parents expected her to go to college, but by the time she graduated from high school, she just wanted a mindless job. "I didn't want to be bothered," she says. "I'd been hanging out in hustler bars for years as a teenager, so when I went into this it was such a small transition. It's where I felt I belonged."

After ten years, Scarlett finally got out, but with little to show. "I know girls who've bought houses," she says, "who've bought cars. I didn't have anything. I didn't travel anywhere. I didn't have any jewels. I made a thousand dollars a week, my rent was only two hundred a month, and when I finally got out, I had eight thousand dollars in credit card debt."

The humiliation visited upon her by a night manager of the Mardi Gras hastened her departure from the business. "This guy's favorite thing in life was making me cry," she recalls angrily. "In front of customers, he'd tell me I was garbage, that this was all I was ever going to be." Her desire to prove him wrong has kept her from returning. "I don't ever want him to be able to say, 'See, I knew sooner or later you'd be back,'" she says. "And that's enough to keep me out."

Entering the legitimate job market with a ten-year gap in her résumé was daunting, but Scarlett came up with an enterprising solution. "I consolidated all the clubs I worked in and called it 'MG Entertainment.' I said that I did payroll, because sometimes I paid off the girls on their drink commissions at the end of the night. I said that I booked entertainment, and that I trained new employees, because when new girls came in I would teach them how to pick pockets, how to hustle drinks, and how to spot cops."

Dramatic as her years in Times Square were, Scarlett is quick to point out that they weren't all bad. "I made some really good friends," she says. "And I loved the get-over, the separation between Us and Them. I had fun with the regulars in the neighborhood—the street hustlers and the loan sharks—because we knew what we were talking about, what we were doing. We were in on the secret. As opposed to the regular customers, the straight johns, who thought they were in on it, but weren't."

But, Scarlett says, "I think I rationalized the get-over to make myself feel good. You have to in order to survive. Or *I* had to." There were times when she imagined she was living a Damon Runyon story. "The reality was different," she admits. "The reality is I learned to dislike and distrust men. I learned to dislike and distrust women. I can't say anything about the way people treated me. I allowed myself to be treated that way."

Now her day-to-day existence is more sane, and satisfying. She's got a good job in publishing, a boyfriend, a better relationship with her family, and a cache of interesting—if sometimes disturbing—memories. "I couldn't go back," she says, "I'm not that person anymore. I'm too shy. I'm even too shy to dance for my boyfriend.

"But I would go back to it in a heartbeat if I needed to in order to survive. It's only within the past couple years that when I have a hard time, I don't turn to the adult pages of the *Village Voice* classifieds and look through them like, 'Okay, now what do I do?' "

I laugh out loud because I *still* do that!

Scarlett drains her coffee cup and I finish my tea. We get into our coats, settle the bill, and step out into the amber morning light on Saint Marks. A young waitress dressed in camouflage baggies and a blue bandeau top is taking orders from the customers sitting at the sidewalk tables. "Put some clothes on!" Scarlett calls to her as we walk past, her breath clouding in the cold air.

The girl's stubby bleached-out dreadlocks bounce as she lifts up her head to look at us. Her face puckers in confusion—she can't tell if Scarlett is joking or not. "No," the waitress says, her expression shifting from indignant to nonplussed as she bends back over her order pad.

Scarlett and I stand on the corner of Second Avenue before parting ways. I'm heading off to pick up my rental car, and she's on her way to the Astor Place Kmart. How, I wonder, after all this time away from dancing, is Scarlett feeling about having done it, about herself? "I like who I am now," she tells me. "I'm more comfortable in my body, I think I'm sexier. I'm glad I did it. There are things I would have chosen not to live through—I didn't need to see people get stabbed, I didn't need to be abused myself, but I'm not going to apologize," Scarlett asserts. "I learned a lot of people skills and a lot of survival skills. It's how I learned to do small talk. And it's how I know how to give a really good blow job. I'll always be grateful for that."

EIGHTEEN

New Jersey

The afternoon before Thanksgiving with my family, I am dancing on top of a bar in Rahway, New Jersey, desperately trying to avoid stepping in a guy's plate of turkey and stuffing. Why am I up here, wavering and acrophobic in my iridescent gold platform heels? Somehow I got into my fool flossy head that if this place allowed dancing *on* the bar, then, by God, I was going to hoist myself up on the beer cooler, step over the compartmentalized plastic tray of drink garnishes— maraschino cherries coddled in their own pink chemical soup, green olives with pimientos poking forth like out-thrust tongues, silky-skinned pearl onions, desiccated wedges of lemon and lime—and rock out. What I end up doing is weaving on a bartop slalom course of beer bottles, shot glasses, sloshes of spilled whiskey and sticky fruit liqueur, and food-laden plates. The man in front of me, strawberry-blond bangs mashed to his forehead by his furnace-repair-company cap, hunkers protectively over his holiday lunch while I gyrate in his face. I'm wearing a bikini—deep pink velvet with a spray of rhinestones, my most elegant one—but the close proximity of food to my sexed-up self makes me feel a few shades past vulgar. I grab an overhead pipe for balance and prepare to swivel past. The man hands me up a dollar, then draws disinterestedly from his Coors. I take the damp bill and tuck it under my gold garter. "Thank youuuuu," I say, in my patented saccharine trill. He doesn't look up.

Thanksgiving Eve is traditionally the busiest day of the year in the go-go clubs, so many places host a uniquely Jersey event called a Go-Go Rama. Instead of booking the usual five or ten or twenty dancers, they declare open season and take however many girls show up. Some clubs promise a hundred dancers or more. It's not killer money for the girls, necessarily, but the gimmick of abundance is a great draw for the house. The upside for the dancers is they can come and go as they please. Instead of being stuck for six to eight hours like on a regular shift, you stay for an hour or two, do a couple sets onstage, then get on down the road to the next club.

The real purpose of my trip to New Jersey is, of course, to spend the holiday with my family. There's going to be a full house, all my siblings are coming, plus Randy and my sister Annette's husband. But I'd planned from the outset to take advantage of this long weekend and see what's up with go-go in the Garden State. I have to pick Randy up at Newark Airport at 11 p.m., which gives me the whole day to bomb up and down the Turnpike in my rental car, 'Rama hopping. At the very least I'll make enough to cover my tolls.

New Jersey, the most densely populated state in the country, has the highest number of clubs per capita—well ahead of the other club-heavy states like Texas, Florida, and California. There are 173 clubs in the 7,419-square-mile area of eight million residents. Aside from a handful of nude places—called juice bars, as that's all they can legally serve— Jersey mostly has go-go bars where dancers have to wear bikinis at all times. Only Utah has more stringent regulations for adult entertainment establishments. Jersey dancers don't typically work in one place. They find a few that they like, book into them a couple times a month, and rotate. My own choices were limited to locations no farther west than Bergen County. Anything past that line is too close to home, literally. I'm trying to keep the Freudian nightmares to a minimum.

My Go-Go Rama marathon is a blur of dingy, grime-impacted bars and off-duty dancers, hair teased high and makeup done heavy, sitting in dressing rooms with turkey dinners from the free buffets resting on their knees. They gossip and maneuver the plastic silverware with long, lacquered talons. The stage is always set behind the bar where a few girls dance for a couple songs, then hop down and "walk the bar," dodging the bartenders hustling to fill drink orders. We present ourselves to the men, one by one by one, as they drink beers and eat, entreating them to slide dollar bills under the outstretched sides of our bikini bottoms. They comply, folding singles from big stacks at their elbows, hoping for a quick peek of something that will make them want to part with another buck. Such low-brow machination isn't what I had in mind the night of the Miss Topless Wyoming contest when I decided to stick with this stripping thing. Maybe a Denver showclub where the image is polished and the rules are strictly hands-off. Maybe some weekend trips back to Dallas with Randy in tow. But not this, where I have to dash off to the dressing room to de-grunge every half hour or so.

In Clifton, a shrunken old black man in a gray Members Only jacket and brown slacks says to me, "I'll give you a dollar for every inch you lower your thong."

I pull the sides of my bottoms down a bit. One dollar. And again. Another dollar. And again. And again. And again. Any lower and he's going to know whether or not I'm a natural blonde. Okay, I got five dollars out of you. That's enough.

279

In her book, *Bitch*, Elizabeth Wurtzel likens stripping to "begging with your body." When I first read that, I fumed, "What the hell does she know. She's never done it." But now, walking the bar, moving from guy to guy, shimmying or winking or tugging at my thong to get him to give me a dollar, begging with my body is precisely what it feels like.

At one bar in Newark, the girls are tough and fast Latinas, with white frosted eye shadow high on the brow bone and lips lined with brown pencil and filled in with pearly pink gloss—steak lips, I call them. They openly flash their pubic hair to capture extra bills, let customers' hands wander to their nipples as they tuck tips in their bikini tops. At another, all the dancers are Russian and Brazilian (the signs in the dressing room are written in Russian and Portuguese, as well as English)—part of the new immigrant class in the industry. The owner begs me to book there. "Keep this under your hat," she tells me, "but we pay more per set for American girls because they're harder to come by." It's a shock that they pay anything at all, regardless of nationality.

Some of the Russian girls are brought over to the States specifically to work as dancers. They are booked into clubs together, then loaded into a van by an agent (or an "agent") and taken to and from work every day. What is it like for them, living in a foreign country and being carted around to bars all over the state? I guess they have one another for companionship, but it seems lonely. Nomads wandering turnpike and parkway, from town to town, booking to booking. I watch them leave when they've finished their sets, dressed in sweat suits, hair pulled up atop their heads in scrunchies, over their shoulders bags full of dirty bikinis reeking of smoke and cheap cologne, nick-heeled pumps, and singles in sweaty rolls secured by a hair elastic or clipped into bunches of twenty each. Today I've met many Russian girls who are clearly free agents grinding their way to the American dream, dollar by dollar, but I wonder how much autonomy is afforded the women who travel in groups. My hope is that they're not going off to yet another loud, dingy bar, but home to pull together something resembling a holiday celebration.

On her way out the door, one of the Russian girls hands a couple of paper tickets to a customer. As a promotion, many of the clubs are holding turkey raffles. Get a winning ticket and garner a twenty-pound Butterball. I wish I could follow all those birds home. What does a guy tell his wife when he comes in with one of those suckers tucked under his arm?

I consider begging tickets off the customers so I can show up at my folks'—the prodigal daughter returneth—with a carload of ill-gotten turkeys in tow.

On Thanksgiving Day, the kitchen is a cacophonous hive of sisters. Kelly puts heat-and-eat dinner rolls on a baking sheet. Barbara spoons two kinds of cranberry sauce—whole-berry and jelly—into a cut-glass dish. Annette sorts silverware and counts napkins while Mom drains the potatoes for mashing. I stand over the turkey, which is cooling on the stove, surreptitiously picking off bits of crispy skin to eat. The men are in the family room, clustered around the game on TV.

I tell my sisters about the turkey raffle and my idea of scamming turkeys to bring home. I figure they'd find the story entertaining, especially the part about my plan to drive up with a turkey propped upright on the passenger seat buckled in a safety belt. Kelly and Annette have always been cool about my dancing. Kelly, an engineer, is a peacemaker by nature. She isn't the kind to judge, and Annette, a chemist, has told me she admires my guts. Barbara, however, is a different matter. As a Presbyterian minister, moralizing isn't just her wont, it's her calling.

When I finish with my story, she asks, "Do you think that when you tell people about being a stripper they think it has something to do with how you were raised?"

The timing and nature of the question are classic Barbara.

Barbara is the one person in my life who can pull my pin, that individual who can completely unnerve me and topple every defense. We're similarly willful and direct, but while I'm the black sheep, she is the dutiful daughter. I adore her, but she's long on nerve and short on subtlety. She will burrow into a sensitive subject at any opportunity, whether it's appropriate or not. When she launches into that line of questioning with me, I feel like a small, flightless bird at the end of a long branch: How did I get here, and, more importantly, how the hell am I going to get down?

Of course, some variation of "why" or "what made you do that" is the question on everyone's lips. It's what people really want to know. But such questions are more easily asked than answered. I never know what to say. Any response would just be an approximated fiction, a right-sounding best guess. While stripping may be an unusual line of employment, the justification is so banal: It really was the best I thought I could do at the time. And I thought whatever dare it implied would be worth taking.

But within "why" there is often a much larger request: Assure me. Make stripping okay. Solve it. Make the enterprise not seem unjust. Make the very idea not catch in my gut. If not that, then at least make its difficulty portable—boil everything down to a kernel of pathology, so that when I am troubled by what I see, I can roll that kernel between my fingers to remind myself, *Ah, this is why they do it. Here's the answer.*

But "why" isn't a tidy singularity, or a linear equation. When asked to explain, we attempt life as straight algebra: A root cause (sexual trauma, violent relationship, crappy parents), and an aggravating factor (low self-esteem, substance abuse, lack of education) equals stripper, but this never works, because there are always women with the same variables who don't end up in the clubs. An authentic reply isn't obedient, it won't shrink down into something you can fit into a pocket, an index of facts, or a list of diagnoses. The truth is much more complicated than that. The truth is so much more of a mess.

I try to fashion the perfect retort, one that makes people shake their heads and smile with relief and knowing. But I rarely succeed.

What can I tell my sister? I could lie, say I was meant to do it, a natural-born stripper. I could appeal to the gods of voodoo science. Pop psychology. Astrology. Numerology. Birth order.

I could tell her about being so mad at the straight world as a teenager that I felt I owed it nothing. Tell her of walking into the kitchen one winter day and seeing my mother leaning on the sink, with her head in her hands, looking absently out the window, yet again. Wondering *Where does she go when she does that?* and thinking that if I engineered my life in a way completely opposite hers, maybe I wouldn't end up standing in a kitchen in a suburb, staring into a bleak arch of naked branches. It was a childish idea, but then, I was a child thinking as a child. Yet surely there was a spasm of individuation in my becoming a stripper.

Would that answer be good enough?

I could tell her that our father asked me, in his own way, the same question years ago. After I "came out" about my life in San Francisco, he sent me a long, pained letter in which he wrote, "If we had held the reins more tightly with you as a child, would you have felt the need to go as far as you did to rebel?" I gripped the letter with both hands, aching with the restraint and love with which he chose his words. I imagined him hesitating, pen over the paper, knitting his bushy brows together as he struggled to come up with a way to tell me what he felt and ask me what he wanted to know without making me feel bad, without making a difficult situation worse.

What I want to tell her is that I don't want anyone to hold Mom and Dad accountable. I certainly don't. What I have done, am doing, isn't punishment or cause for indictment.

"I, I, I don't think they have anything to do with it," I stammer at Barbara, stirring a pot of sauerkraut bubbling on the back burner. "I make it clear to people that I bear the mantle of responsibility." I sound formal and ridiculous, scrambling for dignity in my embarrassment, like a professor speaking before a lecture hallful of colleagues who has just realized his fly is down.

My mother, who has overheard everything from her station in the doorway between the kitchen and dining room, is looking at Barbara with an irritated expression. I can tell she's put off by Barbara's theatrics, that she thinks this is a bit much.

My mother comes over and stands next to me, making a human shield between me and Barbara. She knows I'm upset. She puts her arm around me, her voice even and low, "It's okay. It's o-kay."

I turn into her outstretched arm and hug her, breathing in her special scent of shampoo and cigarettes. I whisper into her sweatered shoulder, "I really don't care what anyone else thinks. Just you."

Which is the very heart of the truth.

I remember a phone conversation with my mother last year, when I said something about every byline being penance for humiliating her for so many years.

"Good heavens, you're not still hung up on that, are you?" she asked in disbelief.

"Kind of."

"Oh, L," she sighed deeply. "In some ways I think your life is my secret fantasy."

I pressed the receiver tight against my ear and my eyes brimmed with stinging tears. This was the first time she'd ever said anything positive about stripping. I doubt she'd remember having told me this, and I'm sure she'd never repeat the sentiment, but I desperately wanted to hear it. Thank you, I thought. Oh, thank you. Papal dispensation would pale in the wake of what she had given me. I had escaped the wrath of Mom, and I was so extremely grateful.

My heart thumps in a deep clutch of love at the memory, but I quickly tamp down the feeling and break out of our embrace. This is a day of Thanksgiving, not a day for breaking down in the kitchen.

Barbara backs off. The family gathers in the dining room. A blessing is offered, dinner is served, and in the foothills of New Jersey, a truce has been declared. I make no mention of the fact that I intend to keep right on dancing.

NINETEEN

Tijuana, Mexico
Los Angeles, California

You know you've reached a milestone of maturity when your Tijuana drug runs aren't for Quaaludes or Valium, but for Retin A. My posse from L.A.—Sue, Jeanette, her friends John and Barb—and I are wandering along Avenida de la Revolución, canvassing the *farmacias*, trying to find the best deal on the skin cream.

The resolution I made the night of the Miss Topless Wyoming contest to go back to stripping has stuck, so I need to prepare myself for the long haul. My original plan was to fly to Los Angeles to get some sun, see friends, and work at the clubs, but now I need to buy stripper supplies, and Retin A is at the top of the list.

Wrinkle-wise, I've more or less been spared so far, but there are a few fine lines coming in around my mouth that I wouldn't mind getting rid of. So here we are, the five of us, among the tequila-puking teenagers from La Jolla careening in and out of open-air

285

discos with names like Señor Frog's Cantina. We stroll among the shops selling knockoff Harley-Davidson T-shirts, ceramic statuettes of cacti wearing sombreros, and dye-bleeding huarache sandals. The air is grayed by the smoke-belching trucks clogging every intersection. Diesel fumes and dust sear our lungs.

Randy doesn't mind that I'm planning to resume dancing full time, but I can tell he's a little tired of me running off without him. His face goes forcibly placid when the prospect of my leaving comes up. I think the crush he had on Barbie has waned and the run-off glamour is gone. "How much more?" he asked when he dropped me off at the airport shuttle, in a not-very-convincing attempt at sounding patient. Not much more, I assured him, rubbing his arm as if to stir up some faith from under his skin. I left him with a kiss and a promise to scope out the very best clubs so we can return on vacation after this is all over.

Practically every other shop on Revolución is a *farmacia*. The white-smocked pharmacists and clerks stand out front touting, in the exact same fashion as the men outside the nightclubs and the souvenir shops. "Best price, best price. Hey, Barbie," they motion to us. Barb bristles at the detested molestation of her name and I jump at the split-second thought that these men might know me from a strip club somewhere. "You come in, Barbie. Best price."

I used to make fun of the women who'd had so many facelifts they looked like their cheeks were stapled to the back of their head. Their vanity seemed ludicrous to me. Did they really think that they looked younger? Or that it looked natural? But somewhere along the way, it stopped being funny.

The window displays are brightly lit paeans to abundance and order. Stacks of three-pack asthma inhalers, rows of five-hundred-count bottles of ibuprofen, antibiotics of all kinds. Boxed tubes of

Retin A are arranged in pyramids right at the front of the store. Six bucks each, American. They're forty dollars at home. I buy two tubes.

We head back out onto the crowded sidewalk. A bedraggled, five-man mariachi band walks slowly by, their brown polyester suits too small, the soles of their shoes cracked and worn. "*Música?*" asks the accordion player, his face drawn and sunburned. We shake our heads no. He nods, adjusts his cowboy hat, and moves on.

"Well, I guess my mission is accomplished," I say to the assembled group. I had envisioned a long, laborious search culminating with a shady back-alley transaction with the illicit tubes handed off in a brown paper wrapper by people who first demanded a secret handshake. "What should we do now?"

The world, or more specifically, Tijuana is our oyster, as John and Barb both speak fluent Spanish. Barb is a droll, athletic strawberry blonde. John, an affable, loudmouth Marine with smiling brown eyes and a buzz cut. The designated muscle of the group.

I scan the street, looking past the men with Polaroid cameras trying to woo tourists to get their photo taken with glitter-encrusted sombreros and burros striped with paint to look like zebras. I see a neon sign advertising topless dancers. "Hey, strip club, dead ahead. You up for it?"

Affirmative from the entire posse. John and Barb are open-minded, up for anything. When John goes off to strip clubs with his buddies in L.A., Barb gives him money to buy rounds of table dances. Jeanette has no issues whatsoever with stripping—after she moved to Los Angeles six years ago, she briefly ran an outcall strip-o-gram service for women. Her boyfriend at the time was scandalized at first, but he got over it. And Sue, well, Sue is the mack daddy of all time. She and I "met" for the first time at the Lusty Lady when our friend Artemis brought her into a corner booth to say hello. Sue thought the big red Tawdry wig was my real hair and instantly fell in love with me. When they picked me up after work and I got in the car with my real, short brown hair, she was decidedly less enamored, but we have been

287

friends ever since. She has a way with strippers, a combination of genuine admiration and rogue flirtation that any male customer would kill to have. Get that girl in a strip club and every dancer in the place, straight, gay, bi, whatever, will make a beeline to her side.

We march into the dank tunnel of an entrance like an invading troop. The linoleum floor is covered with sticky black grit. "Yeesh," Jeanette says, as we enter the club and the noxious tang of dust, beer, mildew, and piss assaults our nostrils.

A host in a penguin suit shows us to a stageside table. The stage is a rickety wooden T-shaped platform about two feet high with a ring hanging from a chain over it. A flabby dancer with kinky hair that was peroxided from black to a brassy orange grabs the ring and goes up on one toe, spinning herself into a blur.

"That's cool," Sue says, excitedly. "We need to get you one of those!"

A waiter comes by and tells us there's a two-drink minimum. We place our order and dig out some singles for the dancer. This is a pretty miserable place and if we're going to be here, we should make it worth the dancers' time.

Two dancers come over to Sue and me. "Do you want a table dance?" asks the shorter one, who has flashing black eyes and a nervous, rabbity energy. Her friend, older and butchy-femme with cropped black hair and a cross tattooed on her hip, clasps her hands behind her back and rocks back and forth, one toe turned inward, as if under instruction to hide her coltishness under a layer of sugary pink frosting.

"No, thank you," I say. Sue smiles her best loveable urchin smile and tells her, "No, I'm sorry. But you're very pretty. Have you worked here long?"

The coltish girl walks away but the nervous girl sits down and curls up in Sue's lap. The bartender comes over and serves us our two-drink minimum drinks, both at once.

I look over at Jeanette. "Would you mind telling me how Sue

does that?" she asks, taking her margaritas from the bartender's tray and shaking her head in disbelief.

John, Barb, Jeanette, and I are chuckling at Sue's magnetism at work, then suddenly, a swarm of waiters is all over us, chattering quickly in Spanglish about how we underpaid and owe them ten more dollars. Barb is clearly annoyed. "What are you talking about?" she says to one of the waiters in stern English. He appears to be the ringleader of the scam, but he isn't a very good liar. He's trying to pretend that we stiffed them on our tab but he keeps screwing up his numbers and his story. The other waiters keep nodding and repeating what the ringleader said.

"Oh, the hell with it," Barb says, thrusting out a ten-dollar bill. "Will this take care of everything?"

"Four dollars more, miss. You owe four."

His grifting technique could stand some refinement. Shouldn't he wait until we're drunk before he tries this?

"No, I do *not* owe you four dollars," Barb says quite loudly. "I am giving you ten dollars and you asked for ten dollars and that is all you are getting from me!"

I have a fleeting vision of police being summoned and the five of us being hauled off to Mexican prison, but the waiter backs off.

Sue disappears into the corner with her new friend to make out. I tip the orange-haired girl onstage and she crawls off the stage and into my lap. I shriek in surprise when she lifts up my shirt and sticks her head underneath, loudly bussing my stomach.

"There aren't many customers in here," I say to Jeanette and Barb. "I wonder how the dancers make their money."

John comes back from his trip to the men's room. "Well, if what the girl who cornered me by the bathroom says is true, you can have sex in that corner over there for forty dollars. Without a condom."

We summon Sue from the corner posthaste and move on down the road. As we leave the club, one of the touts out front looks at

Barb and Jeanette and says, "Why are you leaving? Come back! I dance Chippendales for you!"

On the street, the air is warm and thick with music—from the disco bars, the mariachi bands, the stores. Auditory chaos comprised of the Bee Gees over marimbas over Casio drumbeats. A fat-kneed woman waddles by with a huge donkey *piñata* and her husband, bald and sway-bellied, drags two steps behind. He looks longingly into the stairwell of another strip club. "Come in, cowboy," the touts entice, but he shifts his gaze quickly and shuffles his feet to catch up with the missus.

We drop down the stairwell and find that this club is a little more upbeat. The ceiling is covered in helium-filled red-and-white balloons. The stage is very high—about eye-level with the men who sit around it. Dancers stomp back and forth along the length of the stage, occasionally spinning on the ring or twirling on the pole to unbearably loud heavy metal, their expressions a murk of grim determination and efficient, blasé sexuality that could pass for submission after several beers. The club is purportedly topless, but when taking tips, dancers indifferently pull their g-strings all the way down in front to allow the men to tuck their tips. If a few digits linger, they don't swat them away.

Just like the other bar, it's all big American boys being entertained by small Mexican women.

We order a scam-free bucket of *cervezas* and ten tequila shots for twenty-five bucks and settle in to watch the show. The beer mixed with the almost overpowering scent of air freshener makes me a little queasy, so I trundle up the trash-filled steps to the restroom, which has no running water and is so filthy it makes the nausea worse. I go back downstairs and suck on the limes from my untouched tequila to calm my stomach. The television in the corner is tuned to *Simpsons* reruns.

Around the perimeter of the room, girls are doing topless table dances for the men seated on the vinyl upholstered bench seats along the wall. A plush-bottomed girl with slightly deflated breasts is leaning over a table in the middle of a group of young, loud men in hip-hop clothes. As they rudely grope her ass and dare each other to press their crotches near her mouth, she keeps a patient face, like a noble old cat getting its tail pulled by children and lollipops stuck in its fur.

After dinner, we end up in a humid basement cavern that looks like a medieval dungeon with a stage and a go-go pole in it. A very pretty young dancer gets onstage in thigh-high red vinyl boots and a red bikini. She never looks at the audience. Not once. She dances well, but joylessly. When her set is done, she gets off the stage without so much as a smile or a glance back. She even leaves her tips onstage.

To the left of us sit a couple of retired military-looking guys. They're right at the edge of the stage, resting their elbows on the railing. The younger one pays more attention to his beer than the stage, but the older one, a thick-necked bruiser with a gray flattop, watches the dancers with a mean, rheumy eye. The corners of his mouth turn down sourly. When a dancer comes around to him and bends forward, presenting her buttocks for admiration, he rolls up a dollar and sticks it under the portion of the thong that covers her crotch. He tries to twist his finger inside of her.

He does it over and over, with every dancer.

"You know the fucked-up thing about that," John says, leaning over the table, speaking conspiratorially, "is he doesn't even look like he's enjoying himself."

He's right. The man might as well be putting quarters in a vending machine.

At the table to the right of us is a puppy pile of fresh-scrubbed, freckle-faced teenagers. J. Crew goes South of the Border. Liquored up and ready to roar, one of the girls hops onstage. She tosses her long blonde curls around and dances over to her group of friends. The stripper onstage stays on the other side, collecting tips.

Fists holding dollars thrust into the air from her friends' table. Men all around the bar are craning their necks to look at her. They want to see what she's got. She shyly unzips her jeans and shinnies them down to show her leopard-print thong. Her torso is thick, her hips narrow.

Her friends egg her on, so she takes off her sweatshirt. Her bra matches her panties.

"Oh, Victoria's Secret," Sue says, approvingly.

Jeanette leans over to me. "Now did she wear the matching underwear because she knew she was going to get up and do that, or does she always make sure she matches anyway?"

After the song ends, the girl joins her friends at the table. On my way to the bathroom, I tap her on the shoulder and tell her, Good job.

One of the guys in the group says, "Hey, when are *you* gonna get up there?"

Next thing I know, I am on a strip club stage in Tijuana with a stripper who hates my guts. She is not pleased to share her turf with an interloping *gringa*. The minute I get up there, she stalks over to me, unzips my jeans and yanks them down, then pulls my shirt off over my head. Not exactly the most effective way to embarrass me, but she has a point to make. Her hips switch angrily under her zebra print minidress as she dances to the opposite side of the stage, where she stays for the whole song.

I don't know why she didn't just say no when the manager asked if I could come up with her.

My jeans won't come off over my combat boots, so I pull them back up and keep dancing. The American kids are laughing and clapping. My bra and underwear don't match, but they tip me anyway. I work my way over to our table, where Jeanette, Barb, Sue, and John take turns stuffing dollars down my pants. I dance away, crunching with every step.

When the song ends, I get down and while I'm pulling on my shirt, the angry dancer sweeps up the tips I made and dumps them on our table. When I get offstage and John tells me what she did, I throw them right back on the stage. That'll teach her.

It's late and we've got to get going or I'll fall asleep at the wheel on the drive home.

As we rise from the table, another dancer comes over to me. She's flushed and a little embarrassed, the sweet fat roll of flesh about her hips jiggling with excitement. "Yes, congratulations. Yes, you want I am going up next. You dance with me?"

"I'm sorry," I tell her, shrugging and motioning no with my hands, "we really have to leave."

I would have liked to dance with a woman who actually wanted me there, but I'm tired and too put off by the bitchy dancer.

Well, I shouldn't be too hard on her. Maybe she was trying to make a political statement, something about the encroachment of white, American capitalists in the Third World.

I doubt it.

We cram into a cab that takes us back to the border crossing. John and Barb head off to their car on the Mexican side and Jeanette, Sue, and I wander back over the border to where we parked the car. A paved walkway curves over the highway that joins the U.S. and Mexico, and it's lined on both sides with beggars wrapped in blankets, holding out their hands to us as we pass by. Dirty-faced children in pajamas tug on our pant legs, trying to sell us Chiclets and beaded bracelets. We shower them with coins.

Even though it's obvious who shoulders the emotional and social burden in a strip-club transaction, I'm usually able to see it as more or less a square deal, tit for tat, as it were. But the whole Tijuana scene seemed deeply fucked up, a repository for Yankee sexual aggression. I bet those same men would never, ever treat American strippers so cavalierly. They might try, but they certainly wouldn't get away with it. If they went twenty miles north to San Diego and attempted what they did in Mexico, either the bouncers or the strippers themselves would cuff their ears and toss them out on the sidewalk.

When we get in the car, I clutch my bag of Retin A to my side and breathe a sigh of relief at being stateside.

Los Angeles is the land of the pussy killers—those little booty shorts that you have to wear whenever you're doing a table dance. They give you a frontal wedgie so bad you'd swear it was karmic payback.

I'm trying to find L.A.'s best topless club. I try a club on the west side first. While I'm in the dressing room, a Vietnamese girl wearing a junior prom updo approaches me with a snarl of a smile on her face, as I stand at the mirror applying black eyeliner with a small pointed brush.

"If someone asked you to, would you have sex for money?" She asks the question as if she's simultaneously trying to recruit and accuse me.

What the hell kind of question is that to ask someone you don't even know?

"Um, no," I tell her. "Why?"

"You wouldn't?" Her tone is incredulous.

"I don't think so."

She turns on her spiked heel and click-clacks abruptly out of the dressing room.

Weird.

On the dressing-room bulletin board is a flyer: "Are you working as a stripper and cheating on someone, and want to tell them?
Then call the Jerry Springer show at 1-800 . . ." I'd always wondered
where those guests came from. One mystery solved.

This club is severely bogus. Dead as a doornail. Nothing is
happening except two dancers hanging on either side of a balding,
middle-aged guy doing coke and drinking champagne in the VIP
room. I bail out just before midnight when I see one of the girls
start making out with the customer.

I try Crazy Girls, the Hollywood hotspot of the moment, but
when I stroll in at one a.m., it's too much of a pose—like the Viper
Room with tits. Models and rock stars languish in the booths as imitation White Trash girls and impeccably degenerate drugstore cowboys—faded Levi's, curled-up Resistol brims, Camels tucked into the
corners of their mouths—slouch into the alleyway for a smoke. The
dancers look fabulous, though. They're not generic McStrippers like
me, more like models on a glam-rock bender.

An inked and implanted giantess winds through the crowd on
the way to the small second stage in the center of the room. Her
aluminum-streaked kohl black hair curls over full-sleeve dragon
tattoos. Countless silver rings decorate her ears and fingers. The
hem of her transparent ruby chiffon dress flirts with the ankle straps
on her eight-inch platform shoes. A silver-studded black bikini
embraces her slender body beneath the dress. On her way past, she
fixes her haunted, almond-shaped brown eyes on me, leans down,
and whispers, "You look like you can feel my pain."

This dancer is a specter of Lotusland, one of the city's dark
damsels. I love these girls whose lives were cooked in the crucible
of underground L.A.. Girls like this know that the designer-water
health-consciousness and dogged optimism of this town is a cover-
up, that death and, perhaps worse, obscurity stalk you at every turn.
They know that the glittery orange haze that floats over the freeways
and down through the canyons at night is made of the ghosts of

would've-been stars and hopefuls who never had a prayer. Such morbidity only heightens their beauty.

I grab her hand, strangely flattered that she would pick me out of all the female customers in the place to say this to. With the biggest Honey of the Heartland smile I can muster, I say, reassuringly, "Sweetie, I've known your pain for the last eleven years."

The next evening, Jeanette and I go to Jumbo's Clown Room, which has been a Hollywood Boulevard hangout since the 1970s. It's a tiny dump off of a parking lot, unselfconsciously seedy in a self-conscious way. There's a small stage and a bar surrounded by tables jam-packed with all types of people I wouldn't want to be naked in front of.

Jumbo's has enjoyed a bleeding-edge renaissance ever since it became known that Courtney Love used to work there. But there are a couple of clubs around town claiming to be her ecdysiast alma mater. "Courtney Love stripped here" is the alterna-kid equivalent to "George Washington slept here." I wonder sometimes if there isn't a whole crop of young Hole fans out there, stockpiling their PVC miniskirts and bustiers in preparation for the day that they get up on the strip club stage to emulate their idol. They'd learn quickly enough that stripping doesn't make you Courtney Love any more than doing heroin makes you Keith Richards or wearing a spangly jumpsuit makes you Elvis.

As we shuffle toward the door, slowly, since the club is very crowded, a long-haired guy by the bar presses his business card into my palm with an unctuous, "I'd love to photograph you sometime." I look at the card. It says, ROB SALTER, BARTENDER/PHOTOGRAPHER.

"Gee, which one do you think is his real calling?" Jeanette cracks as I rip the card in two.

Los Angeles is not a lucrative stripping town if you don't dance nude. The girls who are very serious about making money fly to

Vegas or Texas. I can't figure out why there wouldn't be much money in a city this populated, but Jeanette has a theory. "Consider this: Men go to strip clubs because they want to see beauty. But beauty means nothing in Los Angeles," she says. "Beautiful people come here from all over to make it big in show business. Then they don't make it, so they marry another beautiful person and make more beautiful people. You become immune."

"Look at this," Jeanette says, flipping to the back of the *L.A. Weekly*. Page after page of ads for escort services and call girls. "Look at these women," she gestures with a quick swooping flourish of her hand. I scan the photos on the page. They're all gorgeous, it's true.

"And look at the ad copy," she adds. " 'My actual photo. No driver. No agency.' So you can have your pick of any number of model-types, any way you want them. Why would you bother going to a strip club when you could have this? I'm telling you—you really do become immune. You never truly understand what 'just another pretty face' means until you come to Los Angeles."

Still, somebody must be making money stripping in Los Angeles, because the shops on Hollywood Boulevard that used to sell rocker clothes and leather jackets are all dedicated to "dancer wear" now. There are tons of them!

I spend an afternoon shopping for new costumes with Sue by my side. Some people bring a sensible, conservative friend with them when they shop so they have someone to rein them in. Not me. Sue is my fashion enabler. She's just there to "ooh" appreciatively and help me carry the bags.

Within a few hours, we've acquired a pair of pink glittered mules with Lucite six-inch platform heels. Pink patent sling-back platforms. Furry leopard-print platforms. Red-and-white gingham checked sandals. Booty shorts in hot pink, and shiny gold and silver.

A leopard-print bikini. A long, shimmering gold gown with spaghetti straps. A black shortie corset-topped dress with pink roses on it. A white stretch lace slip with gathered puffed sleeves and red rosette trim. And an iridescent bubble-gum-pink backless minidress that matches the glittered mules.

On the north side of the street is Je T'aime, another dance-wear boutique, where I find a canary-yellow long-sleeved mesh romper with a neckline trimmed in yellow feathers, cut all the way down to the navel. Big Bird gone porno. It's too small so Uli, the store manager, offers to make me one in my size. I leave him my measurements and a forty-dollar deposit.

Just up the street Sue and I find a pair of platform Lucite mules with canary yellow marabou poufs over the toe. There's one pair left, and they're my size. And they're on sale! It's kismet.

By the end of the afternoon I have spent over nine hundred dollars. Dolly Parton wasn't kidding when she said, "It takes a lot of money to look this cheap." Not to worry, I tell myself, costumes are tax deductible.

I finally find the best club in Los Angeles. Way down on Hollywood Boulevard, almost in Silverlake. Cheetah's. When I walk in, it's like the fifties brought back to life. The walls are mirrored, the upholstery red. The stage is a little T with a runway and a pole at either end. The border of the stage is lit in tiny white lights. It's small and intimate, total Rat Pack cool.

When the manager takes me into the back office to do my paperwork, I look up at the Polaroids of the dancers. You know a place is going to be great when there are half a dozen Bettie Page look-alikes.

This is a place where a girl can dance to Marilyn Manson one set and Dwight Yoakam the next, and the audience will appreciate both. The crowd is young and trendy, but the lighting is so flattering and the atmosphere so relaxed, I don't mind having an audience of my own at all.

The deejay, a large, ponytailed guy wearing a T-shirt that says, I DO WHATEVER THE LITTLE VOICES IN MY HEAD TELL ME, lets me flip though his collection of CDs. I have to make sure my music is just right; Sue and Julie and a couple other friends of mine are coming in to watch me dance.

By the time they show up, I've watched a full rotation of the girls. My God, what a show! I've seen hiphop mamas in hot pants and eight-inch platforms, pole monkeys in Catholic schoolgirl outfits climbing all the way up to the ceiling to "I Love Little Girls" by Oingo Boingo, and a tattooed supermodel-y girl dancing to "Jesus Built My Hotrod" by Ministry.

I don't know how the money is here, but the stage show is excellent.

You know what's different about this place? The sense that everybody's trickin'. That get-over Scarlett was talking about—Us vs. Them? Here tonight it's all Us. Does this louche equanimity foretell a new wave of striptease? I doubt it—the business survives on skillful manipulation and if everyone were in on the scam, stripping would quickly become obsolete, collapsed by its own knowingness. No, this is an ethereal space—more like a clubhouse than a grindhouse.

My friends gather around the stage when I come on. I'm wearing the silver booty shorts over a silver bikini, and the silver stilettos to match. My music is by Tool, a fierce, driving song. Industrial Strength Barbie. I stalk the stage, pacing and twisting, then smiling serenely at a bunch of customers clustered at the corner of the stage. One by one, the seats along the runway fill up.

I walk deliberately to the end of the runway and kick my legs up over my head and catch my ankles around the pole, like I learned at stripper school. I put my hands on the stage and just hold the headstand, my long blonde hair trailing on the floor. I nod my head as I listen to the music.

Whatever compulsion I've got that makes me love stripping, this is what it sounds like. I don't know if it's skill, comfort, risk, dissociation, or a combination of them all that, in rare moments, makes stripping seem like a borderline ecstatic state. But I know I'm having one of those moments now. When it just feels right. Righteous. At times like this, I can believe that I have all the hearts in the room gathered into the palm of my hand. I will never get old. I will never know harm. As long as I stay on this stage under the benevolent auspices of darkness, everything will be okay.

I suddenly understand what Pillow was describing to me when I was in Alaska. That rush. That blue bolt high. It's like I'm suspended in a narcotic bubble, yet I'm more fiercely aware and alive than I've ever felt. I come out of the handstand and walk toward the center of the stage, loosening the string at the neck of my bikini top. I turn and gaze down at all the faces smiling up at me. They seem very far away, and yet very much a part of the rarefied space I'm in, clearly present and totally gone all at once. It's indescribable bliss resting on the blade of a knife, the most strange and foreign place I was ever meant to be. I would be helpless to try to explain it, but if you had ever known that sensation, you'd never want to leave that warm, wet spot on the lip of the maw.

TWENTY

Gypsy Rose Lee Doesn't
Live Here Anymore

Early the next day, after Jeanette has left for work, I sit at the bat-
tered wooden desk in her living room waiting for my laptop to boot
up. The white-gray morning light shines through the vertical blinds
casting long strips of shadow on the teal carpet. I carefully examine
my face in my compact admiring how nicely the skin is peeling
around my nose and mouth. This Retin A stuff really works! I am
exfoliating my way to protracted youth.

I check my email and there's a message from Pillow. *There's*
someone I've not heard from in a while. I open it right away.

> Hey everybody. Usually I hate "spam" but this situation
> is kinda urgent.
> I hope to get the word out to ALL of my friends in time
> so that they can come visit me at work and catch a last show.
> Please pass this message along.

I'm incredibly sad to inform everyone that I'm leaving PJ's in a few days. I have worked there on and off since 1978, enjoying dancing so much that the sheer kinetic joy and endorphin fix has outweighed any of the "yucky stuff" I've encountered in the club along the way. Many times when I was onstage, the world and its worries would melt away. I guess I took it all for granted, since it was so frequent. I realize ninety-nine percent of you have no idea what I am talking about, but this immediate and ephemeral "high" would carry me over the rough spots in my day to day existence. Sounds like dope? I guess it is. I've kicked a lot of crap that I am not proud of, but this is one jones I am terrified to face. Bone deep? No, soul deep.

Yeah, PJ's is a dive, but it was MY dive, more like my living room than a workplace (okay, so the remote was stuck on some awful cable access channel). I carved a comfortable niche in this obnoxious, smoky cluster of dysfunctional people. I will miss them. I've worked through the years in this "industry," in all its weird, wild incarnations. With red eyes, I witnessed "progress" improve it all to hell, cursing and gnashing my teeth at the great amorphous "Them" as exotic dancing changed from the wonderful thing I've always aspired to— the style of my mentors. Then the compromises, first one thing . . . then another . . . some of the awful changes I could handle, as long as I could maintain my own boundaries and they would just let me dance! I have no illusions that my dancing is technically anything special. Yet it WAS special, to me. But some conditions just are not negotiable. The final showdown is "Me" vs. "The Pole." And I lost.

I will not be able to dance with a pole in the middle of the stage. No traveling spins, half my show incorporates some kind of cape, scarf, or duster work that would be impossible with a physical obstacle in the center of the space. I won't be able to do the "Robot" show (which I did blind, navigating the stage only because I KNEW that stage so well). No, I could not bear to be on that stage, hobbled.

Hence this message. I will be doing some of my shows tomorrow night, and maybe, if I am lucky, that stupid pole they ordered will be late on delivery giving me another few nights to dance. After that, it's over . . .

Please, if you are in any way inclined to come to the club, stop by to say "Hello" and "Goodbye" . . . I really could use some moral support now.

This bites.
Pillow

Oh dear. Oh no. This is a dark day for purists. And for Pillow. What will she do now? I write a quick reply to ask what happened, and to wish her the best. She writes back saying two new girls came down to the club from Fairbanks, and would only stay if Hallie put a pole on the stage. Despite Pillow's protestations, he agreed. And Pillow balked.

This seems like such an unceremonious end—to be chased off the stage by a silly brass pole! But I understand why Pillow finds the presence of the pole untenable—she'd set her standards years ago, only to watch them get challenged, and her options thus narrowed, as the years went by. And now things have changed once again and she's faced with her own personal titty bar Waterloo.

I drive up to Hollywood Boulevard to pick up my Big Bird suit. In J'Ataime, there are two almost identical-looking young blondes pawing though a rack of fluorescent-colored baby-Ts with SLUT written across the front. Their jaw muscles bunch and churn as they talk loudly, working their gum, and their bony shoulder blades poke out like bird wings under the straps of their polyester tank tops.

Uli brings the yellow feathered suit from the back, wrapped in plastic and draped on a wire hanger. "Try it on. See if it fits, please."

I take the hanger from him.

"Oh, that's cute," says one of the blondes, noticing the feathers as I walk by. Her deeply tanned breasts stand out from her ribcage like stiff globes.

On the wall in the dressing room is a poster for a dancewear company. Three girls with teased hair wearing spandex racing check costumes, smiling with their acrylic nails in their mouths and making that "Oooh, baby" porn face.

I pull up the suit and look at myself in the mirror, bright yellow feathers wreathing my neck, then plunging down to my navel. See-through yellow mesh encasing my arms, torso, and buttocks. And sweat socks.

I think of Pillow, imagine her cleaning out her locker at PJ's, sorting shoes and g-strings and gloves. Folding up her capes. My eyes flicker back to the spandex girls on the wall sucking their fingers.

A cheesy heavy metal relic from 1988 bangs out, tinny and aggressive, from the store radio.

Inexplicably, the dressing room goes screwy and twisted. The lights seem too bright, the feathers on my skin too hot. I'm afraid I might pass out.

What am I doing? What the hell am I doing?

You have to stop stripping eventually. At some point you're going to get pushed to the side by something, or someone. That is, if you don't jump first. Jump or get pushed—those are your choices as to how to leave this business. Either way, you can't hang around forever. So take your pick.

I'm in that golden stretch of adulthood—I know where the pitfalls are and I've made enough dumb mistakes to know better than to make them again, but I can still get away with a lot. I can dance around on a stage in a see-through porno Big Bird outfit without someone rolling his eyes and whispering, "Who does granny think she's kidding?" And somehow the realization that the suspended adolescence that is exotic dancing won't last forever makes it all the more fun.

But this new development with Pillow forces me to reconsider my own career mortality—and how hopped up I'd become to defy it. The more I think about it, the less I like the idea of draining this stripping thing to the dregs, of dancing on till the very last. Yes, I've got plenty of time left—probably more than I'd ever want or need. But while I've got health and enthusiasm and gravity on my side, I think I'd rather apply them toward something else, something that feels less brutal. Less finite. There are more adventures to be had. More places to see, more people to meet, more pet theories to test. But, well, so what? None of this changes the fact that if I return to stripping full-time, and forgo writing, I won't be reconciling my past. I'll be living it.

Concerned civilians caution that exotic dancing isn't glamorous. But they're wrong. It *is* glamorous—there are pretty costumes, loud music, the flash of big bills, the affirmation of lingering gazes. To say nothing of the irresistible glimmer of risk. But glamour, by definition, is an illusion. A spell. A state of suggestion. It wears off eventually and you find yourself—peeling skin on your face and all, standing in your old socks in a cheesy Hollywood spandex emporium wearing what looks like an aborted attempt at a Mummer's costume.

A woman playing the role of girl.

You've had a good run, doll. Don't push it.

For whatever may lie ahead, the end seems rather predictable. Suddenly I feel very tired. I don't have much energy but I think I should fix for a jump. Time to go home.

Uli's on the other side of the dressing room curtain. "Miss! Your suit, does it fit?"

This is a custom-made garment. I already put down a nonrefundable deposit, and I have to take it.

"Just perfect, Uli," I yell through the red velvet. "I'll pay for it upfront."

TWENTY-ONE

Hello, Sacred? This is Profane

"What's the matter, baby? You look so sad!"

Randy stands in the entrance to the living room, his wet hair combed back. He drops his black nylon gym bag at his feet.

I sit curled in a lethargic ball on the green velvet recliner. Ever since I came home from L.A. a week ago, I've been feeling out of sorts. I know my decision to stop dancing was the right one, but the change in course was so abrupt I'm a little whipsawed. I've been groping for a conclusion, a way to bring this an elegant close. I'm feeling the impulse to reach out to someone to help me make sense of things but I'm afraid.

I'm fortunate to be surrounded by plenty of sympathetic people. My parents. My mate. My friends. Any of them would be happy to lend some support. But they're not who I want to call. The person who can help me the most is the one who, through it all, understood the least about what stripping means to me.

"Hey," I say when I get my sister Barbara on the phone. "I'm having a minor spiritual crisis. Can you help?"

No sense mincing words.

Barbara laughs for a second, startled. "What kind of spiritual crisis?"

"The dancing thing," I tell her. "I'm finished traveling and I just don't know what to *do* with this stuff. I need to close the deal here."

"Aha." I picture her scratching her chin while she sits back on the couch in her living room, one eye on the television. "I see."

Am I going to regret this? I fight the urge to hang up. The phone feels heavy in my hand.

"So," I ask. "Can I come out for a visit? Can you help?"

Good girl. Keep on. She's blood, not a hanging judge.

"Sure, come on out. I'll pick you up at the airport, it's only five minutes from my house. You can help me with Mom and Dad's anniversary quilt."

"I don't know anything about quilting!"

"Hasn't stopped me yet."

Barbara is eight years older than I. I remember thinking her oddly hip when she was a teenager wearing a Nabokov T-shirt, listening to B. J. Thomas, and getting into arguments with our mother that ended with Mom saying, "But the world isn't always black and white, Barbara!" then drawing deeply from the straw in her take-out diet soda, annoyed. Then Barbara was off at seminary school and living up near Columbia University. The next thing I knew, she was being ordained as a Presbyterian minister in upstate New York, moving into a world largely beyond my reach, as ever. Now she lives in a small Midwestern city, where she teaches a philosophy class at the local university and preaches to two different congregations every Sunday.

• • •

My family is religious but I wouldn't say *strictly* religious, because there isn't much about our stripe of Presbyterianism that's strict. Sinners aren't threatened with damnation, they're broken down with reason.

In the 1970s, blue-jean Christianity hit our church pretty hard. The teenagers would load up rucksacks and march off on youth-group retreats and stage musicals for the congregation. My sisters performed in the musical version of the story of Shadrach, Mesach, and Abednego called "Cool in the Furnace."

My religion is buried deep in the most private memories of childhood, in the same place that people guard their invisible friend or their conversations with trees. Now and then, in some unexpected situation—a trivia game, a discussion of college theater exploits—someone will sing a bit from the *Godspell* soundtrack and cut right into my secret heart. I can unleash an earful of screed about God the Corporation, and thieving, holier-than-thou zealots, but my personal recollections of church and organized religion are actually pretty good.

Barbara's living room floor is covered in colored file folders overflowing with personal papers, boxes, striped throw pillows that have fallen from whatever chair or couch they were sitting on, and back issues of *The New Republic*.

She brings the quilt in from the dining room. It's stunning, a dark emerald green with pink calico and white squares. She shows me the squares she's making, one for each parent, a ring square with their wedding date embroidered on it, and a square for each child with our names embroidered under a flower.

"See, here's a lily for you. A forget-me-not for Tad because that seems like a sort of masculine flower, a pansy for Annette because they're pretty but sturdy, and violets for Kelly because they're dainty and sweet. And poppies for me"—she pauses for a beat—"because religion is the opiate of the people!"

My sister, the original Christian stitch.

Barbara is nearsighted, and often goes without her glasses, so she tends to squinch up her eyes when you're talking to her. But even with her glasses on she looks like she's squinting from a place deep within herself. She gives the impression of constantly exerting effort to get things into better focus, to bring her senses to bear on what someone is really trying to convey. She is a very deep listener. This is what makes her a good person.

Sometimes I'm jealous of Barbara and I don't even know it. I say something fresh when I'm around her, and I'm suddenly taken aback: Hey, where did that come from? I truly envy her clarity regarding right and wrong. She's got guidance, a deeply entrenched system of belief. She doesn't seem to wrestle with ambiguity the way that I do. I've got a definite moral center, but there's a lot of wiggle room around it. I don't envy her everything, though. I think she gets lonely sometimes. She'd like to get married and have children, but it's hard to meet people, surely harder for her than for most. "Mentioning that you're a minister is a pretty effective way to kill a hot tub conversation," she has said.

Barbara wakes me bright and early Sunday so we can get ready for church. It's been a long time since I've attended services. The drive to her first service takes us out of the city and into the next county, endless verdant, Cheeveresque spans of open pasture and horse farms. Humidity is already leaching into the air—I'd never realized how heavily mornings in the Midwest can hang on you.

Atop a pretty knoll stands the one-room church. Inside, the plaster walls glow the color of ancient parchment. There is no stained glass, just tall, simple Palladian windows with slender dark walnut mullions in the form of a cross. The church is empty, so I leave Barbara to put on her vestments and step outside to explore the graveyard.

Amid the graves is a stand of old pines, listing west as the wind blows. The grass makes a lush, barefoot-soft carpet. A weathered headstone, blackened with age, reads, "Remember man as you pass by, As you are now so once was I. As I am now, so you must be." The date on the stone, I can barely make out, is 1767.

The church bell rings—my sister pulling on the rope that drapes down and coils round on the floor of the narthex. I head up the slope and enter the church, where the parishioners have gathered in the pews, all twelve of them.

The third Sunday after Easter is "sheep Sunday," with a call for a sermon about Jesus and his flock, and the need for resistance to false voices.

"What do you get when a minister blesses a flock?" Barbara asks from her pulpit.

The congregation shrugs.

"Pastor-ized sheep."

The congregation groans.

I swear my sister is a bad sitcom waiting to happen.

After joining in the singing of "Savior, Like a Shepherd Lead Us," Barbara begins talking about our need for inclusion.

"My feeling is, we never get beyond third grade. When I was young, my family moved a lot. I remember being in third grade, on my first day in a new school, standing in the cafeteria with my lunch tray. I was thinking, Who will I sit with? Will someone invite me to their table?" She goes on to draw the parallel between our child selves seeking belonging among classmates, and our spiritual selves wandering in search of flock and shepherd. She segues into God's appeal to resist the false voices and bad shepherds that lead people away from the truth.

Everyone sits in rapt attention. I stare down at my church program, biting my lip, cheeks hot, flushing with sisterly pride. This is good stuff. Preaching that's nonpreachy.

Another town, another service. The elderly congregation closes the cloth-covered hymn books and awaits communion. I haven't taken communion since I was twenty. It was at Barbara's ordination, actually. I showed up with spiky orange hair and honored her request to play "Be Thou My Vision" on the flute. I notice that the cover of today's church program is inscribed with Proverbs 31:30. "A woman that feareth the Lord shall be praised." Did she have that put on there for my benefit?

For the second time today, I stand and confess with a churchful of people, "Good Shepherd, we have wandered down the strange pathways of our world. We have ventured into dead-end streets that looked more inviting than the narrow ways marked out by the signposts of your love . . ."

Barbara breaks the bread and the distribution of elements begins—first, a small silver dish containing spongy cubes of white bread, then, clear plastic thimble-sized glasses of grape juice. I roll the bread between my fingers, releasing its subtle smell of yeast and expiation. When Barbara says, "Taste and see that the Lord is good," I tuck the bread under my tongue. There's no bolt of lightning. No voice from on high booming, *You're joking, right?!*

Come dinnertime, my sister and I sit in a booth at a Mexican restaurant with our elbows propped on the table, digging eagerly into our enchilada and burrito platters. A TV in the corner broadcasts a Telemundo soap opera at top volume, which competes with the Top Forty music piped in from the stereo. Latin drama versus bad alternative metal, neither of which appear to be winning. Flustered waiters reel around the tables, dispensing chips and ice water, and salsa verde out of quart carafes.

I wind stringy melted cheese around my fork. "So I spent months and months traversing this fine land of ours and I'm feeling done. But I have this left-over baggage that I don't know what to do with."

Barbara scoops up some guacamole with a half-eaten corn chip. "Have you thought of doing a ritual?"

"No, actually. Is there a decrepit old 'ho ritual that I don't know about that will make this go away?"

"No, but you could create one for yourself. When a woman I know turned fifty, she had a croning ritual with her friends. Whenever you do a ritual, it's important to have people around you so you can share your story."

"Can't I do something by myself?"

"Well, the presence of other people is what gives a ritual its power."

The waiter huffs over, green and red salsa stains on his white shirt, and drops off our check.

"I'll get it," I say, snatching the bill from Barbara's hand.

We sit down in front of the television with the quilt and Barbara teaches me how to "stitch in the ditch," sewing in a single, straight line around the border of a square to create that puffed-up quilted look.

The stitches have to be small and meticulously placed at the very edge of the white squares or else the white thread will show up in the green border fabric. I get halfway around the inside of the wedding ring square when my thread gets tangled in an irreversible knot. I mutter under my breath.

"See, you're learning," says Barbara, rummaging on the cluttered end table to find the embroidery scissors for me. "A major component of quilting is the cursing."

We stitch along in silence, with me working the ditches and Barbara embroidering more names under the flowers. I figure out that small stitches yield the puffiest results.

"That looks really good," Barbara says. She still talks to me like an older sister, as if I need encouragement and extra care. I like it. "So what did you want to talk about?"

"I don't regret dancing," I tell her, cutting fresh thread from the spool. "And I always thought 'ignorance is bliss' seemed really iffy but I wonder if everything I've been exposed to isn't too much for me to handle."

"I know what you mean," Barbara says, "*'I wish my eyes had never been opened.'*"

"Is that from the Bible?"

"No, the Indigo Girls."

"I'm trying to view everything in a positive light, because I don't want to stay as ambivalent as I am. There's this New Age-y philosophy that 'energy follows thought . . . '"

"Yeah," Barbara interrupts, "that's called prayer."

"Really?"

"Really. Do you pray?"

"No. And I'd feel weird praying. I don't want to ask God to help me!"

"Why not?"

Good question. Why not? I guess I'd feel selfish praying for something as trivial as peace of mind when I could be praying for an end to world hunger.

"Think of Saint Augustine. He had problems with behaving himself sexually, so he prayed, 'God, give me chastity but not yet.'"

I don't want to repent. Repent! What a scary word. I always associate it with hateful extremists—fire and brimstone and burning pits in hell. In San Francisco, there's this street preacher, well, not a preacher, exactly, more of a visual proselytizer. He is a clean-cut young white guy, in his mid-thirties maybe, who stands at the corner of Fifth and Market wearing a sandwich board that reads, FALLEN,

FALLEN IS BABYLON THE GREAT. . . . Like the Brown twins or Caffe Trieste, this fellow is a San Francisco institution. He stands, stock still and silent, in the same spot every day, rain or shine, with his laminated forecast of doom for the unrepentant. The tide of the sidewalk churns around him. Skateboarders ripping by. Shoppers juggling bags, slices of pizza, cups of designer coffee. Jabbering tourists fumbling with maps and running for the cable car. Amid it all, his placards entreat: Repent, ye sinners, fags, dykes, tramps, druggies, hippies, and freaks. Basically, my ilk is in for it. Down the street a ways from him, closer to the cable car turnaround, rages an older black guy with a bullhorn, yelling his head off about whores and plague and pestilence. There's something about AIDS in there, too. And he also makes a big appeal to repent. Conformity is the way of the Lord, is the tacit message, so I've always thought of repentance as requiring the complete negation of my identity. The Big Stick school of salvation.

"I don't want to disavow what I did," I say to Barbara, "like, oh, stripping isn't useful to me anymore so I reject it whole cloth, even the things that I liked."

"But that's not what repentance is," she tells me. " 'Repent' comes from a Latin word meaning 'to face another direction.' It means acknowledging that what you've been doing isn't working for you any longer, and trying something else."

So maybe those men trying to save Babylon by the Bay are misguided. And maybe, for me, repentance isn't out of the question.

"I think Jesus always had a soft spot in his heart for women like strippers," Barbara muses. "The people who profit off them is who he had the real issues with."

I picture Jesus in a strip club. Would he get into it? Would he sit at the rail and tip? No, he'd probably be the guy at the bar who's always giving the girls free backrubs.

I had better stop thinking of Jesus like this or God is totally going to kick my ass.

"I don't really think people using each other as objects for gratification is good," Barbara says.

"But it's not always like that," I counter, an unexpected edge appearing in my voice, "sometimes the men who come in just want someone to talk to."

"Hey, how come you can talk about the bad things about stripping, but whenever I say anything bad, you get defensive?"

Welcome to my world, sis.

Later that night after Barbara has gone to bed, I sit cross-legged on the bed in her guest room, reading the Bible. The air is heavy and still, almost oppressive with the scent of night-blooming flowers. Coming through my Walkman is rap bastardization of a Gordon Lightfoot song that depresses me.

When I read a passage like Proverbs 5:3-4, *"For the lips of a strange woman drop as an honey comb, and her mouth is smoother than oil; But her end is bitter as wormwood, sharp as a two-edged sword. Her feet go down to death; the steps take hold on hell,"* something so saturated with fear and hatred of female sexuality, I want to run off and join the Strange Women's Union: Hoydens, Harlots, and Sluts, Local 666-69, pronto.

Clearly, I'm going to have to evaluate and assimilate this Bible thing piecemeal.

I hear the night breeze in the trees outside the window and even though the room is hot I am chilled. I wrap the blanket around my shoulders, and hug my knees to my chest, feeling very alone. Going to church today has something to do with it, I'm sure. Realizing that there's a whole other world out there from which you are totally estranged is always a lonely discovery.

I don't think I'm going to find what I need in these gilt-edged pages.

Prayer, it is said, is the last refuge of the scoundrel, and don't I know it. At five in the morning as I lie flat on my back in the spare bedroom in my sister's house, I say a prayer of thanks that nothing terrible ever happened to me when I stripped. A prayer of comfort for the lonely. A prayer of hope for the lost. And a prayer of well-being for the dancing girls of America, who right now are either out seeking redemption after-hours, or sleeping the sleep of the just.

When I wake in the morning, Barbara has already left for work. The house is quiet and cool.

I pad down the stairs and out the back door. The yard brims with plants busying themselves with the tasks of renewal. Pink roses along the driveway fence itching to burst into bloom, red petunias in white plastic hanging baskets challenging the rim of their container, and stands of hardy purple iris splaying their petals toward the sun.

A good day for a ritual. Maybe the presence of others magnifies a ritual's power, but I would rather do this by myself. Stripping turns the private into the public, and I would like this to be just for me. I don't want any chanting or wax figures or anything else that might make what I'm about to do feel like neo-Pagan corn. I'm self-conscious about this as it is. Organization is my preferred form of sacred practice—everything in its place. Disorganization is the sign of an unquiet mind, as I know very well, and I would like to do what I can to shut things up in there. (*"When I kept silence, my bones waxed old through my roaring all the day long."* Psalm 32.)

On a scrap of paper, I write the three most valuable qualities I developed by being a stripper.

Nerve

Empathy

Charisma

I take this scrap and tuck it into my wallet behind my driver's license, so I'll carry it with me everywhere I go.

On another scrap of paper, I write down the three things that stripping brought me that I would most like to get rid of:

Weight

Defensiveness

Obligation

Oh, the weight. To lose the excess intangible weight, the gross psychic tonnage I've accumulated. All the naked pain I've seen and taken on. And shame. And guilt. How bad I should feel is relative, I know. I'm not Ivan Boesky or Attila the Hun or Doctor Laura. I didn't steal or kill or spread bigotry in the guise of righteousness so I don't have cause to self-flagellate. But for so long, I wouldn't for one second cop to guilt or shame or a sense of wrongdoing and now this residual gunk has worked its way to the surface. These emotions are not all that I am, but they're in there. I'd like to get them out. For good.

I am desperate to get rid of the defensiveness. There are innumerable people at whom I could shake my fist, there's always an attack or a perceived threat from one side or another. But I don't want to leave behind a trail of blame, accusations of who used who, and who had it worse, because that serves no one. Here there is no constructive element to contempt.

And I'd like to bid good riddance to the feeling of obligation. A sense of duty to make the job okay. To reason away the inconsistencies and struggles until I've diluted stripping to prurient pap. Six years of selective focus and one year of concentrated attention, and stripping still won't parse as benign.

I tear the three words free of one another, then take the lighter I keep in my makeup bag for melting my eyeliner pencil and set fire to these three scraps of paper in the sink.

The smoke detector in the dining room goes off, emitting a series of loud, shrill beeps. I jump on a chair waving a magazine in front of it to get the smoke to dissipate enough for the racket to stop.

I scrape the wet ashy scraps from the bottom of the sink basin, carry them to the back door, and toss them into the bed of irises off the side of the back porch.

The popular image of the sex worker is changing. If in more cautious times we needed the "fallen woman" archetype—she who strays from propriety and is socked with shame, regret, and ruin—to keep the family together and the social order intact, now we need the brazen capitalist whore to lead the way toward cannier over-achievement. As she saucily maneuvers to improve her lot, her shamelessness absolves us of our own shame, her pluck affirms our ambitions. Maybe the sense of obligation to act as if I am her is my false voice, and she is my false idol. Or rather, she was. I disappeared her from my life in a blaze of holy purging fire, and her ashy remains I laid to rest among the irises.

The kicker is that I *am* one of the success stories. I entered the sex industry at a young age and came out the other side with a decent career, a home, a stable family life, friends, loyal partner, no sub-stance abuse problem. Such as can be done, I did everything right. And this business still kicked my ass sideways.

I don't want to leave ungraciously, to turn up my nose—"watch the halo, hon"—as I waltz out of this cul-de-sac and on with my life. I don't ever want to disparage a dancing girl. If someone were to tell me that stripping is the best job she's ever had, I'd give her the bene-fit of the doubt. I don't know for sure that I'd be better off had I not done it. I might have been worse. I'm sure I'd be much more of a snob. I hope I never claim superiority to my past.

And I hope striptease sticks around. In his book of interviews with exotic dancers, *Some of My Best Friends Are Naked*, writer Tim

Keefe asks a dancer named Lillith what she thought exotic dance would be like in an ideal world.

She speculates that in the perfect world, dancing wouldn't exploit either party, that it might not exist solely as a commercial enterprise. She ends her conjecture with, "Whatever happens, long live the dance."

Yes. Long live the dance.

I'm starting to think that closure is a lie. And if closure isn't a lie, then it's definitely something that resists appearing on demand. There is no Cathart-o-Matic that you can crank up and watch your unfinished business settle itself while you wait. A couple years ago I was distraught over how quickly time passed. And now here I am wishing I could do something to speed it up. Heal faster, dammit!

I don't feel resolved, but I do feel like it's time to pack it in. I've come to the conclusion that exotic dancing is the hardest work I've ever done. Not the least gratifying, by a long shot—scrubbing toilets and sacking groceries tie for that honor—but it put me through the most contortions, knocked me for the biggest loop. Stripping left the biggest mark on my soul. To me, dancing has been a lot of things, but I can no longer truthfully say it was "just a job."

Had I known at eighteen that I'd still be struggling to sort out stripping more than a decade later, would I have even bothered?

When she drops me off at the airport, Barbara says, "I hope you feel less frustrated soon."

"I'll be all right," I tell her. Which sounds like a crock, but I think it's the truth, pretty much.

Before I get out of the car, Barbara gives me a book on women's Christianity. Published in 1984, before political correctness was even called political correctness, the book stresses inclusive, non-sexist terms for worship.

I browse through the pages while I wait at the boarding gate for my row number to be called. Some of the suggestions for the renaming of "God" are The Source, Lady of Birth, Consoler, Mother, Healer, Giver and Taker, Bakerwoman.

Oh, brother. I am not calling *anything* Bakerwoman, supreme deity or not. But I'm not dismissing faith out of hand. I wouldn't turn my back on God because of an aesthetic technicality.

I could start my own denomination: The Church of Fabulosity. Our Lady of Glam. Post-Punk Jesus and His Egalitarian Crankster Love Posse.

Or maybe I'll take up yoga.

I board the plane and buckle myself into my seat. I put on my headphones until the flight attendant asks that "all portable electronic devices be turned to the off position until ten minutes after take-off." Here we go—cleared and heading home. I gained perspective, but I didn't transcend jack squat, and I can't say I'm not disappointed about that. I wanted an inarguable bottom line, a picture-perfect ending, an epiphanic bang and not a whimper. But right now, what I have instead, courtesy of my Walkman, is the Gospel According to Saint Osbourne. He sings out about two things that don't exist—indisputable truth, and the fountain of youth.

That's for sure, Ozzy. That is for certain sure.

TWENTY-TWO

The Thong Must Go On

If the journey home always seems shorter than the journey out, then why is unpacking harder than packing?

For days, the floor in the extra bedroom has been covered with piles of costumes and shoes—the leopard-print thong is tangled around the black beaded evening gown, a plastic grocery bag stuffed with bikinis and booty shorts disgorges its contents through a huge tear made by an escaped underwire, a gold stiletto nuzzles toe-to-toe with a pink glittered platform mule like they're kissing. The closet doors are obscured by upended luggage. My red satin robe hangs from the back of a chair. A lone false eyelash is stuck to the full-length mirror, its fine, spidery legs matted into spikes. Rhinestone jewelry and errant pots of multicolored body glitter mingle with the dust bunnies under the ocelot-patterned settee in the corner. It looks like Liberace exploded in there.

The truth is I haven't fully unpacked because I don't know where to put this stuff. I'm sure the cosmetics and toiletries will go to good use, as will the bikinis, and the hairpiece is likely to see a few wild nights on the town. But what about the dresses? I definitely don't have a lycra lifestyle. I could pack them in a box for storage but having them tucked away on a shelf would be depressing. Every time I'd see the box, I'd think of the discarded lovers of Miriam, the vampire in *The Hunger*. The men and women Miriam took as her own could have neither her eternal youth nor the release of death, so when they reached decrepitude, she laid them to wither in trunks in the attic, periodically returning to remind them of her pledge of everlasting love. I can't bear the thought of all those garments languishing in disuse, elastic weakening with age, sequins dropping off like rotted teeth.

I'd donate the clothes to the Goodwill, but I'm uncomfortable with the idea of some unsuspecting eight-year-old girl traipsing around in one of my gowns on Halloween. A bonfire would be dramatic, but I'm reluctant to burn anything—that seems too much like destroying critical evidence, a disavowal. I could simply throw them out, but I'm really not inclined to toss what's left of my life as a stripper in the trash. Besides, I don't think spandex is biodegradable.

Regardless of what I do with the rest, I'm keeping the new pieces—the pink shiny minidress, the yellow-feathered ensemble. For what purpose, I don't know. Maybe I'll use them as Halloween costumes myself. I can dress up in them and cover my face in white makeup, then when someone asks what I'm supposed to be, I'll say, "I'm a ghost of my former self." Ha ha.

The weathered cedar plank fence out back is covered in freshly washed, dripping-wet dresses I've hung out to dry. The next-door neighbor's dog sticks his nose through the holes in the graying wood, sniffing and barking. While I was at Barbara's, the lilac bushes in our yard blossomed and now the tight-clustered blooms nod their heavy perfumed heads in the breeze. The air is alive with the happy throating of robins—which are much thinner this spring than last— and now and then, a ruckus from an ornery blue jay.

I've figured out what to do. Once they finish drying, I will fold the dresses and put them in a plastic garbage bag on the front porch. I'm giving them away to another dancer. Autumn is a local girl who works down in Denver. A bitch of a commute, two hours each way, but she thinks it's worth it. I met her at the gym and we sometimes run next to each other on the treadmill. When I bumped into her last night in the locker room, I told her she could have the dresses if she wanted. She's a good four inches shorter than I, and about ten pounds heavier, but I'm sure she can make do. She hasn't been dancing for very long—only a couple months, and as a single woman with a two-year-old to support, I imagine there are more important things than costumes for her to spend her money on.

When we first began talking about dancing, Autumn, then twenty, had just started. She told me she had been looking forward to working as a stripper since she was a teenager, then she had her daughter and got set back for a while. But she didn't grow up under the impression that stripping was a sleazy, dead-end job. Amongst her friends, it was considered an enviable position—almost chic, certainly more so than working at the mall or going to cosmetology school, the other options she and her friends saw before them. Stripping has become pretty cool within a certain subset and I imagine it will only get cooler. But will it get any easier? Probably. Although I doubt it'll ever be genuinely easy.

A decade from now, will Autumn struggle to make sense of her days as a stripper? Will I? After a solid year of scrutiny and self-examination, I'm still not done. I could keep raking it over and over, like currying the stubborn nap of an animal's fur in hopes of getting it to lie flat, but I don't think that would help. If the dancers from previous generations with whom I've spoken are any indication, I'll have this mass of conflicting feelings with me quite a bit longer. I'll take them to the altar, certainly. Maybe I'll take them to the grave.

So I don't feel totally at peace. But I'm pretty well-organized— what's good and bad have become distinguishable. And that counts for something.

Last night Randy and I lay in bed discussing the wedding invitations.

"I've got this idea," Randy said. "The invitation could look like the cover of a romance novel. We could have an illustration of me holding on to you . . ."

". . . and I'm swooning in some tarty dress with a lace-up bodice and you're in your cowboy hat and one of those open-necked Fabio shirts! With a title in gold cursive, like, *The Cowboy and the Showgirl: They Said It Could Never Work.*"

"Exactly! And we'll be against a sunset with a stallion rearing up in the distance."

"I think that is the best invitation idea *ever!*"

"Well, now that you're home for good, we can start working on it."

I looked over at him. He stared up at the slow-turning blades of the ceiling fan, smiling.

I slid my arm under his neck so he rested with his head on my chest.

"So, how were you able to deal with me running around the country half-naked for a whole year?"

"Wasn't a whole year, honey. Just parts of one."

"You know what I mean."

"I do. I'm just teasing."

"Well . . . ?"

"Because ever since I met you, I've known that you have a whole other life. You're a lot deeper than that job. Everybody sees that. Don't you?"

Autumn jumps about a foot in the air when I open the front door.

"I thought you weren't going to be home when I came by!" She holds her hand to her chest trying to regain her composure.

I didn't think so, either. Initially, when I invited her over, I thought I'd leave the bag on the front porch and go out for a drive or something until I was sure she'd come and gone. But then I decided that if this was the end, I might as well have the guts to show up for it.

Autumn is pulling dresses out of the bag and holding them up over her jeans and Nine Inch Nails T-shirt. "These are great! Are you sure you want to get rid of them?"

No.

"Yep, I'm sure," I force the words from my mouth, thinking that the pink-and-white spotted dress she's pressing against herself is what I wore in Dallas. The Tentacle of Love. "They're all yours."

"Well, thank you, thank you!" She does a little bow, which I return.

"Happy to keep them in the family, my dear. Wear them in good health."

We look at each other, unsure of what to say. What do I want to tell her? You've got a hard road ahead of you?

Save your money?

Run while you still can?

Right now, Autumn is in the invincible period where she's over her novice nerves and the money's gotten good enough that the gig seems like a total lark. Blue skies under the black light. There is nothing to be said to a girl in that place.

I know.

The soles of her sneakers squeak on the porch boards. More robins chirp.

"I should go," she says, breaking the ten-ton silence. "My daughter is at my mom's and I need to pick her up." She gives me a quick peck on the cheek and bounds down the front path to her old silver Honda hatchback. The bumper sticker says, STOP INBREEDING. BAN COUNTRY MUSIC.

I lean against the doorsill, watching while she starts the car. I quirk up my lips at the corners and give a half-wave as she pulls away from the curb.

It's going . . .

With a honk and a farewell wiggle of her fingers, she takes off.

"Be careful," I whisper after her.

It's going . . .

At the corner, she signals and turns left, then drives out of sight.

It's gone.

ACKNOWLEDGMENTS

Since anonymity equals courtesy in strip culture, I chose to change the names, stage names, and identifying characteristics of most people who appear in the book. The following people appear in the book as themselves: Randy, Wil, Cathy, Jeanette, Jade, Ann Marie, Jim Hayek, the Pure Talent School of Dance class, Deb, Jane, Atom, Dixie Evans, Carol Queen, Beth Ross, Elliot Beckelman, Jennifer, Jim Mitchell, Lynn Rossman Faris, Scarlett Fever, Pillow, Susan, Barb, John, and Peanut from the Road Dogs.

Many of the aforementioned helped me tremendously in the researching of this book, by being a part of it. I thank them. I also owe huge thanks to Jonathan Burnham and Farley Chase, my agent Tina Bennett and the nice folks at Janklow and Nesbit, my family, Lisa Everitt, Molly Ker, Stony Lonesome, Sherry Britton, Jim Nelson, and Don Waitt and Exotic Dancer Publications.

Additionally, I must express my gratitude to the women with whom I shared the stage. You are the heart, the soul, and the legs of this book. Without you, this book would not only have been impossible, it would not have been worthy of attempt.